The Mantle Site

Issues in Eastern Woodlands Archaeology

Editors: Thomas E. Emerson and Timothy Pauketat

SERIES DESCRIPTION: Issues in Eastern Woodlands Archaeology emphasizes new research results and innovative theoretical approaches to the archaeology of the pre-Columbian native and early colonial inhabitants of North America east of the Mississippi River Valley. The editors are especially seeking contributors who are interested in addressing/questioning such concepts as historical process, agency, traditions, political economy, materiality, ethnicity, and landscapes through the medium of Eastern Woodlands archaeology. Such contributions may take as their focus a specific theoretical or regional case study but should cast it in broader comparative or historical terms.

Scholars interested in contributing to this series are encouraged to contact Thomas Emerson, ITARP-Anthropology, 23 East Stadium Drive, University of Illinois, Champaign, IL 61820; teee@uiuc.edu.

BOOKS IN THIS SERIES:

The Mantle Site: An Archaeological History of an Ancestral Wendat Community, by Jennifer Birch and Ronald F. Williamson

Chiefdoms and Other Archaeological Delusions, by Timothy R. Pauketat

In Contact: Bodies and Spaces in the Sixteenth- and Seventeenth-Century Eastern Woodlands, by Diana DiPaolo Loren

War Paths, Peace Paths: An Archaeology of Cooperation and Conflict in Native Eastern North America, by David H. Dye

Shamans of the Lost World: A Cognitive Approach to Prehistoric Religion of the Ohio Hopewell, by William F. Romain

The Eastern Archaic, Historicized, by Kenneth E. Sassaman

The Mantle Site

An Archaeological History of an Ancestral Wendat Community

Jennifer Birch and Ronald F. Williamson

ROWMAN & LITTLEFIELD PUBLISHERS, INC.
Lanham • Boulder • New York • London

Published by Rowman & Littlefield
A wholly owned subsidiary of The Rowman & Littlefield Publishing Group, Inc.
4501 Forbes Boulevard, Suite 200, Lanham, Maryland 20706
www.rowman.com

Unit A, Whitacre Mews, 26-34 Stannary Street, London SE11 4AB

Copyright © 2015 by AltaMira Press
First paperback edition 2015

British Library Cataloguing in Publication Information Available

Library of Congress Cataloging-in-Publication Data
The hardback edition of this book was previously cataloged by the Library of Congress as follows:
Birch, Jennifer, 1980–
The Mantle site : an archaeological history of an ancestral Wendat community / by Jennifer Birch & Ronald F. Williamson.
p. cm.— (Issues in eastern woodlands archaeology)
Includes bibliographical references and index.
1. Wyandot Indians—Antiquities. 2. Wyandot Indians—History. 3. Wyandot Indians—Social life and customs. 4. Excavations (Archaeology)—Ontario, Lake (N.Y. and Ont.) 5. Ontario, Lake (N.Y. and Ont.)—Antiquities. I. Williamson, R. F. (Ronald F.) II. Title.
E99.H9B55 2012
974.7'9—dc23
2012036746

ISBN 978-0-7591-2100-3 (cloth : alk. paper)
ISBN 978-0-7591-2101-0 (pbk. : alk. paper)
ISBN 978-0-7591-2102-7 (electronic)

Printed in the United States of America

Contents

Figures

Tables

Acknowledgments

Our sincerest appreciation is extended to the Huron-Wendat Nation and particularly to Heather Bastien and Luc Lainé. In the spirit of learning about their past and sharing it: *esk8arih8ateha*, "we will come again to know it."

Our work builds upon that of many other archaeologists who laid the groundwork for research into the ancestors of the Huron-Wendat, who occupied the north shore of Lake Ontario prior to European contact. We would like to particularly acknowledge the life works of Dana Poulton, Peter Ramsden, and Gary Warrick, who constructed the foundation upon which this analysis is placed. William Finlayson directed the mitigative excavations of the Draper site in 1975 and 1978, and in so doing, introduced Ron Williamson to the archaeology of the ancestral Wendat as he was a member of both years' teams. Excavating and analyzing the Mantle site represented an opportunity for him to return to the same, yet reconstituted community.

We are able to tell the story of the Mantle site thanks to the dedication and collaborative efforts of an extensive team of archaeologists, analysts, researchers, and colleagues. Foremost among these is Andrew Clish, who directed the excavations of the site, produced the map of its settlement patterns, and helped unravel the occupational history of the village. With almost thirty years of experience excavating Iroquoian village sites, Andrew is one of the best in the business.

We are also indebted to many regular Archaeological Services Inc. (ASI) crew members who participated in excavations at the site between 2002 and 2005: Eda Ataergin, Amy Au, Katherine Cappella, Andrea Carnevale, Peter Carruthers, Neil Chisholm, David Cooper, Meredith Czaniecki, Jennie Fiddes, Rebecca George, James Herbert, Andrea Jackson, Biljana Jovonovic, Steven Landry, Denise McGuire, Steve Monckton, Charlene Murphy, Matthew Pearce, Aleksandra Pradzynski, David Robertson, Norbert Stanchly,

Debbie Steiss, Annie Veilleux, Bruce Welsh, Brian Williams, and all of the other ASI personnel who assisted in these efforts. As an extension of our crew, Mike and Jack Rooney of Rooney Brothers Gradall Service provided expertise in mechanical soil removal, and Joe Thompson and David Moir provided an opportunity for aerial photography of the site during excavation.

The processing of the artifact assemblage was accomplished by Shawn Bayes, Nicole Beattie, Elaine Cheng, Caitlin Coleman, Laurel Daugherty-Seto, Steve Landry, Elizabeth Matwey, Jessica Paquette, Deb Pihl, Aleksandra Pradzynski, Kayla Reynolds, Doug Todd, Blake Williams, and Rob Wojtowicz under the supervision of Kristine Crawford and Alexis Dunlop.

We are also grateful to the skilled researchers who contributed to the analysis of material culture from the site. The in-house team at ASI includes Andrea Carnevale, Martin Cooper, Rob Pihl, Aleksandra Pradzynski, Debbie Steiss, and Rob Wojtowicz. The human remains in the site's cemetery were analyzed by Crystal Forrest, a longtime research associate of the firm. Thanks to Margie Kennedy and the Toronto and Region Conservation Authority (TRCA) for providing data on the Seed-Barker site and to Holly Martelle regarding the ceramic analysis of the historic Wendat Ball site.

We are particularly indebted to Andrea Carnevale, who assumed the responsibility for researching the biography of the iron object. With determination and innovativeness, she identified its origin and the most likely path from Europe to the eastern coast of North America. It is likely that researchers will henceforth X-radiograph iron objects from sixteenth-century sites due to the potential for identifying forge marks. We would also like to acknowledge George Hoytena and his colleagues at Team Industrial Services in Oakville and Susan Stock and Heidi Sobol of the Conservation Department at the Royal Ontario Museum for their help with radiography and James Bradley, George Hamell, Jim Tuck, and Peter Ramsden for their comments on the discovery of this early piece of iron.

We are also indebted to Rob MacDonald, Jonas Fernandez, and John Sleath for their help in elucidating the factors affecting agricultural productivity in the Duffins Creek drainage; to Rob MacDonald, Thanos Webb, and Peter Popkin for their help in the modeling of deer hide and hunting area requirements; and to Morgan Baillargeon, curator of Plains ethnology, Canadian Museum of Civilization, and David Christensen, historical reenactor, for information regarding the use of hides in Indigenous clothing. John Sleath also provided invaluable research into the origins and distribution of coronet pipes, stone and ceramic vasiform pipes, stone pebble pendants, and steatite beads. Zeeshan Abedin provided research into the distribution of marine shell, copper, and steatite objects on ancestral Wendat sites on the north shore of Lake Ontario.

Stephen Monckton identified the palaeobotanical remains, and the zooarchaeological analysis was conducted by Suzanne Needs-Howarth. Both of these individuals, along with paleoethnobotanist Rudolphe Fecteau and zooarchaeologist Stephen Cox Thomas, have been at the center of archaeological plant and animal studies in southern Ontario for the last three decades. Dr. Needs-Howarth would in turn, like to thank Max Friesen of the Department of Anthropology at the University of Toronto for allowing access to the Howard G. Savage Faunal Archaeo-Osteology Collection; Kevin Seymour of the Royal Ontario Museum, Vertebrate Paleontology, for providing access to recent salmonid vertebrae; Erling Holm of the Royal Ontario Museum, Ichthyology, for tracing records of Atlantic salmon in Duffins Creek; and Nelson Amaral of the Toronto and Region Conservation Authority for facilitating access to fish data for their watersheds.

Linda Howie and Alexis Dolphin conducted petrographic analysis of ceramics from the site, and Brandi Lee MacDonald and Ron Hancock undertook the identification of the origin of the copper beads from Mantle using the facilities of McMaster University. The human isotope data were generated and examined by Susan Pfeiffer of the University of Toronto and Judith Sealey of the University of Cape Town, South Africa.

We are also grateful to Greg Braun, Peter Carruthers, Martin Cooper, Gord Dibb, Bill Engelbrecht, William Fox, Martha Latta, Rob MacDonald, Kostalena Michelaki, Robert Pearce, Rob Pihl, David Robertson, Debbie Steiss, Andrew Stewart, Chris Watts, and Tony Wonderley for thoughtful discussions regarding various aspects of our research.

The production of this volume was aided immeasurably by John Howarth, who photographed the artifacts; Andrea Carnevale, who helped produce the figures and photographs; Caitlin Coleman who prepared figure 6.2; and Jonas Fernandez, who assisted with the agricultural field and deer-hunting-territory modeling and production of most of the GIS-based analyses and mapping. Shady Abbas and Sarina Finlay were also of assistance in this regard. The agricultural field systems and deer catchment figures were drawn using ArcView GIS (GIS software), version 10 (Redlands, CA: Environmental Systems Research Institute Inc., 1992–2012). We would also like to thank Sarah Grant for editorial assistance, especially with respect to organizing the references cited.

Thanks to Jean-Luc Pilon and Stacey Girling-Christie at the Canadian Museum of Civilization for facilitating access to the collections from the Pugh, Best, and Spang sites; Justin Jennings, April Hawkins, and Adrienne Desjardine of the Royal Ontario Museum for access to collections from the Aurora site; Kathy David for access to additional collections and reports on file at the University of Toronto; Dorie Billich and Krista Rauchenstein of the Whitchurch-Stouffville Museum for access to collections from sites in the Holland River drainage; and Gord Dibb for access to his collections from the four sites north of Mantle, to which the community relocated.

The excavation of the site was funded by Lebovic Enterprises, and portions of the research presented were supported by a Canada Graduate Doctoral Scholarship and a postdoctoral fellowship from the Social Sciences and Humanities Research Council of Canada. Jennifer Birch would like to thank Aubrey Cannon, Ron Williamson, and Gary Warrick for supervising her doctoral research and Stephen Kowalewski for his guidance during her postdoctoral work.

Finally, we would like to thank Timothy Pauketat and Thomas Emerson for the invitation to write this volume as part of their edited series.

Chapter One

Understanding Northern Iroquoians

This is the story of the Mantle site, a Northern Iroquoian settlement situated on the north shore of Lake Ontario and occupied in the early sixteenth century. The site was investigated as a cultural resource management project between 2003 and 2005 (ASI 2012a). Its excavation and analysis represented an unprecedented opportunity and challenge to explore aspects of the lives of its occupants. The site resulted from the coalescence of multiple small villages into a single, well-planned and well-integrated community. In this volume, we explore the historical context of the site; the processes that led to its formation; the social, political, and economic lives of its inhabitants; and their relationships to other populations in northeastern North America.

Our analysis is necessarily multiscalar in scope and integrates multiple data sets, including regional and site-specific settlement pattern data, material culture, the modeling of subsistence practices and resource use, and evidence for violent conflict. Together, these various lines of evidence point to changes in the lived experience of communities through time and the historical development of Northern Iroquoian societies, patterns that can only be identified by combining detailed data from large-scale excavations with regional syntheses in an integrated program of research.

When the site was discovered in 2002 it was named the Mantle site in keeping with the established tradition of naming sites after landowners. More recently, the site was renamed Jean-Baptiste Lainé by the Huron-Wendat. Because the site has been registered in the Ontario archaeological database and published in the archaeological literature as Mantle, we have chosen to retain that name for the purposes of consistency in scholarly discourse. Today, ancestral sites are named by the Huron-Wendat soon after their discovery, precluding this problem.

NORTHERN IROQUOIAN SOCIETIES

The term "Iroquoian" refers to both a cultural pattern and a linguistic family, of which Northern Iroquoian is one branch. The Iroquoian language family includes Cherokee, spoken in the southern Appalachians, and Tuscarora, spoken near the mid-Atlantic coast. The term "Iroquoian," therefore, should not be confused with "Iroquois," an Algonquian word adopted by Europeans to refer to the Five Nations of the Haudenosaunee. In the seventeenth century, there were several different dialects spoken by Iroquoian peoples in the Lower Great Lakes.

Descriptions of Iroquoian life at the time of European contact include palisaded settlements enclosing bark-covered longhouses; subsistence based on maize horticulture supported by hunting, fishing, and gathering; a gender-based division of labor; a social structure organized around matrilineal clans; and political organization based on councils and confederacies and warfare, which included trophy-taking and prisoner sacrifice. These traits have often been generalized into a broadly "Northern Iroquoian" cultural pattern. While there were distinct cultural similarities between Northern Iroquoian peoples, there were also significant differences between the nations and even the constituent tribal groups within the nations (e.g., mortuary ceremonies, technological practices and industries, etc.).

The Huron, or Wendat, were the northernmost of the Iroquoians, inhabiting in the seventeenth century the area between Lake Simcoe and Georgian Bay (figure 1.1). Their confederacy consisted of five allied nations: the *Attignawantan* (Bear), *Atingeennonniahak* (Cord), *Arendarhonon* (Rock), *Ataronchronon* (Bog), and *Tahontaenrat* (Deer) (Trigger 1976:30). Their name for themselves, *Wendat*, has been interpreted as meaning "islanders" or "dwellers on a peninsula" (Hodge 1971:24) and may have only come into common use to refer to the confederacy in the seventeenth century (Steckley 2007:25; Thwaites 1896–1901, 5:278). Throughout this volume we refer to the Mantle site as an "ancestral Wendat" community, since at least two of the allied nations were derived from populations living a century earlier on the north shore of Lake Ontario and in the Trent Valley. While the site includes material traits that link it to later Wendat populations, there is no evidence that the people who lived at the Mantle site were, as yet, negotiating with other groups concerning the formation of the confederacy.

The Petun (*Tionontaté*) lived immediately southwest of the Wendat. Their confederacy included two separate groups, the Wolf and Deer (Thwaites 1896–1901, 33:143, 20:43). At the time the Jesuits arrived in Huronia, the Wendat-Tionontaté were allied against common Iroquois enemies, although this had not always been the case. Their combined population prior to the spread of European epidemics in the 1630s has been estimated to have been 30,000 (Warrick 2008:204).

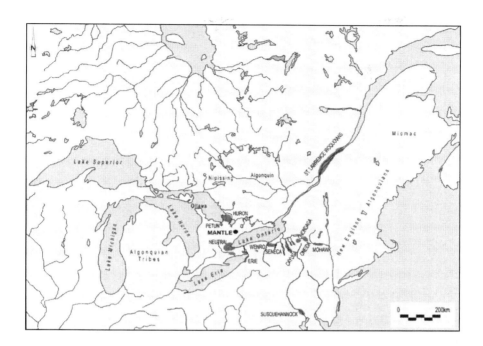

Figure 1.1. Location of the Mantle site with reference to the historic locations of the Indigenous societies of Eastern North America

The Neutral Confederacy (*Attiwandaron*) lived farther south, on the peninsula separating lakes Erie and Ontario. They were called Neutral by the French because they did not engage in the warfare between the Wendat and Iroquois, although they were in conflict with Algonquian-speaking peoples to the west (Trigger 1976:94–96). The Jesuits estimated the *Attiwandaron* population at approximately 12,000; it was likely significantly higher prior to the introduction of epidemic diseases (Trigger 1985:235).

The Erie inhabited the territory south of Lake Erie, possibly as far as the Ohio River. Little is known about the contact-period Erie due in part to the paucity of contact between them and early European visitors (White 1978a). Similarly, little is known about the Wenro (*Oneronon*), another group living south of the Great Lakes, although it is recorded that some joined the Wendat in 1639 (White 1978b).

The Iroquois Confederacy (*Haudenosaunee*) lived in clustered tribal groupings across upper New York State. They included (from west to east) the Seneca, Cayuga, Onondaga, Oneida, and Mohawk. These nations had unique cultural traits and histories owing to their geographic separation and development in distinct tribal territories, which they continued to occupy into the historic period. These differences are reflected in their language and material culture, as well as in their clan organization, kinship terms, and mortuary practices. The Iroquois population was of a similar size to and likely greater than that of the Wendat-Tionontaté (Trigger 1985:236).

The Algonquian-speaking neighbors of the Wendat included the Odawa living in the Bruce peninsula area; the Nippissing, living near the lake of the same name; and a number of small bands on the east shore of Georgian Bay.

These groups defined the geopolitical landscape at the time of sustained European contact. Within a few decades the consequences of the European presence in eastern North America brought about dramatic change. New technologies and economic motivations altered Indigenous lifestyles. Epidemic diseases and famine reduced their populations by more than 50% between 1634 and 1640 (Warrick 2008:222–36). The colonial expansionist agendas of multiple European nations intensified factionalism and conflicts between the Wendat-Tionontaté, the Attiwandaron, and the Haudenosaunee, resulting in the dispersal of the three Ontario confederacies and some of their Algonquian-speaking allies by the mid-seventeenth century. Remnants of these populations migrated to Quebec, Michigan, and Ohio (and ultimately Kansas and Oklahoma), while many others were adopted into Iroquois nations. The Wendat-Tionontaté and Iroquois have since survived four centuries of colonial domination and attempts at assimilation. Archaeological research continues to play an important role in efforts to assert their rights and interests in their ancestral and contemporary territories.

ARCHAEOLOGY AND ETHNOHISTORY

Our understandings of Northern Iroquoian societies are informed by written accounts of the Europeans who visited eastern North America in the first half of the seventeenth century. There are three principal sources for the Wendat. These include the writings of Samuel de Champlain (Biggar 1922–1936), an explorer, cartographer, and soldier who spent a significant portion of his later life supervising the colony he founded at modern Quebec City. In 1615 and 1616, he traveled to Huronia, spending five months living among various Wendat nations with the intent of building trading relationships between the Wendat and the French. In the fall of 1615, he accompanied a contingent of Wendat warriors and their Algonquian allies in an attack against the Onondaga. He was wounded in the raid and forced to winter among the Wendat. His account provides descriptions of Wendat clothing, settlements, military and hunting tactics, and their economy and interpersonal relations.

The second source is that of Gabriel Sagard (Wrong 1939), a Recollet friar who arrived in Wendake in August 1623 and lived there until the following May. His detailed account of Wendat culture and everyday village life may be considered one of the world's first substantial ethnographies (Trigger 1969:4). He also produced a phrasebook and comprehensive dictionary of the Wendat language (Steckley 2009).

The Jesuit Relations and Allied Documents are the third and most voluminous source of information about the seventeenth-century Wendat (Thwaites 1896–1901). These were published yearly in Paris and chronicle the activities and observations of Jesuit missionaries living among the Wendat between 1634 and 1650. Their writings are filled with descriptions of Wendat life and also provide a detailed account of the final Iroquois attacks that eventually decimated the Wendat Confederacy. While the *Relations* as well as the accounts of Champlain and Sagard provide important descriptions and etic interpretations of Wendat culture and society, they were written by outsiders with their own agendas and must be employed in that light (Trigger 1976).

In the twentieth century, these primary ethnohistoric sources, as well as other informative accounts, were synthesized by Elizabeth Tooker (1964) to provide a thorough source for ethnographic references to most aspects of Wendat life between 1615 and 1649. In the foreword to that book, Bruce Trigger presents an excellent summary of the history of archaeological and archival research on the Wendat from the mid-nineteenth to mid-twentieth century. In *The Children of Aataentsic* (1976) and *Natives and Newcomers* (1985), Trigger combined history, ethnography, and archaeology in a unique fashion, to give Wendat peoples their own voices in their struggles with the European colonial enterprise. Conrad Heidenreich (1971) also provided a detailed geographic analysis of Wendat life using the same sources, as well as numerous other accounts and period maps. More recent sources of information were provided by Georges Sioui (1999), who has added a contemporary Wendat voice to the history of his people; Gary Warrick's (2008) ground-breaking demographic history of the Wendat-Tionontaté; and John Steckley's ethno-linguistic analyses of the Wendat language (2007, 2009).

For much of the late twentieth and twenty-first century, the study of the history and archaeology of the Wendat and their neighbors has been dominated by our knowledge of seventeenth-century ethnic groups. The search for ethnohistorical antecedents in the archaeological record has at times led archaeologists to attempt to correlate behaviors and social units of precontact peoples with those defined in historical documents (Harris 1968). This has at times restricted the production of novel interpretations of archaeological materials and the application of critical and contemporary theoretical perspectives (P. Ramsden 1996:105). To completely disregard historic descriptions of Iroquoian societies and history, however, would be in error. Interpretations of precontact Iroquoian societies benefit from judicious use of the ethnohistoric record so long as we do not rely solely on evolutionary and direct-historical approaches. We must allow that while some cultural traits persist for long periods of time, others are changed, given greater or lesser emphasis, or created anew in dynamic processes of social and cultural transformation.

INTERPRETIVE FRAMEWORKS FOR ONTARIO IROQUOIAN ARCHAEOLOGY

Iroquoian archaeology can trace its roots back to the nineteenth century, when antiquarians amassed collections of "Indian relics" that were being plowed up in the fields of Ontario and New York State. Early excavations at a number of important sites helped initially to define the Iroquoian peoples who had occupied southern Ontario and New York State as taxonomically distinct groups (cf. Parker 1922; Ritchie 1944, 1969; Wintemberg 1928, 1936, 1948). When chronology became the dominant concern in American archaeology (Willey and Sabloff 1980:83), seriation and demonstrating that certain types of artifacts had chronological significance likewise became the primary concern of Iroquoian archaeologists (D. Smith 1990:282). In both Ontario and New York State, the typological classification of rim sherds was used to chronologically order sites and assign them to cultural units based on direct analogy with historic societies (MacNeish 1952; Ritchie and MacNeish 1949). From these observations, classification schemes for phases of cultural development were advanced (Lee 1952; Emerson 1954). Indeed, the privileging of ceramic analyses at the expense of attention to other classes of equally informative data still persists to some degree in Ontario archaeology (Williamson 1999:5).

In his seminal volume *The Ontario Iroquois Tradition* (1966), J. V. Wright presented a revised cultural-historical model for Iroquoian archaeology that included many of the ideas and terms already in use at the time, together with new ideas and hypotheses regarding cultural change, radiocarbon dates, and seriated sequences in a broad cultural-chronological taxonomy. For Wright, these chronological divisions were populated by archaeological cultures: the Early Iroquois Glen Meyer and Pickering branches, two cultural groups occupying lands to the west and east of the Niagara escarpment, respectively; the Middle Ontario Iroquois Uren and Middleport substages, representing the increasing homogeneity of material culture and population growth across the region during the fourteenth century; and sociocultural division resulting in the Late Ontario Iroquois Huron-Petun and Neutral-Erie after AD 1400. At the time, it represented an important paradigm shift and dominated the discourse of Late Woodland archaeology in Ontario for the next two decades.

Peter Ramsden was one of the first researchers to attempt to address the shortcomings of Wright's overly generalized model (P. Ramsden 1977). Ramsden utilized ceramic attribute analysis in his attempt to better understand the dynamic interplay of sociopolitical interaction occurring at the local level between communities and the formation of differentiated "local or 'tribal' groups" (P. Ramsden 1990a:381).

Bruce Trigger's considerable influence on the direction of Wendat-focused archaeology is reflected in his own work and that of his graduate students at McGill University, whose studies, grounded in settlement archaeology, addressed a wide range of thematic and conceptual issues relating to precontact Iroquoian societies (see Pearce et al. 2006).

In the last two decades, new frameworks emerged that drew upon contemporary explanatory paradigms such as core-periphery or periphery-margins models (Dincauze and Hasenstab 1989; S. Jamieson 1992), peer-polity interaction (Renfrew 1986; Williamson and Robertson 1994), agency and historical contingency (Ferris 1999), and coalescent societies (Birch 2010a; Kowalewski 2006), among others (cf. Williamson and Watts 1999). The Early-Middle-Late Iroquoian temporal construct nevertheless continues to be used in the discussion and presentation of Ontario Iroquoian archaeology (cf. Ellis and Ferris 1990; Ferris and Spence 1995; Warrick 2000) as convenient temporal referents.

Reconstructions of local precontact sequences have demonstrated the complexity and variability of regional processes of cultural change (e.g., Bradley 1987; Niemczycki 1984; Pearce 1996; Tuck 1971; Williamson 1985). This movement away from generalization led many archaeologists to reject phase-based taxonomies (Williamson 1999) and instead try to account for diachronic change at the local level while situating those changes within broader regional trajectories of cultural transformation (cf. Birch 2010a; Ramsden 2009). Such an approach permits the recognition of distinct local traditions and contingencies at the level of individual communities, as situated in broader historical patterns of social and cultural variability at the regional level. Focusing on the dynamic interplay between these two scales of analysis yields a more nuanced understanding of the complex cultural practices and processes that took place across the Lower Great Lakes throughout the Late Woodland period.

COMMUNITIES AND HISTORICAL PROCESSES

A multitude of sociological and ethnographic studies have shown the local community to be one of the most important contexts for social reproduction (cf. Suttles 1972; Cohen 1985). For many Indigenous peoples throughout

North America, the village community was the center of social and political life (e.g., Boulware 2011:10). This study places the community at the center of historical processes of social, political, and economic change.

The term "community" is frequently used in archaeological discourse yet nevertheless requires definition. Situated between households and societies writ large, the village community is often the largest sociopolitical unit in small-scale societies (Gerritsen 2004; Williamson and Robertson 1994:32). Early perspectives envisioned them as relatively static, homogeneous social units neatly compatible with archaeological definitions of "site" (Flannery 1976; Murdock 1949). A useful redefinition of the community concept by Kolb and Snead (1997) and informed by theories based in political economy viewed the community as serving three broad functions: social reproduction, subsistence production, and self-identification or group association. The emergence of new perspectives on communities, both natural and imagined (Isbell 2000), have enriched our interpretive frameworks for understanding their form and function and encouraged a closer engagement with issues of identity and social practice (cf. Canuto and Yaeger 2000; Gerritsen 2004; Mac Sweeney 2011).

Human communities are dynamic. As archaeologists, our challenge is to use the ephemeral remains of settlements, cultural materials, and the by-products of daily life to demonstrate that practices, identities, and communities do indeed cohere, while at the same time recognizing that they are complex, historically situated, and always potentially in a state of flux. In chapter 2 we provide a broad outline of the historical development of Iroquoian societies and their cultural traits, including the introduction of cultigens and the transition to settled village life; the coalescence of multiple small village communities into large, aggregated settlements; and the development of tribal nations. We then situate the Mantle site both in its local site sequence and in a broader geopolitical context in chapter 3. We first review the evidence for the history of settlement on West Duffins Creek and the origins of the population that came to occupy Mantle and then outline what was happening elsewhere in the Iroquoian world in the early sixteenth century, the period during which Mantle was occupied. Chapter 4 explores the formation of the community that occupied the Mantle site through the coalescence of as many as eight smaller villages. Our reconstruction of the occupational history of the site is discussed, together with a thorough comparison of the built environments of the sites that came before in order to elucidate processes of social and political reconfiguration and the creation of new community-based identities. Here, we are concerned with how communities are given social meaning and how they are constructed in a practical sense through daily interactions, shared culture, and lived experiences. For people to consider themselves members of a community they must consciously see themselves as part of a particular social collective. We discuss how a conscious sense of community identity might arise from geographic and residential proximity, interaction, and the shared experience of historical contingencies and sociocultural practices.

Our approach to understanding the processes by which societies are transformed is informed by the tenets of historical processual archaeology (Pauketat 2001, 2003; Pauketat and Alt 2005), a perspective that bridges a number of theoretical perspectives of the recent past and present (Trigger 2007:497) and situates explanatory power in an understanding of cultural production and reproduction. It is centered on theories of practice (Bourdieu 1977) and structuration (Giddens 1984), albeit in a tangible form where traditions or practices can be understood as the active forces in cultural construction and transmission (Pauketat 2003:45). In this way, the building of houses, the manufacture of meaning-laden objects, the acquisition of traditional foods, and so on, are all moments through which cultures come into being. Identifying the materiality and spatiality of these practices in the archaeological record enables archaeologists to observe historical processes of cultural change by tacking back and forth between various scales of analysis in order to compare significant degrees of continuity and variability within the populations being studied (Wylie 1989).

Chapter 5 thus examines the economic organization of the Mantle community in terms of the production and consumption of the necessities of life such as shelter, food, and clothing. Plant and animal resources are considered, and particular attention is focused on the acquisition of hides, changes in subsistence practices, and the agricultural field systems of Mantle and the sites that this community occupied previously. Chapter 6 focuses on the material culture recovered from the site and the necessary objects of daily life such as ceramic vessels and lithic tools, as well as items used for adornment, smoking pipes, and rare, European-introduced metals. We also discuss the cemetery located at the site and reflect on the complex practices that signified the construction and consolidation of a coherent community identity, as well as evidence for interaction networks that connected the Mantle community to both local and distant populations.

Iroquoian village sites were occupied for a short period of time, approximately ten to fifty years (Warrick 1988), after which they were abandoned and relocated, often nearby—although longer migrations also took place. The reoccupation of sites was rare, and each village site is essentially a slice of time representing the activities of a single generation. The richness of this archaeological record rivals that of any of the early farming societies of the Old or New Worlds (P. Ramsden 1996); it is especially well-suited to exploring how processes of sociocultural change played out in individual communities over time and space. By adopting an analytical approach that focuses on site relocation sequences and the occupational histories of individual communities, our focus of explanation shifts between questions of why and how societies and communities change over time (Pauketat 2001:74). Here, in our discussion of the Mantle site, we explore how one community negotiated change in its social, geographic, and economic circumstances during a period of widespread conflict, community coalescence, and geopolitical realignment in the centuries just prior to direct European contact.

In the concluding chapter, we discuss what happened to the community following the abandonment of the Mantle site. Consideration is also given to the implications of this study for archaeologists studying structurally similar societies and the development of organizational complexity in eastern North America. We recognize that the story of Mantle is not ours, but that of the Wendat, who have played a central role in framing the questions that we have asked and attempted to answer.

Chapter Two

The Historical Development of Ancestral Wendat Societies

The Mantle site is best understood in the context of the long transition to life in permanent villages occupied year-round; the coalescence of multiple small villages into large, aggregated settlements; and their consolidation into allied tribal nations. In an effort to reconcile how daily life in Iroquoian communities was tied to these long-term trends in the development of organizational complexity in Iroquoian societies, we also consider the dynamics between household and community-level organization and the social and political relationships between constituent groups in Ontario and the Lower Great Lakes more broadly.

Because of modern development pressure in the greater Toronto area and the resultant legislative mandate for heritage conservation, archaeological investigations in south-central Ontario have resulted in a far more detailed record of villages and the sequences in which they were situated than exists for southwestern Ontario, the St. Lawrence Valley, and New York State. For this reason, and because our primary aim is to contextualize the Mantle site, our explanation favors the evolution of village life on the north shore of Lake Ontario, one of the most densely populated areas of precontact Iroquoia.

THE ORIGIN OF NORTHERN IROQUOIANS

Early explanations of northern Iroquoian origins and their cultural traits, including maize horticulture, longhouse settlements, and matrilineal descent, focused on migration (Griffin 1944; Parker 1916), while later researchers argued for in situ development from extant hunter-gatherer populations (MacNeish 1952; Ritchie 1944). In the mid-1990s, Dean Snow (1995a, 1996)

11

advanced a new migrationist hypothesis suggesting that Iroquoians entered the Lower Great Lakes region in the sixth century bringing with them the Iroquoian culture. The migrationist hypothesis was rejected by many Great Lakes archaeologists (e.g., Ferris 1999; Hart 2001; Warrick 2000, 2008). It seems more likely that the various components of Iroquoian culture were adopted gradually by local populations and that the full expression of Iroquoian life is not recognizable archaeologically until the turn of the fourteenth century (e.g., Engelbrecht 2003; Williamson 2012).

The antiquity of Algonquian populations in the region has been underscored by recent genetic research. Mitochondrial DNA from the skeletal remains of a number of northeastern precontact sites was compared with several contemporary, descendant Indigenous populations, including Algonquian- and Iroquoian-speaking groups (Shook and Smith 2008). The study demonstrated genetic homogeneity across language barriers and between ancient populations in the Central Illinois River Valley and southern Ontario, suggesting sufficient gene flow among geographically distant populations to maintain regional continuities for at least three thousand years. Shook and Smith suggest that populations were expanding between two thousand and four thousand years ago, perhaps associated with the extension of Proto-Algonquian languages and/or the introduction of maize horticulture into the region, which seems to have involved the flow of new genetic material without replacing existing populations.

Yet there is linguistic evidence for the migration of the Iroquoian language family into the Lower Great Lakes region. Iroquoian languages are completely distinct from Algonquian languages in vocabulary, phonology, and grammar. Stuart Fiedel (1999) has argued that a Proto-Algonquian language emerged in the Great Lakes region by three thousand years ago. The arrival and divergence of the Iroquoian languages were thought by Fiedel to have occurred between fifteen hundred and one thousand years ago.

Given this broad understanding, it is most likely that a small number of Iroquoian speakers introduced the language to resident Algonquian-speaking Great Lakes populations, after which the language gradually gained widespread acceptance. Following Moore (1994), Engelbrecht (1999; 2003: 112–14) has argued for an "ethnogenetic" perspective on Iroquoian origins— a model that can accommodate population movements, acculturation, diffusion of ideas, and continuity, allowing for a more realistic and complex view of Iroquoian development. Peter Ramsden (2006) has even suggested that eastern groups consisting of St. Lawrence Iroquoians, Mohawk, Onondaga, and those Wendats who derive from the eastern part of their territory have in situ origins that differ from the remaining western Iroquoian groups, who were influenced by more recent arrivals, perhaps from the Mississippian world. Possible links with populations to the south can be found in the agricultural complex of Iroquoians, through the symbolic role of bloodshed in the promotion of agricultural fertility. Specific similarities to the ritual systems of Mesoamerica and the Mississippian valley (i.e., the arrow sacrifice ceremony, dog sacrifice, platform torture and sacrifice of victims to the sun, decapitation and scalping of prisoners) (Engelbrecht 2003:37–46; Trigger 1976:73–75) are indicative of cultural continuity between populations throughout eastern North America. The adoption of these practices was no doubt facilitated by the fact that social and ethnic boundaries were flexible and permeable, as they had been for millennia.

FROM HUNTER-GATHERERS TO FARMERS

The Middle Woodland period spans roughly a millennium and a half, from ca. 400 BC to ca. AD 900–1000. Middle Woodland populations were politically autonomous, mobile hunter-gatherers with flexible group boundaries (Pihl, Monckton, et al. 2008:154; Spence, Pihl, and Murphy 1990:143). This flexibility extended not only to group territories but also likely to group membership. Large occupation sites with dense artifact distributions, usually by lakes or major rivers, appear in the later Early Woodland and early Middle Woodland periods.

Several explanations have been advanced for the development of these large sites. William Finlayson (1977) believed that they represented accumulations of material deposited during repeated visits as small groups returned to exploit particularly rich, seasonally available resources, while Wilson (1991) thought that they were base camps used for long periods of the year. Others have argued that they were used by seasonal aggregations of bands, along with more sporadic and informal use of local resources at other times of the year (Spence, Pihl, and Molto 1984). These explanations, while not mutually exclusive, all involve the periodic aggregation of Middle Woodland populations during which there were heightened social and political relations. This in turn may have led people to value a greater degree of sedentism, which ultimately the growing of food surpluses would allow.

In New York State, phytolith evidence suggests that maize (*zea maize*) was being used in New York more than two thousand years ago (Thompson et al. 2004), although its presence does not necessarily mean that the crop was being cultivated locally. In southwestern Ontario, the earliest evidence for carbonized maize comes from fourteen-hundred-year-old sites in the Grand River Valley, most likely introduced from populations in the Niagara peninsula (Crawford, Smith, and Bowyer 1997). In southeastern Ontario, a calibrated radiocarbon date of AD 650 taken on charcoal from a feature in which a maize kernel was found may indicate the concomitant introduction of maize in the Rice Lake region (Jackson 1988), although the potential for contamination from later deposits led Crawford and his associates

(1997:114) to question the date. Recent AMS dating of maize residues on ceramic vessels from Middle Woodland period sites in the westernmost St. Lawrence Valley (Hart, Thompson, and Brumbach 2003), however, reaffirms the potential for multiple origins of maize in Ontario at that time.

The initial introduction of corn into the Lower Great Lakes, likely through exchange systems, initially supplemented rather than dramatically altered traditional Middle Woodland subsistence patterns based on hunting, fishing, and gathering. By fifteen hundred years ago, south-central Ontario was no doubt occupied simultaneously by hunter-gatherers and early horticulturalists (Warrick 2000:423). Indeed, isotopic analyses of bone collagen and carbonate from sites in southern Ontario suggest that maize did not become a nutritional staple until one thousand years ago (Harrison and Katzenberg 2003:241). Over time, it would have been increasingly favored, as it was less prone to variability in productivity and could be grown and harvested close to the village and then stored (Trigger 1985:85). Increasing reliance on corn would have reduced the need for seasonal macroband dispersal and initiated the development of semisedentary settlements (Trigger 1978:59–61; 1985:87).

Although we still have an incomplete understanding of the relationship between changes in settlement and subsistence during this period in southern Ontario, it is clear there was not a simple cause-and-effect relationship between the incorporation of maize into early precontact economies and the shift to a more sedentary lifestyle. These processes unfolded at different rates and times in different parts of the Lower Great Lakes (Hart and Brumbach 2003; Pihl, Monckton, et al. 2008).

In southern Ontario, settlements with evidence for maize and semisedentary habitation have been characterized as "transitional" or intermediate between the preceding Middle Woodland and subsequent Late Woodland communities of the region (Ferris and Spence 1995; Fox 1990; Crawford, Smith, and Bowyer 1997). These sites occur primarily in riverine floodplain environments and include, among others, the Auda (Kapches 1987), Holmedale (Pihl, Monckton, et al. 2008), and Porteous sites (Stothers 1977). These "base camps" are characterized by clusters of hearths and pits associated with small, poorly defined circular or elliptical house structures. Both the Porteous and Holmedale sites were encircled by a palisade, two rows at Porteous and a flimsy fence or single-row palisade at Holmedale, which likely served as a windbreak. The discovery of large, deep pits, probably for storing crops, and the ubiquitous presence of maize on these sites suggest that it contributed considerably to their diet.

Despite our limited knowledge of the period, the events of the Middle to Late Woodland transition are of great significance to the subsequent culture history of the region. The adoption of maize obviously had an important role in reducing the traditional reliance on naturally occurring resources; however, it would seem that this process was much more gradual than previously thought. In some areas, this shift may have been accomplished simply through local populations adopting horticultural practices and associated customs or ritual. In other areas, it is equally possible that the arrival of new peoples was initially responsible for the changes apparent in the archaeological record.

Whatever the mechanisms of introduction, the incipient horticulture of these communities likely led to decreased mobility, as at least some members of the community remained near their garden plots for longer periods of time to tend their crops. It may be easy to overestimate the role of maize in this process, however, as it would also seem that increased sedentism necessitated by population concentration into regional site clusters was already occurring in many areas of the Northeast prior to the widespread adoption of maize (cf. Ceci 1990; Hart 2001; Hart, Thompson, and Brumbach 2003; Wymer 1993). It seems clear, however, that Transitional Woodland sites were intensively occupied, subject to a considerable degree of internal spatial organization, and progressively located in areas suitable for horticulture (Pihl, Monckton, et al. 2008:155).

SETTLING THE VILLAGE

A relatively complete record of Iroquoian village life between one thousand and seven hundred years ago has been documented on the large Caradoc and Norfolk sand plains of southwestern Ontario (Timmins 1997; Williamson 1985, 1990). Similarly, in south-central Ontario, virtually all early Iroquoian sites were located on the easily cultivated sandy soils of the glacial Lake Iroquois Plain on the north shore of Lake Ontario. Unfortunately, most sites in the greater Toronto area have been impacted or destroyed by nineteenth- and early-twentieth-century industrial and urban land development, resulting in a sparse archaeological record of their former presence.

Where they have survived, these sites occur as geographically discrete, regional clusters of semipermanent settlements, together with smaller camps and special-purpose sites (Williamson 1990). Rather than representing a single site relocation sequence, each of these settlement clusters seems to have been composed of two or more contemporary communities that may have shared a hunting territory and a common resource base (Timmins 1997:228). Increasing investment in villages, their immediate environs, and the establishment of clusters of communities in particular localities or drainages may have resulted in an increasing concern for the maintenance of social, physical, or even territorial boundaries. There is enough internal differentiation between site clusters that Early Iroquoian development should be viewed as a multilinear process, with differential adoption of settlement and subsistence strategies and social, political, and economic developments occurring at slightly different times (Williamson 1990). This has also been suggested for contemporary populations in New York State (Hart and Brumbach 2003).

That ceramic design sequences and decorative motifs vary between regional clusters and are more homogeneous within them is consistent with the notion of increasing boundary maintenance (Williamson 1985:289–90). These ceramic data suggest that mates may have been obtained from within the local region, as opposed to intermarriage with peoples from a greater distance away; this practice would have further linked local groups through kinship. It seems likely that intergroup communication and interaction was more frequent within these regional clusters than with groups farther afield (Williamson and Robertson 1994). On the other hand, limited quantities of material culture related to societies to the south and west have been recovered from Early Iroquoian sites and are perhaps indicative of the "waning years of a lower Great Lakes late Middle Woodland symbolic network" (Fox 2008:13).

Early Iroquoian villages are generally small in size, covering approximately one acre or 0.4 ha (Williamson 1990). The settlement patterns of excavated villages often contain multiple structures, averaging 10–20 m in length and 7 m in width (Dodd 1984; Warrick 1996). They are commonly surrounded by a single row of posts, which may be interpreted as a fence or enclosure as opposed to a defensive palisade, owing to their relatively insubstantial construction. Populations based on site size and hearth counts indicate that the earliest Iroquoian communities comprised approximately 75–150 people (Timmins 1997:199), suggesting that they were derived from late Middle and Transitional Woodland yearly territorial band aggregations of 50–150 people (Trigger 1976:134; 1985:86).

Early Iroquoian villages were occupied over a longer period of time than later villages. While the settlement plans of Early Iroquoian villages at first appeared to archaeologists as somewhat disordered, they are in fact, palimpsests of multiple episodes of rebuilding involving multiple reoccupations over many decades, sometimes for a century or more. Peter Timmins (1997) has reconstructed the occupational history of the Calvert site, an Early Iroquoian village in southwestern Ontario, showing how it developed from a seasonal hunting camp into a semipermanently occupied village between AD 1150 and 1250.

Social organization in Early Iroquoian villages likely revolved around autonomous households. There is no evidence that the appearance of semisedentary villages marked the incorporation of matrilineal descent and residence patterns or formal village political organization (Hart 2001; Williamson 1990). Their small size also suggests that leadership remained informal, perhaps limited to an individual who acted as an intermediary in dealings with neighboring groups (Trigger 1981a:24).

Warrick estimates that the population of south-central Ontario grew steadily from approximately 3,000 to 9,500 persons during this period (2008:171). An increasing reliance on maize as a dietary staple is suggested by isotopic data, though it likely comprised less than 20% of the diet until the end of the thirteenth century (Harrison and Katzenberg 2003:241; Katzenberg, Schwartz, et al. 1995; Schwartz, et al. 1985). During most of the period, corn clearly augmented a diverse and regionally differentiated subsistence economy in which populations chose to reduce the risk of crop failure through the continued exploitation of naturally occurring resources (Williamson 1990). Toward the end of the thirteenth century, it appears that some of these local networks came together into fully sedentary village aggregates and intensified their horticultural production to accommodate the larger populations.

FOURTEENTH- AND EARLY-FIFTEENTH-CENTURY TRANSFORMATIONS

The turn of the fourteenth century marks a transformational point in Iroquoian cultural evolution. A fully developed horticultural system; large, year-round-occupied villages; new socially integrative institutions; and distinctive material culture are all for the first time recognizably "Iroquoian" as described in early European descriptions of their life.

There is demonstrated continuity between the location of sites and the regional clusters that characterized the preceding three centuries. Notably, the shift to a horticultural subsistence economy brought about profound changes in the size and structure of settlements and human-environment interaction. While previous interpretations of Iroquoian life during the fourteenth century indicated that this was a period of widespread cultural homogenization, with similar settlement patterns, subsistence strategies, material culture, and socioeconomic networks being adopted throughout southern Ontario (Dodd et al. 1990; J. Wright 1966), new data resulting from multiple complete village excavations suggest that life in Iroquoian communities was in fact much more variable than previously thought. Individual communities underwent a series of transitions in different ways and at different times, depending on local contingencies and the structure of the social and economic networks of which they were a part (Williamson and Robertson 1994).

It has been estimated that by AD 1330, the population of southern Ontario had increased to almost 11,000 people (Warrick 2008:174). Increased fertility and decreased infant and juvenile mortality owing to a more stable food supply are thought to have been responsible for this growth (Warrick 2008:171–72). There is no evidence for a similar demographic expansion in New York State, although this may be a function of the limited amount of data available on precontact Iroquois settlements and it is possible that similar demographic trends and developmental processes were occurring throughout the Lower Great Lakes region.

In the early fourteenth century, Iroquoian settlements in south-central Ontario begin to shift off the sand plains and onto more drought-resistant loams, such as the South Slope till plain north of Lake Ontario. This shift in settlement corresponds to an increasing commitment to horticulture. Isotopic analyses of human remains from the turn-of-the-fourteenth-century Moatfield ossuary, located approximately five kilometers north of Lake Ontario in the city of Toronto, indicate that for at least one generation, maize comprised 70% of the diet (van der Merwe et al. 2003). Such horticultural intensification may have been a necessary, temporary response to the subsistence needs of the larger populations inhabiting late-thirteenth- to early-fourteenth-century Iroquoian villages.

This same population growth may have been a major factor influencing the northward and westward expansion of Iroquoian settlement. There is no evidence for permanent human settlement in the Simcoe Uplands, immediately south of Georgian Bay, for example, prior to the turn of the fourteenth century, after which there is evidence for multiple agricultural communities migrating into the region (MacDonald 2002; Sutton 1999). At the same time, a similar expansion was occurring east into the Trent Valley (P. Ramsden 1990a; Sutton 1990). While a number of hypotheses have been advanced for the reasons behind the colonization of the Simcoe Uplands and Trent Valley (MacDonald 2002; Sutton 1999; Warrick 2008:177–80), population pressure and increased opportunities to trade with Algonquians along with ecological considerations provide the most likely explanation for these early-fourteenth-century migrations. The establishment of new villages no doubt involved significant communication and negotiations between the Iroquoians on the north shore of Lake Ontario and Algonquians from the surrounding area, broadening the base for future sociopolitical interaction.

While migration to unpopulated areas seems to have been one strategy adopted to cope with regional population growth, amalgamation was another. In the early fourteenth century, settlement patterns from a number of village sites (e.g., Uren [M. Wright 1986] and Myers Road [Williamson 1998]) indicate the union of previously discrete Early Iroquoian communities into larger villages.

The groups that came together to form Middle Iroquoian villages are very likely the same peoples that formed regional clusters of sites during the preceding Early Iroquoian period. This shift in settlement prompted changes in sociopolitical and economic organization and interaction both within communities and throughout the region in which they were located.

Early-fourteenth-century villages average 1.5 ha in extent, twice the size of the earlier base settlements. Most appear to have been occupied for approximately twenty to thirty years and exhibit less rebuilding and structural change than Early Iroquoian villages (Dodd et al. 1990; Warrick 2008: 135; Williamson and Ramsden 1998: 201). The amalgamation of two or more Early Iroquoian communities would have created villages that were on average greater than the normative threshold of 300–400 persons that permit informal sociopolitical organization (Forge 1972: 370–75; Warrick 2000: 439–41) and would have exceeded the capabilities of band-level social institutions (Trigger 1985: 93). These larger populations would have required more elaborate means for social integration, conflict resolution, and decision making.

The average length of longhouses increases dramatically in the fourteenth century, although there was a great deal of variability in house length both within and between villages. The relatively large sizes of longhouses have been interpreted as representing the appearance of formal matrilineages and the beginnings of clan organization, both in Ontario (Pearce 1996; Trigger 1985:92–94; Warrick 1984:66) and in New York State (Engelbrecht 1985:174). Attempts to pinpoint when the reckoning of descent through the matriline and/or the shift to matrilocal residence began have been fraught with difficulty (Richards 1967; Trigger 1978), in part because of the difficulty in inferring kinship relations using archaeological evidence alone (Birch 2008; Harris 1968). It has been suggested that matrilocal residence developed in the context of an increasing commitment to horticulture and the consolidation of village life as women remained in villages for longer periods of time, helping each other tend crops and care for children, while men were increasingly absent from communities hunting and fishing (Trigger 1985:89). The division of labor and of social spheres seems to have been further reinforced over the next three centuries as the village increasingly became the domain of Iroquoian women, whereas men dominated affairs regarding trade, war, and "external" affairs (Trigger 1978; see also Hart 2001).

Between AD 1330 and 1420 a veritable population explosion occurred. In less than a century, the population of south-central Ontario jumped from 10,000 to 24,000 persons, representing the doubling of the population every third generation (Warrick 2008:141–42, 182). This late fourteenth-century surge in regional population resulted in larger villages and the establishment of new villages, together with the continued migration of groups from the early Iroquoian heartland into adjacent areas.

There was a great deal of variability in the size and structure of later fourteenth- and early-fifteenth-century settlements. It may have been the case that after a period of initial aggregation some communities fissioned, opting for a more dispersed settlement strategy. Some sites are comprised of single clusters of three or four aligned longhouses, or less structured groups of houses, with estimated populations of approximately 250–350 persons. Other sites contain two or more clusters of aligned houses and would have supported larger populations of up to 500–600 persons. Villages were not palisaded, although some sites featured internal fences that seem to represent visual barriers separating house clusters or segments of a community, perhaps both symbolically and physically.

The fourteenth century also witnessed the development of new mechanisms for integrating and ordering social segments within communities and facilitating ties between populations in the Lower Great Lakes more broadly. Village amalgamation, long-distance migration, the emergence of segmented matrilineal clans practicing village exogamy, and a heightened degree of interregional interaction resulted in the appearance of a relatively homogeneous distribution of material culture in the early fourteenth century (Dodd et al. 1990; Warrick 2000:441; Williamson and Robertson 1994). Ceramic and smoking pipe assemblages show both a continuation of earlier trends and the development of new formal characteristics.

The increasing size of some longhouses during the period may reflect the growing importance of the social, economic, and political unit formed by the coresidential household group (Dodd 1984; Warrick 1996). MacDonald (1986:177–78) has discussed how the formation of larger villages and the emergence of community politics may have favored the growth of large residential corporate groups along kinship lines, which would have served to cushion the effects of breakdowns in group hierarchies. In some cases, household groups became very large, as evidenced by the enormous longhouses of the early fifteenth century, which commonly reached over 50 m in length (Warrick 2000:447). These longhouse groups may have become so large they were prone to fissioning (Sahlins 1963), and a new political strategy emerged based on representation by clan segments in village politics and the ranking of leaders within lineages. While matrilineal descent and marriage into longhouse-based lineages may have initially emerged in response to the shift to a horticultural economy, increasing emphasis on a clan system that bound lineages together by ties of real or fictive kinship may have arisen in response to the need for more formalized sociopolitical organization within amalgamated villages and between communities now separated by greater distances.

Another integrative mechanism that appears in Wendat and Neutral villages in the fourteenth and early fifteenth centuries is semisubterranean sweat lodges. These features appear in the archaeological record as shallow, keyhole-shaped pits within or attached to longhouses. They were likely used for ritual, curative, or sociopolitical purposes, an inference supported by robust ethnographic and historical data. Over 230 of these features have been documented across forty sites in southern Ontario, dating to between the late thirteenth and early fifteenth centuries (MacDonald 1988; MacDonald and Williamson 2001:66–67). The frequency with which these structures appear after the turn of the fourteenth century suggests that they played a fundamental role in Iroquoian households by providing a venue for men to host their kinsmen for social and ritual events. These kinsmen may have been from within the village or longhouse itself or may have been visiting members of wider social networks, including Iroquoians or Algonquian-speaking trading partners (Kapches 1984; Robertson and Williamson 2003). The fact that these features appear at a time when we see the amalgamation of formerly discrete populations suggests that their function extended beyond the social sphere of the village itself. They are conspicuously rare, however, on sites dating to after AD 1450, suggesting that the practice by groups fell out of use and was replaced by aboveground sweat lodges that accommodated far fewer people.

The most conspicuous integrative mechanism of the period is ossuary burial. Ossuaries are large pit features containing the disarticulated remains of hundreds of individuals who were buried in a ceremony called the Feast of the Dead, one of which was witnessed in 1636 by Jean de Brébeuf in Huronia (Thwaites 1896–1901, 10:279–303). At the time of village relocation, the remains of those who had died and been placed in bark huts or buried during the tenure of the village were disinterred and their remains redeposited and commingled in one or two mass graves (see chapter 6).

The appearance of semisubterranean sweat lodges and ossuary burial throughout southern Ontario in the early fourteenth century suggest that there was an increasing commitment to community-building both within individual settlements and larger social networks. While mortuary practice differed from the ancestral Wendat, few sites in New York State dating to the period between 1300 and 1450 have been excavated in sufficient detail to comment on whether or not semisubterranean sweat lodges or other similar integrative mechanisms were developed in ancestral Iroquois communities. Snow has noted that there seems to have been a seemingly contradictory pattern of widespread interaction occurring at the same time local clusters of villages were diverging from one another as "cultural variants on a common theme" (1994:37).

FIFTEENTH-CENTURY COALESCENCE AND CONFLICT

Beginning in the mid-fifteenth century, the Iroquoian societies of the Lower Great Lakes experienced a period of rapid and sweeping change, which included increased evidence for violent conflict, the coalescence of multiple small communities into villages of unprecedented size, and increasing regionalization thought to represent the initial development of "tribal" groups or "nations."

While these phenomena occur throughout the entire Iroquoian world between the mid-fifteenth and early sixteenth centuries, there is evidence from specific site relocation sequences that these trends began somewhat earlier in southern Ontario than in New York State. These events resulted in dramatic social and geopolitical realignments that altered the precontact Iroquoian world. While these transformational changes have long been noted at the regional scale (P. Ramsden 1990a; Snow 1995b; Tuck 1971), the site sequence on West Duffins Creek, including the Draper and Mantle sites, provides an opportunity for a detailed perspective on how this process unfolded within an individual community.

By the mid-fifteenth century, the surge in population had slowed considerably, and by the end of the fifteenth century it had stopped altogether, stabilizing at approximately 30,000 persons (Warrick 2008:185). The pattern of population increase followed by a lagged increase in violent conflict has been documented cross-culturally by Turchin and Korotayev (2006). The regional context for violent conflict and coalescence extended from southwestern Ontario to the Trent and St. Lawrence Valleys and into Upper New York State, however, suggesting that population pressure alone cannot explain the dramatic increase in violence evidenced in the archaeological record. As in many other societies, aggregation was one strategy adopted by the Wendat when threatened. The Jesuit Relations note that, in 1635, when the northern Bear Nation felt endangered by an Iroquois attack, five villages discussed moving to a single, fortified settlement—a plan that was abandoned when threat of attack was diminished (Trigger 1969:17).

Indirect evidence for conflict includes the defensive situation of villages at the top of slopes and away from navigable water. Palisades with multiple rows of posts are present on most sites, and evidence for their maintenance and expansion suggests an ongoing concern for communal defense. Middens on late-fifteenth-century sites have been found to contain hundreds of charred and otherwise altered human skeletal elements. There is a dramatic spike in the presence of modified human bone on sites dating to the late fifteenth century (Jenkins 2011; Williamson 2007). Such finds have been interpreted as evidence for prisoner sacrifice, trophy taking, and the manufacture of objects for use in ritual performances.

While it has traditionally been assumed that the endemic conflict that characterized Late Iroquoian society was played out over long distances (e.g., Pendergast 1993:25–26; Warrick 1984:63), in some regions it would seem more likely that feuding was taking place between neighboring communities (Dupras and Pratte 1998; Robertson and Williamson 1998). However, given the likelihood that both alliance formation and conflict between individual communities was highly dynamic, it may be expected that both occurred at a broad range of scales.

The accumulation of status by young warriors in newly aggregated communities, blood feuds, or disputes over political alliances may have also driven warfare (Birch 2010b; Snow 2007; Trigger 1976:68-69). Also, the formation of these coalescent communities corresponds to the decades in which we see the possible alliance of the Oneida, Onondaga, and Mohawk (Engelbrecht 2003:130) to the south and the initial confederation of Wendat populations living in Simcoe County to the north. It is noteworthy that conflict, alliance building, and the formation of large aggregated communities are roughly coterminous phenomena.

This coalescence of multiple households and communities resulted in domestic settings considerably more complex than those experienced during the preceding two generations and almost certainly involved drastic transformations in sociopolitical relationships and the use of domestic and public spaces. These new social environments would have required more formal structures for political organization and decision making, and considerable negotiation related to access to resources and public spaces. It is likely that identities based on clan membership became as significant as those based on lineages. Structuring social relations through village councils and the clan system rather than households and lines of descent likely aided social integration within coalescent communities and dampened tensions between emerging tribal nations across the wider region (Birch 2008; Williamson 2012).

Mechanisms for social integration common to Iroquoian cultures identified ethnohistorically include ceremonialism tied to seasonal rhythms, communal feasting, sodalities, medicine societies, death and burial, and rituals of intensification (Fenton 1978; Tooker 1964). These practices may not have been present in their full-blown historic form in precontact societies, but it is almost certain that variations of at least some were in place as early as AD 1300—certainly by the mid-fifteenth century—and developed, at least in part, to facilitate the integration of larger communities than existed previously.

SIXTEENTH-CENTURY CONSOLIDATION AND REALIGNMENT

By the early sixteenth century, expansion of populations into the uplands of Simcoe County and the Trent Valley waned, and settlement on the South Slopes Till Plain consolidated into two large village communities. The increasingly well-planned and integrated layouts of a coalesced village such as Mantle suggest that a new level of decision making had emerged in these communities that influenced aspects of village planning and the organization of production, and superseded the various social segments that existed within the village as a whole. Yet the increasing homogeneity in village-level production but heterogeneity between local sequences and interaction with or incorporation of other, far-distant groups suggest that there was a complex interplay between the crystallization of locally based identities, interaction between communities, population movements, and the reorganization of networks of interregional interaction. It is significant that while the Mantle site is heavily palisaded, only trace amounts of human bone were found in non-burial contexts at the site, suggesting a decrease in violent conflict from the preceding fifty-year period, at least on the north shore of Lake Ontario.

Elsewhere in Iroquoia, there is evidence of the formation of large, amalgamated villages in the mid-sixteenth century on the lower St. Lawrence River and among the Mohawk, Oneida, and Onondaga. By the late sixteenth century, the Lower St. Lawrence Valley was abandoned entirely, and there is evidence that these populations were eventually incorporated into communities and site clusters in the Trent Valley and Jefferson County (Abel 2001; J. Jamieson 1990:403; P. Ramsden 1990a:383; Warrick 2000: 454–57). The initial colonization of the Nottawasaga Highlands, homeland to the Tionontaté, also occurred at this time.

Some mid-sixteenth-century sites contain limited amounts of European metal. The presence of two European-derived copper beads and a single iron object in secure contexts at the Mantle site (see chapter 6) suggest that early-sixteenth-century populations were also accessing European goods through indirect contact. After ca. AD 1550, European metals become relatively common on Iroquoian sites, and copper, brass, and iron objects predominate, often reworked or cut into smaller pieces; iron tools were reworked into miniature celts or awls, and brass or copper sheets rolled into beads. Nearly all seventeenth-century village sites contain European materials (Fitzgerald 1990a), and documented historic accounts indicate that the European presence in eastern North America was being strongly felt by the end of the first decade of the seventeenth century.

The final shift and consolidation of communities into the confederacies subsequently encountered by European explorers and missionaries occurred in the late sixteenth and early seventeenth centuries. In the same way that contacts between communities led to the formation of individual nations, contacts between nations, presumably to conclude political alliances, led to the confederacies. For ancestral Wendat populations, by the end of the sixteenth century, the northward migration that had begun in the thirteenth century approached its final stage, as groups coalesced to form the Wendat tribal confederacy in the northern uplands of Simcoe County—historic Huronia—and the Tionontaté nation in the Nottawasaga Highlands.

Chapter Three

Situating the Mantle Site

In this chapter, a series of local community relocation sequences are reviewed to better understand how the historical development of the Mantle community was related to the histories of other contemporary sites and site sequences in the Iroquoian world. In both Ontario and New York State, site relocation sequences have been documented that represent hundreds of years of occupation by contiguous communities (e.g., Bradley 1987; Niemczycki 1984; Pearce 1996; P. Ramsden 1977; Tuck 1971). Violent conflict, settlement aggregation, and the consolidation of populations into emergent tribal nations characterize the mid- to late-fifteenth- through early-sixteenth-century archaeological record of Northern Iroquoian societies. While delineating each of these sequences in detail is beyond the scope of this volume, examining these conditions and developments is best accomplished through a multiscalar analytical framework that strives to understand how change in individual communities related to both specific local contingencies and macroregional trends.

The Mantle site is one of a dense cluster of precontact Iroquoian settlements that occupied the north shore of Lake Ontario (figure 3.1). The Lake Ontario drainage system comprises a series of rivers and creeks that follow roughly parallel southeasterly courses from their headwaters in the Oak Ridges Moraine to Lake Ontario. The major watersheds from west to east are the Humber River, Don River, Rouge River, and Duffins Creek drainages. These watersheds traverse four physiographic zones (Chapman and Putnam 1984) including, from south to north, the Iroquois Plain, a narrow band of sandy soils bordering the north shore of Lake Ontario; the South Slope Till Plain, which stretches between the Iroquois Plain and Oak Ridges Moraine and contains highly fertile, drought-resistant, loam-based soils; the Peel Plain, an island in the South Slope that has heavy clay soils and poor drainage; and the Oak Ridges Moraine, a high landform composed predominantly of sand and gravel that acts as the watershed divide between Lake Ontario and the Georgian Bay and Lake Simcoe drainages.

The Mantle site is part of an unbroken sequence of community relocations on the Duffins Creek and Rouge River drainages that span at least five hundred years. The majority of settlement on the Rouge and its tributaries is clustered within twelve kilometers of the shore of Lake Ontario and predates the formation of large community aggregates. These populations contributed, however, to the large late-fifteenth- and early-sixteenth-century village communities on the adjacent Duffins Creek. As such, the Iroquoian village relocation sequences on the Rouge River and Duffins Creek are considered together.

DUFFINS CREEK

The Earliest Rouge-Duffins Drainage Sites

There is evidence of a long, largely unbroken sequence of occupation along Duffins Creek and its tributaries. A significant cluster of Early Iroquoian settlements has been documented on a portion of the Iroquois Plain, north of the urbanized lands along the lakefront. Between the Rouge and West Duffins drainage systems, nine Early Iroquoian villages (and a number of ancil-

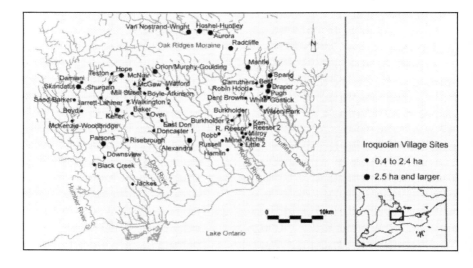

Figure 3.1.   All Known Iroquoian Village Sites on the North Shore of Lake Ontario ca. AD 1350–1600

lary sites) have been identified that are estimated to occupy areas of 0.5 to 1.0 ha. Walter Kenyon's (1968) excavations at the Miller site revealed a small, palisaded thirteenth-century village consisting of six longhouses. Limited excavations at the twelfth-century Boys site resulted in the documentation of portions of two longhouses, a single-row palisade on the north side of the site, and several middens along the steep ravine slopes that defined the south and east limits of the settlement area. It is likely that other houses are present within those portions of the compound that were not investigated (Reid 1975). The settlement pattern and material culture assemblage from these sites, along with test excavations at the others, helped define our understanding of Early Iroquoian occupations in south-central Ontario.

There are a number of fourteenth-century sites on Duffins Creek, including the Pearse, Peter Webb 1, Peter Webb 2, and Hoar sites (Poulton 1979), all of which have only been subject to minor investigations. It is possible that these sites represent the footprint of two or three distinct but closely related community groups, whereby each of the earlier sites is relatively small, and its antecedent larger. The Wonowin (ASI 2011a), Sebastien (ASI 2011b), and Miindaamiin (URS 2011) sites form another early-fourteenth-century sequential cluster of 2 ha-sized sites two to three kilometers to the east. The nearby mid- to late-fourteenth-century, 2 ha Carl Murphy site was occupied subsequently by one or two of these communities. These site data, along with evidence of other contemporary special-purpose sites (AM Archaeological Associates 1997), suggest that there were at least three separate communities occupying the Duffins Creek drainage in the fourteenth century.

Fourteenth- and early-fifteenth-century sites are also located on southern portions of the Rouge River and Highland Creek, a small drainage immediately west of the Rouge Valley. Because of their proximity, the sites in these two adjacent watercourses were likely related both to each other and to the fourteenth-century communities on Duffins Creek. We believe that the descendants of these groups relocated eastward, contributing to the populations that eventually came together at the Draper site and later formed the Mantle community.

The New site has been excavated in its entirety (ASI 2006a). The village covers 1.2 ha and consists of six houses, four of which are arranged in pairs. Not all of the houses are necessarily contemporary, although none overlap. Settlement data and ceramic serration suggest that this site dates to the first half of the fourteenth century. The poorly documented Thompson, Woodland Park, and Elliot sites also date to the first half of the fourteenth century and are located on tributaries of Highland Creek (Kapches 1981; Konrad and Ross 1974). The Thompson site is located approximately two kilometers from the Tabor Hill ossuary, with which it is provisionally associated and which comprises two ossuary pits that together contain the remains of 523 burials (Churcher and Kenyon 1960). Williamson and Steiss (2003:102) suggest that these may represent the collective dead of two communities, who buried them concurrently while choosing to keep them in separate pits. Unfortunately, subdivision development in the immediate area may have destroyed evidence of any additional contemporary settlements.

Sites in the lower Rouge River drainage that have been provisionally dated to the late fourteenth century include the Hamlin (MPP 1988), Faraday (Kapches 1981), Russell Reesor (Konrad and Ross 1974), Sewell (Berg 1976) and Archie Little 2 sites (ASI 2002), all of which have only been documented through surface collections and limited test excavations.

The Robb, Alexandra, and Burkholder 2 sites, on the other hand, are all thoroughly investigated, late-fourteenth-century villages. The Robb site is a roughly 2 ha village consisting of nine longhouses and an extensive midden on a slope above Milliken Creek, a tributary of the Rouge River (Kapches 1981:110–31; ASI 2010a). None of the longhouses overlap, and variability in the density of house wall posts as well as varying house orientations precludes ascertaining their contemporaneity. The nearby Fairty ossuary is thought to be associated with Robb; it was excavated in the 1950s and found to contain the remains of 512 individuals (Gruspier 1999), likely the deceased of more than one community, perhaps also those of the nearby Faraday and Alexandra sites.

Alexandra is located adjacent to a minor tributary of West Highland Creek. The 2.5 ha village consisted of seventeen house structures, of which fifteen represent permanent or year-round dwellings. The village has two overlapping phases of occupation, including eight houses in the southern portion of the site and nine in the northern segment. The southern houses were likely occupied first, as they yielded the earliest ceramic vessels and their walls exhibited evidence of rebuilding, while those in the north had not been rebuilt (ASI 2008a:124), perhaps a reflection of an early aggregation of two communities, one joining after the initial settlement of the village. Twenty-nine semisubterranean sweat lodges distributed between houses at the site suggest a focus on integration of the site inhabitants.

Burkholder 2 is a 1 ha village consisting of four parallel, contemporary longhouses situated on a high point of land between two tributaries of the Rouge River (ASI 2005a) (figure 3.2a). Limited investigations of the Burkholder 1 site, located less than a kilometer to the north, revealed evidence of a palisaded village, also approximately 1 ha in extent, likely postdating Burkholder 2 (ASI 2004). The Milroy site is a 0.8 ha village located on a tributary of the Little Rouge River. Limited excavations yielded high frequencies of Black Necked ware in the ceramic assemblage, suggesting that the site is late in the Rouge River sequence and dates to the early fifteenth century (Kapches 1981:71, 189).

There are no sites that postdate the early fifteenth century on the southern portions of the Rouge River and Highland Creek, the communities having likely relocated east to the Duffins Creek drainage, or possibly elsewhere.

Fifteenth-Century Occupation of West Duffins Drainage

In the early to mid-fifteenth century, there were at least eight Iroquoian villages occupying an area of twenty-five square kilometers on the Duffins drainage system. Most fifteenth-century sites are known primarily from surface collection and/or limited test excavations related to the New Toronto International Airport (NTIA) survey, which took place in the mid- to late 1970s (Poulton 1979). By the mid-fifteenth century, all of these small village sites were abandoned, their populations presumably coming together to form the large, heavily fortified Draper site (Finlayson 1985; Warrick 2008:136; see chapter 4).

The largest village sites in this cluster are the Pugh and Best sites, which are 2.8 and 1.8 ha in area, respectively. Because of its relatively large size, there is a chance that Pugh represents the fusion of two smaller, earlier communities. Both sites are defensively situated between two severe slopes. A continuous midden was identified in the eastern portion of the Best site. The 2 ha Wilson Park site lies just outside the boundaries of the NTIA survey area and has been subject to detailed test excavations to define its extent (ASI 2012b).

We know the most about the .5 ha Robin Hood and White sites, both of which have had most, if not all of their settlement plans exposed. The Robin Hood site was partially excavated in 1979, revealing four longhouse structures (Williamson 1983). The presence of numerous exterior house features and what appeared to be open-ended houses initially led to its interpretation as a series of sequential cabins constructed in the agricultural fields of a larger village and occupied in warmer weather only. Subsequent regional investigations have revealed that the early- to mid-fifteenth-century occupation of the area included numerous sites that contained four to five houses. An additional locus of high artifact density on the opposite bank of the creek suggests that another area of occupation is likely present. The White site encompasses two stream terraces, each with a cluster of longhouses (Tripp 1978), which on the basis of settlement and ceramic data, were interpreted to represent separate components. While possibly concurrently occupied at some point, the lower terrace appears to have been occupied longer than the upper. These and the other sites on West Duffins Creek were all abandoned during the mid- to late fifteenth century, their populations coming together at the Draper site over a period of ten to twenty years.

Coalescent Communities: The Draper and Spang Sites

The Draper site is situated on an open, flat terrace overlooking a steep western bank of West Duffins Creek. The site covers a total of 3.4 ha (see chapter 4, figure 4.1) and ceramic seriation and three radiocarbon dates (see chapter 4, table 4.2) place its occupation in the mid-fifteenth century. A defining characteristic of the village is the clear evidence that the main village palisade was expanded five times to incorporate new groups of aligned longhouses. There is evidence that Draper was embroiled in a significant degree of violent conflict with other communities during its occupation. The site's palisade was constructed with three to four rows of posts, and 287 pieces of scattered human bone were recovered, primarily from middens. Of these, 71% were cranial elements, 6 of which had been smoothed or perforated, presumably in order to manufacture skull rattles (Cooper 1984; Williamson 2007). One of the houses contained an interment of an aged male who had been scalped and speared in the chest and was found with the tip of a chert arrow point embedded in his right femoral neck (Forrest 2010a; Williamson 1978). These remains have been interpreted as those of a man who was attacked, mutilated, and his remains returned for burial within the village.

The Spang site is a partially undisturbed village approximately 3.4 ha in area. Little is known about its internal settlement pattern. Seven middens were located during the initial survey of the site. Preliminary excavations also revealed five rows of palisade posts adjacent to the steep break-in-slope along the site's eastern edge (Carter 1981). Based on analyses of the Spang site ceramics (Pihl, Birch, et al. 2011), it seems most likely that the site immediately predates the early-sixteenth-century Mantle site (see chapters 4 and 6).

There are at least four likely descendant villages north of Mantle, one in the upper Rouge and the others north of the Oak Ridges Moraine in the East Holland River watershed. These are discussed in chapter 7.

OTHER NORTH SHORE OF LAKE ONTARIO COMMUNITY SEQUENCES

Lynde and Harmony Creeks

Approximately twenty kilometers to the east of the Duffins Creek drainage is Lynde Creek, on which at least three villages have been documented. Joseph Picard is an unpalisaded, mid-fifteenth-century village that features at least nine longhouses distributed across an area of 1.5 ha.

To the west of Joseph Picard by a few kilometers is another 1.5 ha fifteenth-century village discovered in the summer of 2012. About eight kilometers south of it is the Waltham site, a fourteenth-century village for which only limited data are available. No late-fifteenth- or early-sixteenth-century successor villages have yet been documented in this drainage system, although there are late-fifteenth-century sites situated about forty kilometers further north.

To the east by another twenty kilometers is the Grandview site, a 0.8 ha village estimated to date to the late fourteenth or early fifteenth century. It was fully excavated in 1993 and was found.to contain twelve longhouses and three midden deposits (Williamson, Austin, and Thomas 2003). The site was not palisaded. The settlement patterns and ceramic distribution suggest three major building phases, involving the construction of four, five, and three houses in each phase. The likely successor to the Grandview community is the McLeod site, a 1.6 ha Late Iroquoian settlement. Limited excavations by Reed (1993) revealed portions of two longhouses; the fact that this site is twice the size of Grandview suggests that it resulted from the amalgamation of Grandview and another community. The antecedents of these communities are unknown. One Early Iroquoian settlement, the Short site, is situated about fifteen kilometers east on Bowmanville Creek (Williamson, Austin, and Thomas 2003:47).

Don River

The Don River drainage is located immediately west of the Rouge-Duffins Creek drainage (see figure 3.1). Most of the sites in the Don River drainage were occupied during the fourteenth and fifteenth centuries on the northern branches of the river. Only two village sites have been identified in the lower Don Valley (Moatfield and Jackes). It is almost certain that more settlements existed in this part of the drainage; however, many of these have undoubtedly been lost to urban development in the City of Toronto.

The earliest documented village is the turn-of-the-fourteenth-century Moatfield site. While the village itself has only been subject to test excavation, the associated ossuary was located on the perimeter of the site (Williamson and Pfeiffer 2003). It contained the commingled remains of eighty-seven people and represented the earliest community ossuary yet excavated; the remains have since been reinterred elsewhere. Much less is known about the Jackes site (Noble 1974) as it has been lost to urban development. Jackes, as well as the poorly known Doncaster 1 and East Don sites in the middle drainage, have been provisionally dated to the late fourteenth century (Konrad 1973; MPP 1986b).

A number of fifteenth-century sites in the Don Drainage have been subject to partial or complete excavation, including the Mill Street (ASI 2006b), Baker (ASI 2006c), Walkington 2 (ASI 2010b), and Hidden Spring (ASI 2010c) sites. With the exception of Hidden Spring, all featured single clusters of three to four longhouses, with one longhouse significantly longer than the others, perhaps representing the sociopolitical cores of the villages. The late-fifteenth-century Hidden Spring site, on the other hand, featured two overlapping longhouses each with a substantial midden, and several exterior activity areas suggesting a special-purpose site.

The ShurGain and Jarrett-Lahmer are two village sites, 1.0 and 1.2 ha in size respectively, located approximately three kilometers apart (DPA 1994, 2003). Both are situated defensively, on tableland whereby slopes form the site limits on three sides. Both sites feature palisades. At the Jarrett-Lahmer site, two extrapolated palisade lines located ten meters apart suggest the village may have at one point been expanded. Test excavations in the midden on the western slope of the site yielded sixty-four human elements, suggesting engagement in conflict and prisoner sacrifice (ASI 2001). The sizes of both sites as well as their ceramic assemblages suggest mid- to late-fifteenth-century occupations.

The McGaw site (ASI 2003; Pihl 2002) is a relatively undisturbed 1 ha early- to mid-fifteenth-century village. Limited test excavations have revealed seventeen mounded middens and densely occupied longhouses. Teston is a 1 ha village that has only been subject to test excavations. An ossuary associated with the site was discovered during roadwork in 2006 and was thought to have contained several hundred individuals (ASI 2005b). The Boyle-Atkinson site is also thought to have been approximately 1 ha in size. While incompletely excavated prior to its destruction, portions of eleven houses with various orientations were recorded (MPP 1987).

The Over site (DPA 1996) dates to the early to mid-fifteenth century and comprises two aligned clusters of longhouses, one with three houses and the other with four, both of which have one longhouse that is significantly longer than the others (figure 3.2b).

The Watford site is located in the upper reaches of the Rouge River but is spatially associated with the settlements in the Don River drainage. The village consisted of six houses surrounded by a single-row palisade, and a seventh house located northeast of the palisaded enclosure (Pearce 1997). Within the palisaded enclosure, four houses formed one aligned group in the eastern portion of the site (two of which overlap and could not have been occupied concurrently), and the two western houses form another aligned pair. The house outside the palisade may also be associated with this aligned pair, particularly if the palisade was constructed after the site's initial occupation, isolating this house, which at that point may have been abandoned. Palisades are rare on early- to mid-fifteenth-century sites, and the insubstantial nature of this palisade suggests that it may not have served a defensive function.

The McNair site (ASI 2012c) was a 1.0 ha village occupied during the middle of the fifteenth century. It was organized into two discrete loci separated by a large open area. The south locus consisted of three spatially separ-

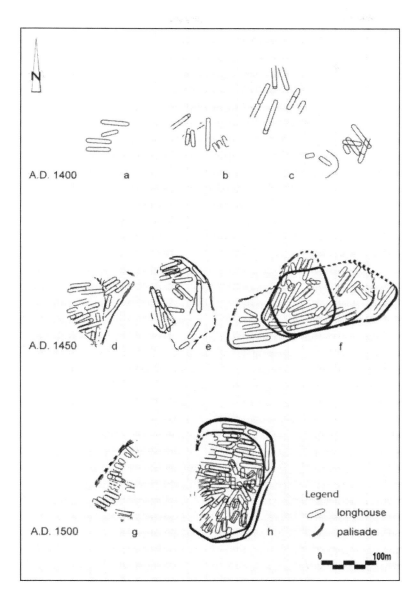

Figure 3.2.   Comparison of the size and layout of selected excavated Iroquoian villages on the north shore of Lake Ontario, ca. AD 1400–1600: a) Burkholder 2 (ASI 2005a); b) Over (DPA 1996); c) Hope (ASI 2011c); d) Damiani (ASI 2012d); e) Keffer (Finlayson et al. 1987) ; f) Draper (Finlayson 1985); g) Seed-Barker (Burgar 1993); h) Mantle (ASI 2012a)

ated and lightly constructed houses, perhaps occupied seasonally or for special purposes, while the other locus comprised five houses and two middens. Both loci featured open-air activity areas and fence-row formations. No evidence of a palisade was detected. It is possible that the occupation of the McNair site proceeded in phases, perhaps involving an initial brief occupation of the south locus followed eventually by a more substantial reoccupation. The four modified human cranial fragments recovered likely represent fragments of a human skull rattle and suggest the site was occupied during the initial period of heightened hostility in the fifteenth century.

The latter three settlements (Over, Watford, and McNair), and perhaps McGaw, ShurGain, and Jarrett-Lahmer, would appear to be early-stage amalgamations of groups of the size and composition of the Baker and Walkington 2 sites described above, or the White and Robin Hood sites in the Duffins Creek drainage to the east. As such, they may have necessitated more complex organizational structures in order to regulate decision making functions between constituent social segments. These sites may also represent the beginning of a settlement trend that set a cultural precedent for the large-scale amalgamations that occurred in the next generation.

The Hope site is distinctive in that rather than being composed of closely spaced pairs of aligned longhouses, it is composed of adjacent clusters of longhouses, separated by a seventy-meter-wide tract of land (and a stream) suggesting social or conceptual, as opposed to chronological, separation (figure 3.2c). The site is relatively large, covering 3 ha, 1.6 in the north and 1.6 in the south (ASI 2011c). The northern component contains six houses, arranged in pairs sharing a similar orientation. The southern component is slightly more complex and contains seven houses. The westernmost two houses are fairly small and contained within a semicircular fence line. Of the easternmost houses, two seem to have been occupied intensively though not concurrently, as they overlap. The remaining three structures appear to have been less intensively occupied; two of these overlap. The ceramic assemblages of both components are consistent with an early-fifteenth-century occupation, and there is no reason to suspect that the two components were not contemporary. Each group may have retained political autonomy while sharing a locale and together represent another form of small-scale coalescence prior to the larger-scale amalgamations of multiple communities.

The Orion–Murphy-Goulding site is situated on a branch of the upper Rouge River headwaters, in close proximity to the Don River drainage and its group of sites. It comprises two clusters of six and four houses respectively, separated by two hundred meters of unexcavated land. Originally registered as two separate sites, the close similarities in settlement patterns and artifact assemblages suggest that they may constitute the northern and southern extremes of a single village (ASI 1998, 2008b). The large size of the village led investigators to suggest it may represent an early coalescent site similar to Draper or Parsons (Andreae, Pihl, and Williamson 1998:9), although the site lacks a palisade and does not exhibit the compact village layout that characterizes those sites.

The Keffer site is a 2.5 ha village and has yielded the clearest evidence for significant levels of violence and village expansion among all sites in the Don watershed. Dating to the late fifteenth century AD (Finlayson et al. 1987), the initial village was composed of two clusters of aligned houses, which was then expanded to accommodate three, possibly four, new longhouses, arranged more or less parallel to the palisade (see figure 3.2e). Houses were simultaneously added and lengthened in the original core area, and the palisade was strengthened from one row to two.

Significant amounts of butchered and modified human bone were recovered from midden deposits at Keffer—more than a thousand pieces in total (Rainey 2002; Williamson 2007:200, 205). Of all the sites on the north shore of Lake Ontario, only Parsons (see below) had more scattered human bone recovered from nonburial contexts. More than 50% of the scattered human bone (excluding teeth) recovered from Keffer were cranial components, suggestive of the taking of trophy heads, and many of these cranial elements exhibited evidence of modification (polishing or perforating), further suggesting their use as items for personal adornment or ceremonial use (Williamson 2007:205).

While the site is certainly larger than others in the Don River drainage, it is smaller than the contemporary Draper and Parsons (Humber River) sites, which also constitute coalescent communities. The alignment of structures at Keffer suggests it is composed of three or four of the smaller fifteenth-century communities that occupied the drainage, having perhaps aggregated in response to pressures created by the formation of the larger Draper and Parsons communities to the east and west. With the abandonment of Keffer near the turn of the sixteenth century, the Don drainage was abandoned, concurrent with the main period of occupation at the Mantle site. While there are insufficient data to determine where the Keffer population relocated, it is possible that they amalgamated with populations from the Middle Humber drainage.

Humber River

In the Humber River valley, century-long settlement sequences have been reconstructed for at least two communities (P. Ramsden 1977; Williamson, Cooper, and Robertson 1998) (see figure 3.1), one spanning the fifteenth century in the middle Humber–Black Creek area and the other in the headwaters, spanning the mid-fifteenth to late sixteenth centuries. Each appears to have had a discrete ceramic manufacturing tradition in place for at least one hundred years (Robertson and Williamson 1998:149).

It appears that a number of small communities came together in the mid-fifteenth century to form a large, palisaded village aggregate at the Parsons site, in the middle Humber–Black Creek area. Our knowledge of the site sequence that led to the formation of the Parsons community begins with the late-fourteenth-century Black Creek site. This village was subject to limited excavations in the 1950s, revealing an unusual double palisade straddling two terraces adjacent to Black Creek, a tributary of the Humber River for which the site was named (Emerson 1954:123, 142). It is possible that upon the site's abandonment, the community relocated two kilometers upstream to the late-fourteenth- to early-fifteenth-century Downsview site (Emerson 1954:101–2; J. Wright 1966:101) and from there to the Parsons site in the mid-fifteenth century.

The nearby Riseborough site, encompassing an area of approximately 1 ha, is also a possible contributor to the Parsons community, as is the Emery site, a poorly known village located approximately four kilometers west of Parsons.

The 3.2 ha Parsons site is the largest and best-documented site in the Middle Humber sequence (Williamson and Robertson 1998). Based on settlement pattern data, ceramic seriation, and radiocarbon dates, Parsons was most likely occupied in the mid- to late fifteenth century. The portion of the site that has been fully excavated consists of an eighteen-meter-wide corridor traversing the core of the settlement. The relative position of structures in this area suggests that the village was laid out in a well-planned manner but had a complex occupational history, as not all structures were contemporaneous. Three structures were erected and inserted between the original longhouses, suggesting population growth and/or an influx of new inhabitants. The site is defensively situated on a broad promontory overlooking Black Creek and was surrounded by a formidable palisade. At the western edge of the site, the palisade consists of at least two rows of posts, one along the top of a fifteen-meter slope and the other on a terrace midway up the slope, similar to that documented at the Black Creek site. On the eastern edge of the village, the palisade consisted of seven rows. More than twelve hundred fragments of human bone were found inside and adjacent to midden areas (Robertson, Williamson, and Welsh 1998:52), many of which were burned cranial fragments (Williamson 2007:200). Perforated skull fragments that may have been worn as pendants (gorgets) or used as skull rattles were also found.

The ceramic assemblage and other aspects of the material culture, such as the recovery of a catlinite pendant, suggest either direct or indirect links to peoples originating farther afield. Nine percent of the vessels have been identified as having attributes originating among St. Lawrence Iroquoian populations to the east, a relatively high percentage compared with contemporaneous sites along the north shore. Interestingly, 75% of these eastern-style vessels originated in House 8 and associated refuse deposits along the inner eastern palisade (Robertson and Williamson 1998:147). These same deposits (House 8, associated middens, support posts, and one semisubterranean sweat lodge) produced the highest frequencies of scattered human bone from the site (75% of the total scattered human remains) (Robertson and Williamson 1998:148). Two intact adult crania were excavated from a refuse-filled depression in the area of the eastern palisade (Robertson, Williamson, and Welsh 1998:40–41). A craniometric analysis indicated that they closely resembled others from the Uxbridge site (Dupras and Pratte 1998), an ossuary situated to the northeast, considerably north of the Lynde Creek cluster, which points to feuding between the communities.

The earliest known settlements on the northern Humber River, where its headwaters flow south from the Oak Ridges moraine, date to the late fifteenth to early sixteenth century, concurrent with the period of widespread settlement aggregation and warfare on the north shore. This group represents the later occupation of the Humber River drainage.

The late-fifteenth- to early-sixteenth-century Damiani site encompassed an area of 1.5 ha and included a total of twenty-three house structures surrounded by a two-to-three-row palisade (ASI 2012d) (see figure 3.2d). The village was expanded from an original core settlement of sixteen aligned houses to incorporate seven more longhouses. The midden also contained scattered human bone, including burned cranial fragments.

The Boyd site is thought to be an early-sixteenth-century village estimated at 1 ha in extent. While Boyd has been subject to long-term small-scale excavations associated with field schools (Burgar 1990) and early investigations by the Ontario Archaeological Society (Donaldson 1962), little is known about its internal structure. Peter Ramsden (1977:216) thought Boyd was ancestral to Seed-Barker and contemporaneous with Mackenzie-Woodbridge.

The Mackenzie-Woodbridge site is thought to be an early- to mid-sixteenth-century village located slightly south of Boyd and encompassing an area of approximately 2 ha. It too has only been subject to limited test excavations; portions of seven houses and a multirow palisade have been documented (D. Johnson 1980:78). There is possibly one large continuous midden running outside of the palisade (similar to that found at the Mantle site; see chapter 4) and another interior midden that does not overlap houses or the palisade (D. Johnson 1980:83). An ossuary was reported less than a kilometer from the site (J. Wright 1966:1969), and a village cemetery was excavated on a sandy knoll at a distance of one hundred meters from the palisade (Saunders 1986; Williamson and Steiss 2003:108).

The Seed-Barker site is an approximately 2 ha village occupied in the early to mid-sixteenth century (Burgar 1993). While only 25%–30% of the settlement has been excavated, twenty houses have been identified, along with a seven-row palisade along the northwest boundary of the site (see figure 3.2g). Two segments of two rows and one of three suggest at least three reconstructions of the palisade. The well-planned organization of the settlement and lack of evidence for any expansions suggest that Seed-Barker may be more similar to the Mantle community than any other site on the north shore. As such, it is likely a consolidated community aggregate—the second generation of a community that may have initially come together elsewhere, perhaps at the Mackenzie-Woodbridge site, and then relocated to Seed-Barker. The multirow palisade surrounding the village suggests a concern for defense; no data are available on scattered or modified human bone from the site. The close spacing of the houses suggests a high population density. The presence of European metal and exotic ceramic vessels is discussed in comparison to the Mantle site assemblage in chapter 6.

The latest site in the Humber sequence is the Skandatut site, an early-contact-period village (ca. AD 1570–1610) encompassing some 2.3 ha (ASI 2012e) and situated approximately three kilometers north from Seed-Barker. Skandatut is the latest site in both the Humber and Don River drainages. The Kleinburg ossuary, situated across the river from the site, is thought to be associated with Skandatut and contains substantial numbers of European trade items of the same age as those found on the surface of the village site (Williamson and Steiss 2003:111). These two sites therefore represent one of the final moments in the ancestral Wendat occupation of the north shore prior to the migration of these communities northward to Huronia. On the basis of the first collections from the site, it was suggested that Skandatut's primary external ties were oriented toward the Neutral of the Hamilton-Niagara region, given the predominance of plain collarless vessels, which occur in large numbers on contact-period sites in that area. It was also suggested that it may have been through such terminal Toronto-area sites as Seed-Barker and Skandatut that the historically attested close relations that existed between the Tionontaté (Petun) and the Neutral were facilitated. Indeed, it is also possible, based on some of the ceramic vessel trends, that the Skandatut community represents a population that enjoyed external ties with those communities that relocated to the Tionontaté area along the shore of Georgian Bay.

Summary of North Shore Community Sequences

At the turn of the fifteenth century, Iroquoian settlement on the north shore of Lake Ontario was characterized by clusters of 1 ha sites scattered along major drainages. These villages were composed of three to five aligned longhouses (e.g., the Baker and Burkholder sites). Some sites have more than one aligned group of houses (i.e., the Robb, White, and Over sites), which may or may not have been occupied concurrently (see figure 3.2a,b,c). It may be that these villages were home to more than one lineage-based group. The Hope site represents one form of possible intermediate stage between smaller communities and the large, coalescent communities of the late fifteenth century (see figure 3.2c). Its settlement plan suggests that two populations shared a location and field systems but preferred to maintain spatial separation of their house groups. The settlement may have begun with that structure or resulted from immigration, either by populations from the local area or a neighboring drainage.

The initial development of larger village communities greater than 2.5 ha in area occurred in the mid-fifteenth century AD with the formation of the Parsons and the Draper sites, which appear to have been occupied concurrently (see figure 3.2f). The occupation of the Damiani and Keffer villages may have occurred slightly later, in the late fifteenth century AD, with their occupations possibly extending into the sixteenth century (see figure 3.2d,e). The lesser-known Mackenzie-Woodbridge site may be another example of mid- to late-fifteenth- and early-sixteenth-century aggregation. Permanent settlement on the Don River appears to have ceased at about the turn of the sixteenth century. In relation to broader historical processes of coalescence on the north shore, the precontact settlement trajectory in the Don River drainage differs from the pattern shared by communities on the Humber and Duffins Creek drainages. Nowhere in this drainage did communities reach the size of those documented on watercourses to the east and west. Yet, direct evidence for violent conflict in the form of butchered, burnt, and scattered human bone, interpreted as evidence of trophy-taking and prisoner sacrifice, is abundant on the mid- to late-fifteenth-century Draper and Parsons sites, as well as the Damiani and Keffer sites. While it is still unclear with whom these communities were engaging in conflict, feuds and raiding between villages on the north shore is a distinct likelihood, although the presence of ceramic vessels with design sequences originating in New York State and the St. Lawrence Valley may indicate either alliances or enmity with groups to the east and south. The scant evidence for scattered or modified human remains at Mantle as well as on the Mackenzie-Woodbridge site (Saunders 1986; Williamson 2007) suggests that large-scale violent conflict ceased on the north shore shortly after the turn of the sixteenth century, coinciding with the consolidation of large, aggregated villages that formed during the previous several decades. It would seem that, here, the consolidation of coalescent communities and the cessation of conflict were linked.

It is unclear what became of the people who lived at the Parsons and Keffer sites after their abandonment; they may have contributed to the populations aggregating in the headwaters of the Humber River and/or West Duffins Creek, or they may have joined groups living to the north in historic Huronia.

We also know of no settlements in Durham Region that postdate the mid-fifteenth century, although the presence of the late-fifteenth-century Uxbridge ossuary in northwest Durham suggests that there must have been similar-aged settlements in that region. It is also possible that portions of the populations that occupied the Grandview, McLeod, Joseph Picard, and Waltham sites migrated out of that region, perhaps north to Uxbridge, west to Duffins Creek, or east to the Trent Valley, another locus of late-fifteenth- to early-sixteenth-century settlement.

Finally, it should be noted that there are a number of Iroquoian sites on the lower reaches of the Credit River drainage about thirty kilometers to the west of the Humber drainage (figure 3.3). That sequence begins with the turn-of-the-fourteenth-century palisaded Antrex site, which has been completely excavated (ASI 2010c) and includes a number of fourteenth- and fifteenth-century villages and small, temporary, special-purpose sites that have had little to no investigation (Konrad 1973; Williamson and Pihl 2002; Robertson 2010). These include the fifteenth-century Pengilly site, which on the basis of limited test excavations has been interpreted as an overlapping series of camps or hamlets, if not a village, and the River site (MPP 1986a). The sequence ends with the Emmerson Springs (Hawkins 2004) and Wallace sites (Crawford 2003), both of which have yielded European items and date to the sixteenth century. The enigmatic 1 ha palisaded Beeton site is situated in southwestern Simcoe County on the Oak Ridges Moraine (Latta 1980). Subject to only limited test excavations in the 1960s and 1976, it yielded considerable quantities of modified human bone from middens and features a ceramic assemblage characterized by vessels with decorated necks. Thus, while the site appears to date to the mid- to late-fifteenth century, the apparent recovery of European trade era iron and brass materials from the site has led to confusion as to the site's date of occupation.

After the mid-sixteenth century, the only settlements remaining on the north shore of Lake Ontario are very large villages ranging from 2 to 4 ha in size in the northeast and northwest limits of the study area, including perhaps Emmerson Springs or Wallace in the upper Credit, Skandatut in the Humber headwaters, and Van Nostrand–Wright on the East Holland River. By shortly after the turn of the seventeenth century, the north shore of Lake Ontario was devoid of permanent settlement, these populations having relocated north to join the Wendat Confederacy and/or the allied Tionontaté nation.

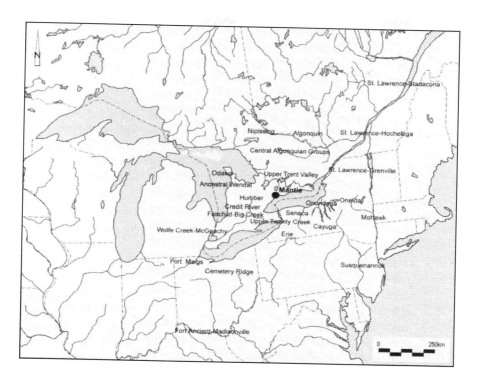

Figure 3.3. Locations of archaeological site clusters occupied contemporaneously with the Mantle site, ca. AD 1500–1550

OTHER ANCESTRAL WENDAT SITE SEQUENCES

Trent Valley

The Trent River drains a large portion of south-central Ontario, including most of the Kawartha Lakes and the supplying watersheds (see figure 3.3). By the early sixteenth century, there was a large ancestral Wendat presence in the Upper Trent Valley, which appears to have been a product of in situ cultural development (from sites lower in the valley) and perhaps also immigration from the Toronto and St. Lawrence Valley regions. A few eleventh-through fourteenth-century sites have been found along the shore of Lake Ontario (Kapches 1987; MacDonald and Williamson 1995), as well as two late-fourteenth-century villages in the Middle Trent Valley that are likely the result of in situ development from these and other earlier Iroquoian populations in the Rice Lake region (Sutton 1990:50).

The lower Trent Valley, between Rice Lake and Lake Scugog, features a number of villages that date to the late fifteenth century, including the Payne (Pendergast 1963; Emerson 1967), Waupoos (Pendergast 1964), Hillier (P. Ramsden 1977), and Lite (Pendergast 1972) sites. The ceramic assemblages from all of these sites are similar to those in the Toronto area (Sutton 1990:3), and while little is known about the former three sites, they are all smaller than the Lite site, which encompassed an area of 3 ha. While no settlement pattern data were recorded for the site, Pendergast reported that the remains of a multirow palisade were found at the brow of the hill on which the site is situated and that the presence of deep middens indicated a lengthy occupation. That intensified conflict and concern for defense might have influenced the location and fortification of this village was further underscored by the recovery of three skull gorget (rattle) fragments and a significant quantity of human bone scattered in the undisturbed middens (Pendergast 1972:35). Clearly, this community was also involved in the widespread conflict that characterized the mid- to late fifteenth century on the north shore of Lake Ontario and elsewhere.

There are also a number of fifteenth-century sites in the Upper Trent Valley, including the Hardrock site, located on the east side of Balsam Lake (P. Ramsden 1977:207, 255); the Jameson site (Sutton 1990:45); and the Quackenbush site, a 1.5–2 ha village located east of Stoney Lake in the eastern Trent Valley (P. Ramsden 1977). Limited excavations at Quackenbush revealed portions of two longhouses, two midden deposits, and a mass grave of individuals within one of the longhouses, all of whom displayed signs of interpersonal violence (Helmuth 1993), indicating that sites in this region were also embroiled in the widespread conflict of the period.

The primary occupation of the Upper Trent Valley took place in the late fifteenth through sixteenth century, in the vicinity of Balsam Lake. Thanks largely to the work of Peter Ramsden and his colleagues, we have a detailed record of excavated village sites, including the aggregated communities of Kirche (C. Ramsden 1989) and Coulter (Damkjar 1990), which are 2.5 and 3.3 ha in size respectively. Given the concern for defense and village expansion at both, a late-fifteenth-century date for their inception would better situate these sites in the macroregional processes of coalescence and conflict occurring to the west, although an early-sixteenth-century date would fit the patterns of conflict and village expansion to the east in the St. Lawrence River Valley. Moreover, the presence of European metal artifacts on the sites also points to a sixteenth-century occupation. While it is not known if the sites are coterminous or sequentially occupied, it is certainly possible that they are contemporary paired villages, a pattern observed in the Tionontaté, Onondaga, Cayuga, and Seneca regions.

The late-sixteenth-century Benson site has also been documented in detail. It was fully excavated in the late 1970s and has been subject to extensive, microscale analyses of its occupational and sociopolitical history (Fogt and Ramsden 1996; Ramsden 1978; 1988; 2009). The village covers 1.5 ha and contains twenty-three structures, meaning that it is not large enough to house the combined populations of the Coulter and Kirche sites. However, the gap in dates between these sites and largely unsurveyed tracts of land in the Kawartha Lakes means that other intermediate or contemporary as yet unknown communities may be located nearby.

Ceramic styles originating in the St. Lawrence River Valley appear on most sites in the Upper Trent Valley, suggesting that these village aggregates may have included populations derived from there, as well as from the local area and possibly the Toronto area. At the Benson, Coulter, and Kirche sites, some vessels were decorated with an amalgamation of Wendat and St. Lawrence Iroquoian attributes. Wendat vessel types were inscribed with attributes characteristic of St. Lawrence Iroquoians—large circular punctates, corn-ear motifs, and frontal lip notching were added to otherwise typical Wendat sherds (P. Ramsden 1990b:90). As such, it seems appropriate to believe that some potters were literally inscribing a new, hybrid identity into their ceramics, a practice that is also evident in assemblages from the Toronto area (see chapter 6).

Wendat accounts provided to early Europeans suggest that the abandonment of the Trent Valley occurred circa 1590, implying that the area was unoccupied after the occupation of the Benson site.

Huronia-Wendake

The land historically inhabited by the Wendat Confederacy, called Huronia by Europeans and Wendake by the Wendat, was also occupied in the early sixteenth century by a number of ancestral communities who had begun to form what would become the Wendat Confederacy. Huronia is generally defined as the lands between Lake Simcoe and Georgian Bay, corresponding to modern Simcoe County. Since research has focused on the late-thirteenth- to early-fourteenth-century colonization of Huronia and the postcontact period in attempts to identify historically documented villages and missions, we know less about fifteenth- and sixteenth-century settlement in Huronia.

By the early fifteenth century, there may have been as many as twenty-seven ancestral Wendat villages in Simcoe County (Warrick 2008), including completely excavated sites such as Wiacek (Lennox, Dodd, and Murphy 1986; Robertson, Monckton, and Williamson 1995), Hubbert (MacDonald and Williamson 2001), and Dunsmore (Robertson and Williamson 2003), all of which were unpalisaded, had complex occupational histories, and featured large numbers of semisubterranean longhouses. The late-fourteenth- to early-fifteenth-century Loughheed site (Haxell 2002) does have a multirow palisade—but no additional evidence for conflict was identified, nor have other sites yielded evidence of hostility. While Warrick estimated that by the early fifteenth century, there were more people living in Huronia than in the Toronto area and that more than half (some 7,300 people) were recent immigrants from the Toronto area (2008:182), the discovery and investigation of more than a dozen new sites in the Toronto region since his research was undertaken suggest that the population may have been more balanced than originally thought.

Despite the absence of evidence for hostility in fifteenth-century Huronia, the ethnohistoric record suggests that the initial alliance-building and confederacy formation occurred during the mid-fifteenth century, some two hundred years before the arrival of the Jesuits (Thwaites 1896–1901, 16:227).

THE ST. LAWRENCE VALLEY

Jacques Cartier encountered Iroquoian-speaking peoples living along the St. Lawrence River when he made his journeys in 1534, 1535–1536, and 1541–1542. He found them inhabiting two principal villages called Hochelaga and Stadacona, located near the modern cities of Montreal and Quebec, respectively. When Samuel de Champlain returned in 1603, these populations had disappeared, their former village sites reportedly no more than grassy fields (Biggar 1922–1936; Thwaites 1896–1901, 9:159). Their relocation was a regular feature of the larger processes of sociopolitical realignment that characterized the Northeast in the late precontact and early contact periods.

The settlement-subsistence system of the easternmost Iroquoians was adapted to their location on the St. Lawrence River, on the edge of one of the largest estuaries in the world (Chapdelaine 2004:66). St. Lawrence Iroquoians possessed distinct styles of material culture, which included finely made ceramic vessels, often decorated with circular punctates; a paucity of stone tools; and a well-developed bone and antler industry (J. Jamieson 1990:389).

There are six regional clusters of St. Lawrence Iroquoian sites in southwestern Quebec, southeastern Ontario, and New York State (Jamieson 1990), although artifacts associated with the St. Lawrence Valley can be found as far east as northern New England (Petersen et al. 2004) and as far west as the Toronto area (Powis and Williamson 1998).

That these populations also experienced the mid- to late-fifteenth-century period of hostility is evident at the Roebuck site, a 3.5 ha village protected by a three-row palisade and a semicircular earthwork (Wintemberg 1936:7). Within the palisade were no fewer than forty longhouses ranging in length from eighteen to forty-one meters, which could represent a peak population of 1,500–2,000 persons (J. Wright 1979:69), consistent with population estimates for the Draper and Mantle sites. More than three hundred pieces of butchered, broken, and burnt human bone were recovered from midden contexts at the site, including artifacts made of human bone such as perforated cranial rattles or gorgets, awl-like hairpins, and beads (J. Jamieson 1983:166–72). The settlement pattern data and evidence for conflict suggest that the Roebuck site likely dates to the mid- to late fifteenth century.

Sites that are contemporary with Mantle include the Mandeville site, an unpalisaded village situated on a terrace of the Richelieu River near its juncture with the St. Lawrence River (Chapdelaine 1989:50), and two village sites in the Grenville cluster, the Maynard-McKeown and McIvor sites, both of which exhibit evidence of village expansion and the amalgamation of two or more communities. At Maynard-McKeown, the initial two-row palisade was expanded at least once, and likely twice, including some rebuilding of the second multirow palisade, the excavation of a borrow trench, and construction of a strengthening embankment (Pendergast 1988). Recovery of a single European copper bead is in keeping with the small numbers of European-introduced goods that characterize other early- to mid-sixteenth-century sites in the region.

The McIvor site was expanded once and enclosed aligned longhouses in the excavated portion of the site, suggesting it was contemporary with Maynard-McKeown (Chapdelaine 1989:181). Scattered and modified human bone was recovered from the site, including a bowl manufactured from a human cranium (Chapdelaine 1989:211).

The evolution of the Wendat and Iroquois confederacies during the time that Iroquoian populations in the St. Lawrence Valley and northern New York were realigning suggests that these populations may have found it difficult to maintain an independent existence in opposition to larger confederacies (Engelbrecht 2003:143). Their only option was likely to join one or the other, an assertion supported by artifactual evidence for a strong St. Lawrence Iroquoian presence on some early and mid-fifteenth-century sites in the Trent Valley and Toronto area (P. Ramsden 1990b; Pihl, Birch, et al. 2011) and a northern New York/Jefferson County presence on Onondaga and Mohawk sites in the same period (Bradley 1987:85–87; Engelbrecht 2003:125; Snow 1995b).

THE NEUTRAL

The ancestors of the Neutral, called *Attiwandaron* by the Wendat, once occupied most of the north shore of Lake Erie and Niagara Peninsula. There is a long and rich history of settlement in southwestern Ontario, which involved the in situ development of ancestral Neutral populations for at least seven hundred years, starting in the Early Iroquoian period (Pearce 1996; Williamson 1985). Pearce (1996) has documented a site sequence spanning the fourteenth to sixteenth centuries, terminating in the coalescent, heavily defended mid- to late-fifteenth-century Lawson site.

The Lawson site is a 1.8 ha, partially excavated, largely undisturbed village situated on the Thames River. Exposed sections of the village defenses suggest that the original core village covered 1.4 ha and was surrounded by a three-row palisade, which included an earthwork or strengthening embankment on the northwest and southeast ends—those sides of the village not afforded additional protection by the break-in-slope and watercourses to the east and west. The village was later expanded an additional 0.4 ha to the north, and the palisade and earthwork reconstructed. Nineteen houses have been partially or fully excavated within the village, nine of which are located within the expanded portion and are closely spaced and arranged in a single parallel row. An additional eighteen houses have been estimated (Anderson 2009:39), although there may well be more present in the unexcavated portions of the village if the tightly packed, parallel pattern identified in the expansion continues throughout.

Wintemberg (1939:58) found more than 500 human bones or bone fragments scattered throughout the site. More recent excavations (as of 2004) identified 342 additional fragments. Recent reanalyses of all of this material, including refitting, suggests that these bone fragments derive from at least thirty-four individuals (Fontaine 2004:59–60). While nonviolent causes have been advanced for the deposition of remains in middens, such as material left behind when primary burials are processed for secondary burial (Anderson 2009:45), the fact that almost all scattered human bone and artifacts manufactured from human bone are found only on late-fifteenth-century sites is simply too robust a pattern across Iroquoia to ignore. Nine of the Lawson cranial pieces had been polished, ground, perforated, and otherwise modified into gorgets or rattles. Other similar fortified communities in southwestern Ontario include the fifteenth-century Southwold village site, which contained at least eighteen houses (not all of which were occupied at one time) surrounded by a palisade and earthen embankment (D. Smith 1977).

The Van Oordt Site is a late-fourteenth- to early-fifteenth-century special-purpose cemetery located in the city of Kitchener, containing up to thirteen young men, all exhibiting signs of interpersonal violence (Molto, Spence, and Fox 1986). One of the individuals had portions of three projectiles embedded in his skeleton. His remains also indicated the severing of both arms and one leg and beheading. On the basis of the arrangement of the bones and their condition, it was suggested that the burials were primary inhumations of dismembered individuals. The special care taken in the interment of these individuals, at some distance from their home community, seems to be consistent with the burials from the Draper (above) and Cameron (Wray, Sempowski, and Saunders 1991:211) sites, perhaps representing people discovered by their own villagers and provided with proper interment in accordance with Iroquoian beliefs that those who died violently could not be interred with the general population (Thwaites 1896–1901, 39:31; Williamson 2007). The discovery of so many individuals thought to have suffered from personal violence, perhaps resulting from one encounter, points to a critical level of hostility, possibly in a single attack, early in the fifteenth century.

By the early to mid-sixteenth century, ancestral Neutral populations had all moved east of the Grand River and settled in eight or nine major clusters in the western Lake Ontario and northeast Lake Erie basins, where preexisting ancestral Neutral populations were already well established (Lennox and Fitzgerald 1990:410–11). While this contraction may relate to the hostilities documented between the Neutral and the Algonquian Fire Nation to the west in the seventeenth century, it also coincides with the appearance of aggregated, heavily fortified villages and is in keeping with geopolitical processes unfolding throughout the Iroquoian world at this time.

Sites that were occupied concurrently with Mantle include the early-sixteenth-century Wolfe Creek and McGeachy sites on the Thames River near the western Lake Erie Basin (Foster 1990; Lee 1952); the mid-sixteenth-century MacPherson site in the Fairchild–Big Creeks cluster, consisting of a core village of at least six houses surrounded by a multirow palisade that was expanded and rebuilt at least twice to incorporate more than ten new structures (Fitzgerald 2001:39); the 2.5 ha Ivan-Elliot site; and a possible hamlet, the Raymond Reid site (Fitzgerald 1990b). In the Niagara Peninsula, the 1.2 ha Steele site may also date to the early-mid sixteenth century. Its palisade was expanded twice to incorporate a total of twenty-seven longhouses (Archaeologix 2006).

THE IROQUOIS

The precontact development of the Iroquois was not unlike that described for ancestral Wendat peoples living on the north shore of Lake Ontario. There was a gradual adoption of maize-based horticulture and a millennium-long transition to year-round settlements and longhouse dwellings (Hart and Brumbach 2003). Beginning in the fourteenth century, the archaeological record indicates increasing geographical separation and differentiation of discrete village relocation sequences into distinct local cultural traditions. These may be the early forms of the tribal nations that would go on to form the Iroquois Confederacy described in early European accounts. In the seventeenth and eighteenth centuries, the strength of the League of the Iroquois came in part from their political confederacy and from the fact that by the mid-seventeenth century, they had defeated or dispersed all of the other Iroquoian-speaking peoples in the Lower Great Lakes, including the Wendat-Tionontaté, the Neutral, and the Erie.

The fission and fusion of Iroquoian communities (Bradley 1987; Niemczycki 1984; Snow 1995b; Tuck 1971) and languages (Lounsbury 1978:336) suggest that the Iroquois nations developed in a complementary fashion, with repeated convergences, separations, and recombinations over the course of the fourteenth to eighteenth centuries (Engelbrecht 2003:112–13).

Seneca and Cayuga

While data on site size and relative chronology are lacking for delineating clear community sequences, these two nations seem to have strongly influenced one another's histories and are thought to have undergone parallel or convergent development during precontact times (e.g., Niemczycki 1984:37). Prior to the mid-fifteenth century, villages were less than 1 ha in size and were located on hilltops, perhaps suggesting an early concern for defensive siting. After the turn of the sixteenth century, site distribution narrows to traditional Seneca and Cayuga territories, and an increasing divergence of ceramic traditions suggests a distinct separation of each sociopolitical group (Niemczycki 1984:77).

There is provisional evidence for interaction between the ancestral Seneca and Neutral that may have involved occupation of the Alhart site, a village in western New York, by a population that originated in southern Ontario (Lenig 1965:71–72; Niemczycki 1995), although it is thought they were eventually destroyed or absorbed by the Seneca (Engelbrecht 2003:115). Excavations at the Alhart site (ca. AD 1440–1510) demonstrated that this community met a violent end, its houses burned and at least some of the inhabitants massacred. Fifteen skulls were found in a pit, all of which appeared to be male (Wray et al. 1987:248). Distinctive physical anomalies observed on the Alhart skeletal material also appear on human remains from the late-sixteenth-century Seneca Adams site, suggesting the incorporation of Alhart females into the Seneca population (Sempowski, Saunders, and Cervone 1988). The destruction of the Alhart site and absorption of a portion of its population might relate to the expansion of proto-Seneca populations into the territory between the proto-Cayuga and the region that the Ontario population inhabited, together with the increasingly hostile macroregional climate of the late fifteenth century.

The Seneca historically occupied two major villages with one or more satellite villages; each of these major villages is represented by an eastern and western site relocation sequence, beginning with Belcher and Richmond Hills, ca. AD 1525–1550, and continuing into the eighteenth century (Niemczycki 1984; Wray and Schoff 1953). At the Adams site (ca. AD 1560–1575), demographic, osteological, ceramic, and mortuary data suggest that the site was a product of the aggregation of several small local populations. The presence of defensive earthworks at Adams and the contemporary sixteenth-century Tram site suggest a concern for collective defense (Engelbrecht 2003:98).

The first distinct Cayuga settlements appear in the mid-fifteenth century, and the Klinko, Payne, Schempp, Indian Fort Road, Parker, and Carman sites may represent a single community moving south along the southwest side of Cayuga Lake (Niemczycki 1991). The late-fifteenth-century Fort Hill site includes an earthwork that is still visible today (Engelbrecht 2003:120), suggesting that the Cayuga were also embroiled in violent conflict as early as the late fifteenth century. Indeed, some of the earliest instances of defensive positioning of sites and other evidence for violent conflict occur in Seneca-Cayuga territory in the early to mid-fifteenth century and continue through the early sixteenth and seventeenth centuries. It is tempting to suggest that the early evidence for conflict at the Black Creek and Parsons sites in the early and mid-fifteenth centuries may be related to similar occurrences among the western Iroquois nations, potentially indicating that these two groups were engaged in hostilities.

Onondaga

Tuck (1971) and Bradley (1987) reconstructed the in situ development of the Onondaga from the eleventh century to the contact period. Oral accounts of Onondaga history speak of the consolidation of small, dispersed sites within the historic hunting territory of the Onondaga (Engelbrecht 2003:121; Fenton 1998:60; Tuck 1971:216). This territorial claim to ancestral lands may have also been the case among proto-Wendat populations on the north shore of Lake Ontario, whose site catchments often included previously occupied village sites (cf. MacDonald 2002).

Six mid- to late-fifteenth-century Onondaga village sites have been identified, all of which were defensively located and heavily fortified (Engelbrecht 2003:121). These sites include the Bloody Hill, Schoff, Keough, Christopher, Carley II, and Burke sites, most of which are 0.8 to 1 ha in size, with the exception of the Burke site, which may be up to 1.5 ha in area and an example of early aggregation of two or more communities (Bradley 1987:26). Tuck similarly suggests that the Christopher site may be an amalgamation of the Bloody Hill and Keough sites (1971:212). At the Bloody Hill site, a large cooking pit with the disarticulated skeletal remains of a middle-aged male has been interpreted as evidence of cannibalism (Engelbrecht 2003:44; Tuck 1971:113–14; Sublett and Wray 1970:17). The combination of defensive site location, aggregation, and evidence of hostility suggests the escalation of violent conflict in the mid-fifteenth century. While coalescence of previously distinct communities seems evident in Onondaga territory, their size is considerably smaller than those forming at the same time in the Toronto area (e.g., Draper and Parsons).

Five village sites have also been identified that are potentially contemporary with the Mantle site, of which three are relatively small (0.4 to 1.2 ha). The McNab and Barnes sites, however, may represent villages of unprecedented size, suggesting that they resulted from the coalescence of a number of villages. While McNab seems to cover 2.0 to 2.4 ha (Bradley 1987:34; Tuck 1971:161), the palisaded Barnes site has been estimated to be 2.4 to 3.2 ha in area, equivalent to other sixteenth-century sites in southern Ontario. Bradley (1987:34) suggests that these sites may represent the same community moving through time. Small quantities of human bone appear in midden deposits at the Barnes site (Bradley 1987:37), which together with evidence of a palisade might indicate their involvement with conflict. The Barnes site marks the first appearance of human face effigies on ceramic vessel castellations in Onondaga territory (see chapter 6), which, along with more diverse and elaborate smoking pipes, bone and antler combs, beads, and effigy pendants, represents the elaboration of material culture through interregional interaction, a characteristic of contemporary Mohawk (e.g., Cayadutta) and Seneca (e.g., Richmond Mills) sites.

Oneida

While a few sites predating the fourteenth century are adjacent to historic Oneida territory, thereby hinting at a possible in situ development, spatial proximity with the Onondaga and linguistic evidence of close ties to the Mohawk (Lounsbury 1978:335–36) suggest a diverse ancestry for the Oneida (Engelbrecht 2003:123).

Prior to the turn of the sixteenth century, site sizes were less than 0.5 ha, but by the early to mid-sixteenth century, a single large village aggregate formed at the 2.7 ha Olcott site. The slightly later Vaillancourt site covers 3.4 ha (Jones 2010a; Pratt 1976; Whitney 1970) and, together with Olcott, likely represents the footprints of a single community moving through time. Scattered human bone has been found in the middens of both Olcott and one of the antecedent sites (Pratt 1976:19), suggesting that warfare preceded coalescence.

Mohawk

The in situ development of the Mohawk Valley site sequence has been documented in detail by Dean Snow (1995b). In the early sixteenth century, the small, dispersed communities of the previous century amalgamated, and clustered site locations shifted from open, level lands to highly defensible positions protected by steep, elevated terrain and water (Kuhn 2004:159). Some sites were also protected by palisades and earthen embankments; modified skull fragments were found at one (Engelbrecht 2003:43).

These mid-sixteenth-century sites average 1 to 1.5 ha in area and are relatively small compared to contemporary communities throughout Iroquoia. They are typically composed of nine to twelve long longhouses thought to have housed between 1,500 and 2,000 persons (Snow 1995b), which suggests that while site sizes are smaller than the Draper and Mantle villages, for example, they may have housed equivalent-sized populations.

SUMMARY OF IROQUOIAN SITE SEQUENCES

This examination of local site sequences from across the Iroquoian world demonstrates that while general patterns that affected the greater region are apparent, each community also had a history tied to its specific local context. Three important trends emerge in all contexts and inform our understanding of the formation of the Mantle community: increasing levels of violent conflict, settlement aggregation and the consolidation of populations into integrated communities, and perhaps formative tribal nations. Settlement aggregation and consolidation of the Mantle community are discussed in detail in the next chapter, while at least one possible cause of violent conflict is explored in chapter 5. The relationship between these three trends is summarized in chapter 7.

Chapter Four

Community History

The formation of the community that occupied the Mantle site represented a process of population aggregation and sociopolitical transformation that, prior to the late fifteenth and early sixteenth centuries, had never before been seen in Iroquoia. Over a period of less than a century the inhabitants of many small villages came together to form large, aggregated settlements. In the Duffins Creek Drainage, as many as eight small villages coalesced at the Draper site. The community later relocated to the Mantle site. The social integration of these groups did not occur simultaneously with their physical aggregation. By comparing the built environment of the Draper site to that of Mantle we can see how, over two to three generations, the people occupying these sites went from thinking of themselves as members of distinct communities with discrete sociopolitical identities to thinking of themselves as members of a single, well-planned, and well-integrated community. While this volume frames these processes of settlement aggregation and social integration in the context of the historical development of Northern Iroquoian societies, a discussion of how this process compares to other examples of coalescence cross-culturally is presented elsewhere (Birch 2012).

This chapter will focus primarily on the occupational histories of the Draper and Mantle sites that have been reconstructed from settlement patterns: the distributions of post molds, features, and midden deposits, which reveal the layout and spatial organization of each village. Our ability to delineate large-scale patterns in settlement change through time derives from the systematic excavation of total settlement patterns, which have been recorded for many of the precontact villages on the north shore of Lake Ontario (see chapter 3), including the Draper and Mantle sites.

Architecture, or the built environment, is both a class of material culture and a symbolic expression of a larger cultural framework. As such, built forms both reflect and influence the social interactions that take place in and around households and communities (Bourdieu 1970; Hillier and Hanson 1984; Lawrence and Low 1990; Rapoport 1990). Changes in the way that people planned, constructed, inhabited, and transformed domestic and public spaces in their communities reflect the reproduction and negotiation of social relationships during the process of coming together. In this way, we can use changes in the size and placement of structures and spaces to help understand the social and political transformations that accompanied the initial coalescence and eventual consolidation of this aggregated community through successive generations.

These occupational histories also reveal how widespread social and political transformations visible at the regional scale were ultimately enacted through changes in practice at the community level. Evidence for changes in practices such as longhouse construction, the spatial organization of the built environment, and refuse disposal can be used to reconstruct social and political transformations in communities that had profound implications for large-scale, long-term transformations in Iroquoian societies.

Much of this discussion necessarily focuses on the reconstruction of the occupational history of the Mantle site. The Mantle community plan is a palimpsest; it contains many layers of overlapping structures, features, and palisades and is considerably more complex than any village site excavated to date in the Lower Great Lakes. This necessitated the development of a methodology for elucidating the occupational history of the site to determine construction sequences and diachronically record changes in the arrangement and composition of the built environment. The early phase of occupation is characterized by a highly organized village plan that emphasized the integration of the community, including an open plaza in the center of the village and two very large longhouses that had enduring and prominent presence in the community. Over time, this original community plan was altered, including a major contraction of the palisade and the infilling of the plaza with new residential structures. Comparing features of the Draper and Mantle sites helps in understanding the specific ways in which people constructed, inhabited, and transformed domestic and public spaces and the ways in which they reproduced and renegotiated social relationships during this process of community coalescence.

BEFORE DRAPER

As described in chapter 3, there is evidence of an unbroken history of Iroquoian settlement in the Rouge–Duffins Creek drainage beginning as early as the first millennium. By the early fifteenth century, there were eight village sites on West Duffins Creek and its tributaries. These include (from west to east) the Dent Brown, Robin Hood, Wilson Park, Best, White, Carruthers, Pugh, and Gostick sites (Poulton 1979). This increase in local site density was a part of the general pattern of regional population growth occurring during the late fourteenth to early fifteenth century (Warrick 2008:181–85; see chapter 2).

At this time, the distribution of Iroquoian village sites on the north shore of Lake Ontario began to exhibit an increasing east-west geographical division. Settlement focused on the Humber and Don River drainages to the west and Duffins Creek and its tributaries to the east, with the Rouge River drainage forming an unoccupied buffer zone between two clusters of sites (see figure 3.1). This clustering foreshadows the coalescence of local populations into large communities on the Middle and Upper Humber River, the West Don River, and West Duffins Creek in the late fifteenth and early sixteenth centuries.

Close ties almost certainly existed between the West Duffins Creek communities. All lived within an area of twenty-five square kilometers, with some villages located less than two kilometers apart. Their proximity and that of their horticultural fields suggests that these people would have had overlapping hunting and fishing territories and shared the same favored areas for collecting wild plant resources. In terms of personal relationships, affinitive ties of kinship and marriage, exchange and gift-giving between communities, and the possibility of cooperative trade and/or procurement of resources only available some distance from the local area (for example, Onondaga chert from the Niagara Peninsula) could have created close ties between these populations (Spence 1999). Shared religious practices and a common ideology that included ossuary burial (Williamson and Steiss 2003), a distinct ancestral Wendat mortuary practice, would have also helped ameliorate tensions that may have arisen in amalgamating these populations into a single village community. Each village, wholly or in part, may also have identified as being part of an imagined community (Isbell 2000) on the basis of their shared experiences and concerns within the local settlement landscape. This peer polity interaction and, perhaps, the formation of a particular local identity may represent an intermediate stage of sociopolitical organization between Middle Iroquoian populations and the coalescent communities and emergent tribal nations that characterized the late fifteenth and early sixteenth centuries. These interactions and associations undoubtedly would have laid the foundations for negotiating coalescence. By the late fifteenth century, these small villages were all abandoned, their populations presumably aggregating at the nearby Draper site (Finlayson 1985; Warrick 2000:449).

THE DRAPER SITE

The Draper site is composed of a main village covering 3.4 ha and a satellite longhouse cluster of 0.85 ha. An isolated structure, House 42, was located seventy meters south of the main village and fifty meters east of the south, exterior cluster (figure 4.1). The Ontario Archaeological Society carried out the first excavations at Draper in the 1950s, and a number of other investigations sampled portions of the site (Finlayson 1985:26; Hayden 1979:6). The first site plan was formulated by Peter Ramsden (1968), who indicated the location of all known middens, which were tested and compared for ceramic differences. Brian Hayden conducted detailed excavations at the site in 1973, including the exposure of two longhouses, one of which was systematically explored (Hayden 1979). The site was excavated in its entirety under the direction of William Finlayson in 1975 and 1978 (Finlayson 1985). At the time, it represented the largest salvage excavation of an Iroquoian village ever conducted; many of the techniques employed there, including using heavy machinery to systematically remove topsoil to reveal a total settlement pattern, influenced the methods used in Iroquoian village excavations today. This method of excavation results in a more or less two-dimensional site plan, though superposition of house walls, palisades, and features can often be discerned in the field, recorded, and used to reveal temporal relationships between features and built forms.

A report on the Draper site settlement patterns, including detailed house-by-house descriptions, was produced by Finlayson (1985). Unfortunately, material culture analyses were never integrated with the settlement pattern data but were produced separately, including reports on the ceramic artifacts (Pearce 1978a, 1978b, 1978c; Pihl 1984), flaked and ground stone (Pearce 1983; Poulton 1984), smoking pipes (von Gernet 1982, 1985), worked bone (McCullough 1978), faunal remains (Burns 1979), and plant remains (Fecteau 1978). Human interments were also documented (Forrest 2010a; Williamson 1978).

Formation and Growth of the Draper Village

The Draper village had its beginnings when one of the early-fifteenth-century communities on West Duffins Creek relocated to the site. Later, through a gradual process of settlement aggregation, the remaining communities joined the Draper settlement, one or two at a time, until the village reached its maximal form in the late fifteenth century. The main village underwent a

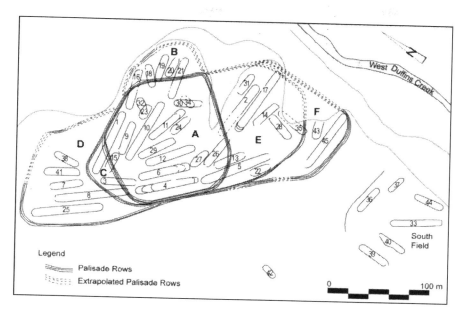

Figure 4.1.   Draper Site Settlement Plan. Redrawn from Finlayson (1985, figure 14)

total of five expansions following the construction of the original palisaded "core." Field observations noted that rows of palisade posts were obliterated where houses crossed them, meaning that all alterations to the main village were expansions rather than contractions. The letters A–F as shown in figure 4.1 were assigned to each segment of the main village (see Finlayson [1985:67–70] for a full description of each segment). Based on the relationships of segments to one another (e.g., it is obvious that segment C preceded segment D), estimated densities of house wall post molds, aboveground sweat lodge post molds, interior post molds, and pit (feature) density, Finlayson proposed that the relative order of segment additions was A (core), C, D, E, B, F. Segment E, or expansion 3, may have included the addition of two longhouse groups, one comprised of Houses 5, 13, 22, 26, and 27, and another cluster comprised of Houses 2, 14, 17, and 31. Interestingly, the east end of House 45, the longest house in the final expansion, lies beneath the final palisade (Finlayson 1985:385), meaning the house was contracted before the palisade was constructed, suggesting that the longhouse was built prior to the palisade's extension.

Similar wall post densities in the houses in each village segment indicate that they were added in groups, as opposed to being constructed one at a time. The density of post molds in the outlines of house walls has proven to be an effective method for estimating the duration of Iroquoian villages. The walls of Iroquoian longhouses are constructed using rows of either single or paired posts. The average number of posts per linear meter of wall is a direct measure of the effort expended on the construction, rebuilding, and repair of houses and is therefore an indirect indication of the relative longevity of the structure (Warrick 1988).

At the Draper site, the houses in the central portion of the village had the highest average wall post densities and were occupied longest. The average wall post densities in each subsequent expansion decrease in the order in which each expansion was added (table 4.1). Within each segment, houses that had been lengthened during their occupation (e.g., 4, 6, 10, 11, and 15) exhibited higher wall post densities in the longest-occupied portions (Finlayson 1985:178–79).

In the case of the south field, low wall post densities coupled with the fact that ceramics from this area seriated to late in the sequence supports the notion that the houses in the south field were added late in the occupational history of the site and could be considered to be the sixth village expansion. A choice was made not to expand the main village palisade to incorporate these additional houses. This decision may have been practical in that relocation of the village was imminent and the expansion of the palisade seen to be impractical or strategic in the sense that the group was socially or politically distant from the others.

Each house cluster is of a size consistent with one of the neighboring early-fourteenth-century communities. Warrick suggested a sequence of village additions based on the size of palisade expansions and corresponding

Table 4.1.   Draper Site Settlement Data

Expansion (Segment)	Size (ha)	No. Houses	Wall Post Density (posts per linear m)
Core (A)	1.19	9	5.9
Expansion 1 (C)	0.12	3	4.6
Expansion 2 (D)	0.76	5	4.1
Expansion 3 (E) (N + S groups)	0.77	9 (4 + 5)	4.1
Expansion 4 (B)	0.18	5	3.7
Expansion 5 (F)	0.39	4	2.9
South Field	0.85	6	2.8
Total	4.2	41[a]	4.0 average

[a]The isolated House 42 excluded.

sizes of contributing villages (Warrick 2008:136–37). His approach considers only the total size of villages and not the nuances of how much of that area was occupied at one time or other inferences derived from material culture or intrasite settlement patterns. This is problematic when one considers, for example, the two sequential phases of occupation at the White site or the suggestion that two previously distinct villages contributed to the third expansion of the Draper village. Moreover, the presence of black pebble pendants frequently associated with populations originating on the north shore of Lake Erie (Fox 2004; see chapter 6), together with significant quantities of ceramics associated with populations originating in the St. Lawrence Valley (approximately 2.5% to 5% of the total assemblage) (Pendergast 1981a), suggests that the population of the Draper site may have included peoples from distant communities.

As the village expanded, the palisade was extended and new groups of aligned longhouses were added to the village. We believe it is significant that each cluster of houses retained a form similar to those that characterized precoalescent villages, in that each segment contained a small number of aligned longhouses and each expansion remained spatially distinct. The residents of the Draper community retained a spatial separation between house clusters, even when it would have been more practical, in terms of the length of houses themselves as well as the additional palisade that needed to be constructed, to construct smaller houses and arrange them in a parallel fashion within the palisaded enclosure. The desire to retain spatial separation between groups of longhouses is most evident in Segment E, the third village expansion. In that case, two clusters of longhouses were added to the village, both with similar wall post densities and coinciding with a single episode of palisade expansion. These two groups of houses were, nevertheless, constructed fifty meters apart. While it would have been far more energy efficient to build these houses closer together, the perceived benefits of social or spatial separation seem to have outweighed the costs of the extra labor invested in constructing them farther apart. If one considers the two clusters of longhouses in Segment E and the southern satellite group as previously distinct communities, then all eight of the preexisting, early- to mid-fifteenth-century villages in the Duffins Creek sequence could be accounted for at the Draper site.

Given the emphasis on retaining the spatial separation of longhouse groups, it follows that the inhabitants of each longhouse cluster were more closely related to one another than they were to the inhabitants of the other segments. This is consistent with our interpretation of the Draper site not as a single village community, at least not in its initial form, but rather as a settlement composed of multiple small groups sharing a palisaded compound. The areas between the house clusters were interpreted as plazas (Finlayson 1985), but these areas were most often used for refuse disposal. There is no evidence that they should be regarded as public spaces in any other sense. Each segment of the Draper village may have retained a distinct social and political identity. The village inhabitants would have had to negotiate how to live together in a settlement considerably larger than any of them had experienced previously. They would have had to develop social and political mechanisms for reaching decisions regarding the challenges and opportunities in making the new, much larger village "work." This may have initially involved representatives of each house cluster meeting as a council when necessary. A formal village council, with all of its attendant rules, rankings, and protocols may have developed gradually over time. The social and political relationships between community members and social units would thus have developed over time with repeated negotiations that, given the multiple episodes of village expansion, would have involved increasingly complex discussions as new populations were added to the mix.

It is also possible that, for a time, each segment continued to farm the fields associated with their previous village. The establishment of new fields around the Draper site, fields expansive enough to sustain the large amalgamated population of the village, would have taken many years to clear and plant. There may have been a transitional time in which women returned to their natal villages (possibly accompanied by males for protection if the threat of raids was significant) in order to continue to plant, tend, and harvest their previous fields.

Indeed, the process of community relocation would have been exceedingly complex and as such subject to detailed planning and implementation. Such moves would have involved scouting for and evaluating potential new village locations. While not visible in the archaeological record, supernatural factors such as omens, dreams, and the presence or significance of particular plants or natural features may have also played a role in decisions about where and when to relocate. Preparation of the site, clearance of agricultural fields, felling timber for houses (the latter two tasks being mutually beneficial), construction of houses, and eventually, the movement of people and their possessions would have required a significant expenditure of time and effort. It is likely that young adults, the strongest members of the community, would have made the move first, with others following when the new village was ready for habitation. While this would have been a significant undertaking for a single community of 200–250 people with a relatively simple political structure, perhaps organized around one or more lineages, the scale and complexity of the decision making processes would have increased with any corresponding increase to the size of the community. It would seem unlikely that the eventual aggregation of groups from the local area had been firmly decided prior to the construction of Draper, given the ever-expanding palisade to accommodate new additions and the construction of an initial palisaded core.

As discussed in chapter 3, this settlement strategy was adopted through-out southern Ontario and New York State in the late fifteenth and early sixteenth century and correlates with other evidence for violent conflict. What is of considerable importance here is not only why people came togeth-er into larger social formations, but how these newly aggregated populations learned to live together in a single large village community. Once the deci-sion had been made to aggregate with one or more other groups, new strate-gies for facilitating and maintaining larger coresidential populations would have had to be devised and incorporated. The larger size of communities would have affected decision making in individual households and sociopoli-tical relationships with other communities across the Lower Great Lakes. These peoples may have struggled to balance the advantages of living in larger communities, such as mutual defense or a richer social and ceremonial life, with the disadvantages, such as pressure on local resources and the deleterious health effects (i.e., environmental contamination, communicable diseases, pests) of densely populated settlements. The aggregated community that formed at the Draper site appears to have met these organizational chal-lenges and remained together as a single, consolidated community through several village relocations. The Draper site itself was abandoned after ap-proximately twenty-five to thirty years of continuous occupation. There is no evidence that the site was reoccupied. The presence of middens overlying some of the houses in the central portion of the site, however, suggests that the core was abandoned while other areas of the site continued to be occu-pied.

THE SPANG SITE

Understanding with confidence the place of the Spang site in the West Duf-fins Creek sequence is challenging because so little of the site has been excavated. Spang is a large, 3.4 ha village located approximately 2.5 km north of Draper and 2.5 km south of Mantle, on a tributary of West Duffins Creek (see figure 3.1; Poulton 1979). The site was subject to surface collec-tion and limited excavations in 1978 and 1979 that exposed sections of a multirow palisade, portions of five longhouses, and a hillside midden deposit (Carter 1981). The site location straddles an agricultural field and a woodlot. As a result, approximately one-third of the site remains undisturbed.

There are three possible hypotheses regarding the position of Spang in the local site sequence, including its being contemporary with Draper, its post-dating Draper and being settled by a portion of the Draper population, or its being the village to which the entire Draper population relocated. A reanaly-sis of a sample of 1043 rim sherds from the site indicates it is most similar to the latest expansion at Draper, seriating to the late fifteenth century between

Draper and Mantle (Pihl, Birch, et al. 2011; see chapter 6). St. Lawrence Iroquoian and Iroquois vessels are present in smaller quantities at Spang than at Draper, which may signal changes in interregional interaction in the late fifteenth century but may also be a function of the small size of the assemblage recovered in the 1978 and 1979 excavations.

The possibility that the site was contemporaneous with Draper is unlikely, as there are no known villages that could have contributed to its formation. All of the local precoalescent communities are required to model the formation of Draper. It should be noted that this is unlikely to have resulted from incomplete survey coverage, since the entire region has been subject to intensive survey in advance of a large planned commercial airport (Poulton 1979). Even had villages been available to model its formation, there are serious questions about the ability of local resources to sustain two large populations concurrently in such close proximity (Carter 1981:8; Heidenreich 1971). Given the similar extent of the site to that of Draper and Mantle, Spang could have been home to as many as 1,500 persons. It is, therefore, most likely that Spang postdates Draper, as has been suggested by other researchers (Finlayson 1985:434; Warrick 2008:136). The similar sizes of the three sites and the fact that 95% of the estimated Draper population is accounted for at Mantle (see below) suggest that these are three consecutive sites occupied by the same population.

The presence of a multirow palisade situated at the top of a steep break-in-slope, which we assume completely enclosed the Spang site, indicates that defense was a concern for the community. Moreover, sixteen pieces of human bone were recovered from the 1978 and 1979 excavations, including fourteen skull fragments, one of which has a smoothed edge suggesting it may have been part of a skull rattle (Carter 1981:37). The distribution of human remains is similar to those recovered from Draper and suggests that captive sacrifice and the taking of trophy skulls was practiced by community members, indicating their continued involvement in widespread conflict.

Warrick (2008:137) suggested that the Draper site was occupied from AD 1470 to AD 1500. Now that we have radiocarbon dates from the Mantle site (table 4.2) along with ceramic seriation suggesting Mantle was occupied at the beginning of the sixteenth century, the Draper, Spang, and Mantle sites have to be accommodated within an eighty-year period between AD 1450 and AD 1530. This suggests that the three sites were each occupied for twenty-five to thirty years. Within this scenario, the Draper community relocated to the Spang site and then to the Mantle site around the turn of the sixteenth century or shortly thereafter.

THE MANTLE SITE

The Mantle site is located on the east bank of Stouffville Creek, a tributary of West Duffins Creek (see figure 3.1), 2.5 km north of Spang and five km northwest of Draper. The total area of the site covers 2.9 ha. Two radiocarbon dates on carbonized maize kernels (table 4.2), together with ceramic seriation (see chapter 6), indicate that the site was likely occupied in the early sixteenth century, which is consistent with the settlement pattern data. While admittedly provisional at best due to the problem of multiple intercepts at this general time period, these dates can be interpreted to be consistent with the period during which we believe the site was occupied. The presence of a single wrought metal object, an iron celt of Basque origin, and only two European copper beads, suggests that the site could not have been occupied any later than the mid-sixteenth century, when European trade goods became

Table 4.2.   Radiocarbon Dates

Site Name, ^{14}C Lab No., Sample	^{14}C Yrs ± σ B.P.	δ^{13}C ‰	cal AD Yrs (1σ)	cal AD Yrs (2σ)
Draper site, S-860, charcoal	405 ± 65		1435–1521 (0.73)	1421 −1639 (1.0)
Draper site, S-861, charcoal	570 ± 95		1299–1369 (0.60) 1380–1428 (0.40)	1257–1512 (0.99)
Draper site, S-862, charcoal	430 ± 85		1414–1522 (0.74)	1390–1649 (0.96)
Draper site, S-863, charcoal	495 ± 65		1392–1458 (0.83)	1377–1518 (0.74)
Mantle site, Beta-217158, carbonized maize	340 ± 40	-9.6	1487–1527 (0.34) 1554–1604 (0.44)	1462–1642 (0.95)
Mantle site, Beta-217159, carbonized maize	370 ± 40	-7.6	1453–1521 (0.67)	1446–1530 (0.53) 1539–1635 (0.47)

Notes: Sample info for the Draper site obtained from the Canadian Radiocarbon Database (CARD) (Rutherford, Wittenberg, and Wilmeth, 1979). Calibration by CALIB 6.0.1, calibration data set: intcal09.14c (Reimer, Baille, 2009).

more common and abundant on Iroquoian village sites (Fitzgerald 1990a). More details about this iron object and its implications regarding regional interaction and exchange networks are explored in detail in chapter 6.

A significant difference between Mantle and its antecedents is the limited presence of scattered or modified human bone from Midden 1 or posts and features. Compared to the hundreds of skeletal elements found on sites dating to the previous half century, only twenty cranial fragments with some evidence of modification in addition to a few postcranial elements were found at Mantle. This suggests that hostilities lessened at least for this community at this time.

Discovery and Methods of Excavation

The Mantle site was not documented until 2002, when the presence of a large Late Iroquoian site on two lots slated for development immediately south of the town of Stouffville was made known to personnel from Archaeological Services Inc. (ASI 2012a). As with most Northern Iroquoian villages, much of the Mantle site lay in an area that had been cultivated for the last 150 years. Aside from a strip of land approximately ten to fifteen meters wide running north-south along the western edge of the site, the entire area of the village had been subject to repeated plowing, resulting in a disturbed layer of topsoil some 25–30 cm deep, which obliterated most of the living floors and primary contexts in the plow zone. Below the plow zone, posts and pit features remained well preserved and their contents intact. The unplowed western portion of the settlement along the creek was also disturbed to varying degrees, first by a nineteenth-century mill, including a dam and millpond located adjacent to the northwest portion of the site. When the mill ceased operation in the 1920s, the property was converted to a farm. The twentieth-century farm complex included a laneway leading to the house, barn, and drive shed. Prior to the beginnings of the cultural resource management project, these structures were demolished, further impacting the western edge of the site.

Several surface collections resulted in the recovery of 18,000 artifacts. The next stage of investigation involved the sampling of one-meter units in areas of high artifact density referenced to a grid covering the estimated site area. Once the site limits, some settlement patterns, and areas of high artifact density were identified, the topsoil of the entire site was systematically removed to just above the undisturbed subsoil using heavy machinery. These excavations resulted in the documentation of ninety-eight longhouses, one large midden feature on the slope adjacent to the creek (Midden 1), a multi-row perimeter palisade that was constructed in three separate phases, and a linear trench midden situated parallel to the late phase palisade (figure 4.2). More than 150,000 artifacts, 60,000 individual palisade and house posts, and over 1,500 features were recorded. All subsurface features including post molds, pits, and hearth features were mapped with reference to the site grid. All features and post molds greater than 15 cm in diameter were excavated by hand and recorded in profile or in quadrants depending on the nature of the feature. The site turned out to be rather shallow in character, leaving fewer hearth features than might be expected. The high density of post molds, features, and artifacts recovered from both surface and excavated contexts, nevertheless, suggests a very intensive occupation relative to many other excavated Iroquoian villages.

Unraveling the Occupational History of the Mantle Site: Methods

The complexity of the site settlement patterns necessitated the development of a creative methodology for elucidating its occupational history. The sheer number and degree of overlapping longhouses and other features meant that houses could not be numbered in the field. The identification of individual houses, palisade phases, and interior and exterior activity areas took place postexcavation, using maps of the settlement plan prepared by Andrew Clish, cross-referenced with records of each five-meter square and feature excavated. While not all structures may have been houses in a strictly domestic sense, they were labeled as houses in accordance with common terminology used in Iroquoian archaeology.

As demonstrated in chapter 3, many Iroquoian villages have multiple identifiable phases of occupation. At Mantle, the identification of occupational phases is complicated by the sheer volume of overlapping structures. In some areas as many as five houses were constructed in a single location (figure 4.3, Houses 48, 49, 50, 51, and 52). In order to understand transformations in the occupational history of the Mantle site as a whole, sorting the entire village into "early" and "late" stages based on the first and third (or final) phases of the palisade was the logical way to approach how the layout of the site changed over time. The second palisade phase was omitted from this phasing because no structures or key features crossed it and because the first, outermost palisade constructed on the east side of the village was contracted very early in the site's occupation. Because the construction, deconstruction, and relocation of structures would have been ongoing processes, some longhouses were assigned to both the early and late phases, early-mid, or mid-late, reflecting their occupation throughout or partway through the total duration of the village's life (ASI 2012a).

We acknowledge that the "early" and "late" phases of occupation are archaeological constructs. The actual temporal rhythms of construction, maintenance, and deconstruction of structures and palisades would not have followed these abstract phases. The early and late phases of the Mantle village are schematics that permit comparisons between the village plan as it

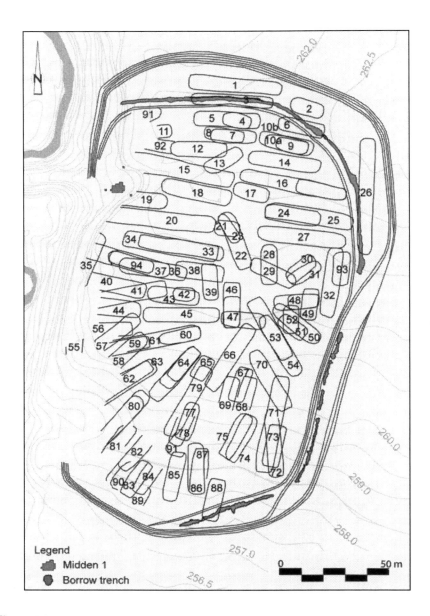

Figure 4.2. Mantle Site Settlement Plan

was originally conceived and constructed, and how it came to be after more than a decade of sustained occupation. These schematic plans also facilitate

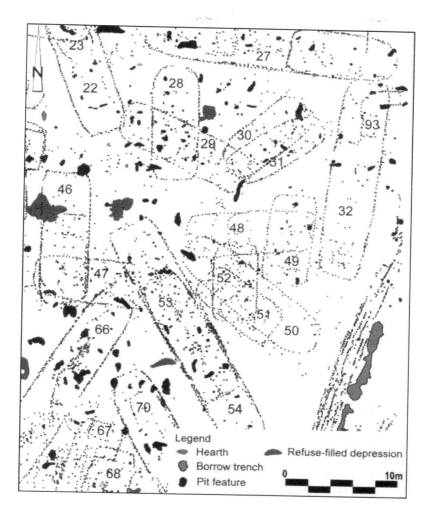

Figure 4.3. Section of the central portion of the Mantle village illustrating the complex nature of the site's settlement pattern

comparison between the Mantle and Draper sites within the West Duffins Creek site relocation sequence, as well as between other Iroquoian sites and site sequences in the Lower Great Lakes.

Multiple criteria were used when assigning a longhouse to a particular phase, including superimposition and fit within palisades, house walls that crossed over or lay under features, longhouse alignment and distance from adjacent houses, and the density of wall posts and features, both of which are known to be time dependent (Warrick 1988). When possible, longhouses with similar orientations and consistent spacing were grouped together and placed in the same phase. The superimposition of longhouses was used to determine the order of construction or deposition (particularly when one structure had already been assigned to a particular phase based on a combination of other factors, as outlined above). The insights of Andrew Clish, the field director who supervised excavations at the site for three years, were invaluable in this endeavor.

As noted with regard to the Draper site, the density of posts used in the construction and repair of houses can be used as a relative measure of how long a structure was in place. The average wall post densities of the longhouses at Mantle were important in reconstructing and interpreting the occupational history of the village. The density of house posts per linear meter of house wall was calculated by measuring undisturbed wall segments deemed representative of the entire structure, counting the number of posts in those segments, and dividing by the meters in each segment to produce a figure for the average number of posts per meter. This reduced the potential for counting errors where house walls overlapped or were disturbed. House ends often contain fewer posts than walls and therefore do not provide an accurate measure of post density. The average wall post density could not be calculated for some houses, particularly in the southern part of the village where soil qualities were poor.

When house sizes, sorted by length, are compared to the average wall post densities, and examined on a house by house basis, certain patterns emerge(table 4.3). Some of the longest houses exhibit considerable evidence for rebuilding or maintenance (figure 4.4). Houses 15 and 20, both estimated to exceed 50 m in length, have the highest wall post densities at the site, 6.8 and 7.9 posts per meter, respectively. Conversely, many of the smaller houses at the site, those less than 30 m in length, have uniformly low post densities. For example, House 21, a very small structure (only 11.4 m in length) has a wall post density of 2.7 posts per meter. Houses 48 through 52, all of which are superimposed and range between 13 and 25 m in length, have wall post densities between 2.2 and 3.2 posts per meter. This suggests that they were not occupied for as long as the houses that were rebuilt and may have been only seasonally or temporarily occupied.

A comparison of wall post densities for some of the longest-lived houses at each site (Draper site Houses 6 and 12 had 7.5 and 7.4 wall posts per meter, respectively [Finlayson 1985:183], Mantle site Houses 15 and 20 had densities of 6.8 and 7.9 wall posts per meter, respectively) suggest that these two villages may have been occupied for a similar length of time, although evidence that midden deposits overlay house walls and living floors in the Draper village core suggest they were unoccupied prior to the abandonment of the site. It may also have been the case that some houses at Mantle were

Table 4.3. Mantle Site House Lengths and Wall Post Densities

House Length	No. Houses	Average wall posts per m	STDEV
Greater than 40 m	15	4.4	1.75
30 – 39.9 m	13	3.9	1.23
15 – 29.9 m	39	3.3	0.97
Less than 14.9 m	7	3.2	0.52

Note: Incomplete or heavily disturbed houses omitted (*n*=74).

occupied before others in the same phase of occupation. These contingencies make definite estimates of village duration difficult based on wall post densities alone.

Advance Occupation at the Mantle Site

There are two structures that stand out as possibly being among the first constructed at the site. House 13 (see figure 4.4, upper right) is a relatively small structure (18.9 m long) located in the northern portion of the village, and on the highest topographic ground. The orientation of House 13 (56 degrees east of north) does not correspond with the other houses in the area (90–99 degrees east of north), and it is superimposed by Houses 15 and 12, two of the longest-occupied structures in the village based on their wall post and feature densities. Both a large feature and a living floor in House 12 superimpose the north wall of House 13; all of the House 13 wall posts were identified in the subsoil below the features, not in their fill or cutting through the living floor of House 12. As such, House 13 predates House 12, suggesting that House 13 was constructed early in the village's occupational history. It may have been used by advance work teams or scouts. House 13 had a relatively high wall post density (5.4 posts per meter) which suggests repair or rebuilding, indicating that it may have stood in place for some time prior to being dismantled.

The second structure that is early in the village's occupation is House 26 (figure 4.5). It is oriented 2 degrees east of north, adjacent to the palisade in the northeast corner of the village. While House 26 is among the longest houses (54.8 m), it is completely devoid of internal features, suggesting a temporary occupation. This longhouse may have functioned as a sort of "construction trailer" used for housing work parties or possibly storing building supplies. Two gaps in the early phase palisade are positioned at either end of this house and may have functioned as entrances to the early village. A large, exterior hearth feature in the center of one of the gaps may be related to this entrance. House 26 lies outside the late village palisade; wall posts were

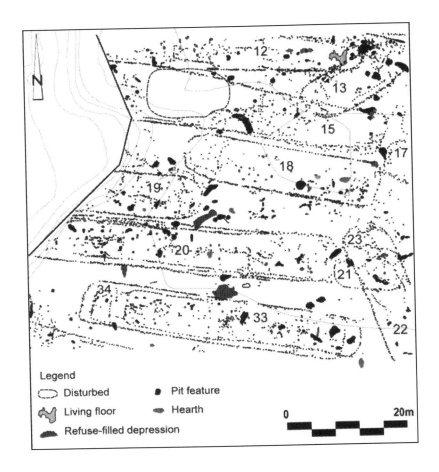

Figure 4.4.   Houses 15 and 20 and adjacent structures

identified under the borrow trench that surrounded the village in its final
iteration, but not in the fill of that trench, suggesting that it was dismantled
prior to the contraction of the late phase village.

For the entire duration of its occupation the Mantle village was surrounded by a palisade. In contrast to other late-fifteenth- to early-sixteenth-
century sites in southern Ontario, which expanded during their occupation,
the palisade surrounding the Mantle site was contracted twice. We know this
because houses associated with the early village are obscured or overlain by
later phases of palisade construction and by the borrow trench that surrounded the third and final phase of palisade construction (e.g., Houses 3, 6,
26, and 88). In some sections there appear to be as many as seven rows of
palisade posts, though this is the result of maintenance and successive phases

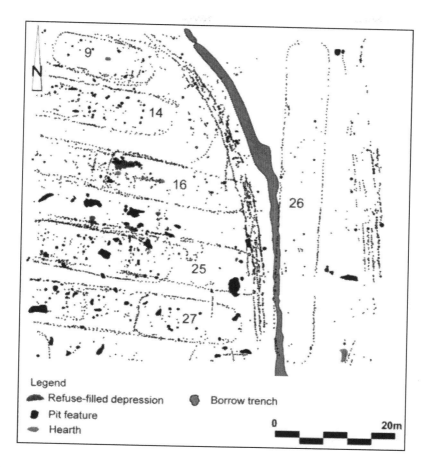

Figure 4.5. House 26 surrounding structures and Context, Mantle Village

of palisade construction. Engelbrecht (2009:180) has suggested that any more than three rows would likely have been redundant. The earliest phase of the village was surrounded by a palisade that was comprised of between one and three (or four) rows of posts. It seems possible that the palisade surrounding the village was constructed prior to the majority of the houses, in that the initial palisade, in the southeast corner of the site (see figure 4.2), did not stand very long in its original location. This section of palisade is very irregular in construction; there are between one and four rows of posts, and some are spaced irregularly. The soil in this area was very gravelly, making it potentially unstable and not well suited to anchoring the palisade firmly in place. It was likely moved relatively soon after construction, reducing the size of the palisaded enclosure by 460 m^2 from an initial size of 2.9 ha to 2.5

ha. Throughout the village, houses are built approximately ten meters from the palisade, creating sufficient space to protect the houses should any enemies have attempted to set fire to the palisade. It also created a space for movement and defense from within the palisade.

The Early Village Plan

The most striking feature of the layout of the early phase of the Mantle village is the high degree of structural organization and integration in the arrangement of longhouses (figure 4.6). In the northern two-thirds of the site, where the topography is relatively flat, houses were constructed perpendicular to the creek in parallel and paired rows. Although the houses vary in length, they generally conform to the same roughly east-west orientation. As one moves counterclockwise around the village, this parallel arrangement continues to about two-thirds of the way southward, where house orientation begins to shift to a more north-south alignment. Taken as a whole, the arrangement of structures in the village is radial, with longhouses arrayed around a central area where the footprints of a number of small, superimposed houses were identified. This shift from an east-west to a north-south orientation corresponds to a change in topography. The east-west-aligned houses in the northern portion of the village are situated on relatively high, flat ground, whereas the houses in the southern portion of the village are situated on a six-meter drop in slope. Excavations in this southern, sloping portion of the village were hampered by gravelly soil conditions that made the identification of posts, and therefore the identification of structures and phasing, difficult. The large number of superimposed houses in this southern area may have been due in part to these poor soil conditions, which made post placement difficult and caused wall posts to shift over time, requiring the frequent replacement of structures.

Houses 15 and 20 (see figure 4.4) were likely very prominent structures in the village from the time of their initial construction, as there is no evidence of either having been extended. They are also favorably situated on the highest elevation. This height would have given them a commanding presence in the village, and the roofs of these houses would have been visible from beyond the southern limit of the palisade. The very high wall post density in Houses 15 and 20 indicates that they experienced significant rebuilding. This would have involved the dismantling of entire house walls and their reconstruction in precisely the same location. This was not the case for most other houses in the village, which were dismantled between the early and late stages and new houses constructed on the same location but with slightly or dramatically different footprints. The persistent presence of Houses 15 and 20 implies an enduring significance in the community for the structures, their location, and perhaps the lineages that occupied them. The

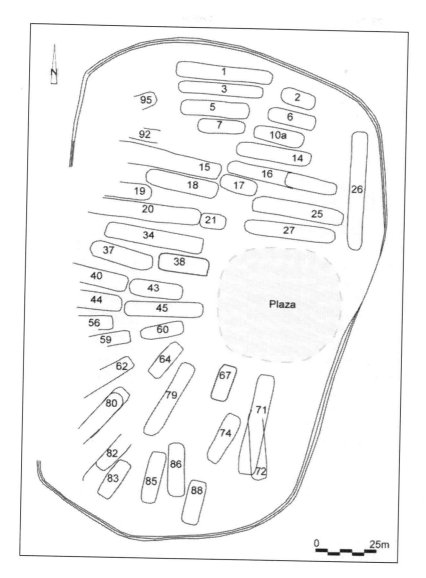

Figure 4.6. **Reconstruction of the Mantle early village plan**

smaller Houses 12, 18, and 19 flank Houses 15 and 20 and also have relatively high wall post densities. They too may have been part of the same social
unit that dominated the high ground in the Mantle community.

In the west-central portion of the site, the arrangement of structures end-to-end (e.g., Houses 40 and 43, 44 and 45, and 59 and 60 [which later merged into House 61]) could suggest a desire for ease of access between the ends of adjacent houses, particularly in winter months when it is possible that snow accumulation made passage between the house flanks more difficult. These centrally located houses are all regularly spaced and tightly clustered.

The shortest houses in the village had uniformly low densities of posts per linear meter of house wall, their short occupations precluding the need for maintenance or rebuilding. In many locations in the village, these houses are superimposed, implying that they may have been temporary or short-lived structures. They may have only been in place for a season, a few months, or a few years, possibly constructed to fill a short-term purpose and then disman-tled. Small longhouses have been interpreted as "cabins" (Kapches 1984; Robertson and Williamson 2003) and may have been constructed to house nonlocal visitors such as Algonquian speakers from the north who would winter with Iroquoian communities, as was common in the historic period (Thwaites 1896–1901, 21:239). While we acknowledge that these structures were an important part of community life, particularly in light of the fact that the sole iron object from the site was found in one of them (House 28 or 29; see chapter 6), their absence from both the early and late plans provides a sense of what the more stable structure of the village would have looked like.

When these houses are removed from the early village plan (see figure 4.6), it becomes apparent that the arrangement of structures, as originally conceived, was laid out with the intention of leaving an open space at the center of the village. We believe that this central, 1,500 m^2 space can be interpreted as a plaza. There are many large refuse and ash-filled depressions in this area, likely related to its use for outdoor activities. An open plaza at the center of the village could have served as a socially integrative space (Lipe and Hegmon 1989). It would have provided a venue for community-wide events such as feasts and ceremonies, and it also increased visibility and interaction between households as people went about their daily domestic tasks. The construction of houses in a single, radial alignment around an open space might also be interpreted as not only an integrative strategy but also as a projection of the cohesive nature of this community—an expression of a single, community-based identity. While a radial arrangement of houses was documented at the contact period Wendat Bidmead site in Simcoe County (Merritt 2001), to the best of our knowledge this feature of the built environment is otherwise unique in the Iroquoian archaeological record.

Ultimately, buildings were erected in the plaza. In the early phase of the village, six small, temporary structures were placed in this area, three of which (Houses 48, 49, and 52) are superimposed. In the late stage of the village's occupation, this area became completely filled in with houses, some small (e.g., Houses 28, 30, 31, and 51) but others that were larger and were occupied for a longer period of time (Houses 22 and 54). This suggests that the plaza may have been part of the village plan as originally envisioned but did not survive as an integral feature of the community.

Isolating short-lived houses also revealed that the houses in the northern-most portion of the village (Houses 1, 2, 3, and 6) were not occupied for long, or at least not long enough to require rebuilding that would have raised the density of wall posts over 3.5 per linear meter. This suggests that the early village plan as originally conceived during the initial phase of construction was not long-lived. There are less of these short-lived houses in the late stage of the village, and those houses with wall post densities of less than 3.5 posts per meter are clustered in the central and southern portions of the site. The average wall post densities for houses in the early phase is 3.6 posts per meter and for those in the late phase 4.2 posts per meter. This suggests that the early village structures were not occupied as long as those of the later phase.

The Late Village Plan

After approximately a decade of occupation, a decision was made to reduce the size of the Mantle village's palisaded precinct (figure 4.7). The third and final phase of palisade construction involved a total rebuild of the village's defenses and reduced the size of the palisaded enclosure from 2.5 ha to 2.0 ha. The third-phase palisade also employed a new style of construction. Whereas the rows of the first- and second-palisade phases in the early village were somewhat irregular in form and spacing, with gaps ranging from 1 to 1.5 m between posts in some places, the gaps in the third-phase palisade rarely exceed 1 m and there is an overall impression of tighter, more uniform construction. More significantly, a trench was excavated around the perimeter of the late village palisade, and the fill presumably used to create a strengthening embankment at its base. Cross-culturally, defensive fortifications are the most costly and largest-scale pieces of preindustrial military technology (Keeley 1996:55). The construction and maintenance of palisades and earthworks would have required a significant investment of time and effort, with implications for the organization of communal labor in large communities. The construction of defensive earthworks is a feature of a number of late-fifteenth-century sites in Ontario and New York State (see chapter 3) and was employed at the early- to mid-sixteenth-century Aurora site (Emerson 1954), one of the villages to which the Mantle community relocated. It is tempting to speculate that this development might be related to the arrival of one or more persons who was skilled at palisade construction and familiar with earthworks.

The rebuilding and contraction of the palisaded enclosure required the dismantling of a number of structures, including Houses 1, 2, 3, 6, 16, and 93 in the northern half of the village and House 88 in the southern half. The contraction of the palisade appears to have put a new premium on space within the village precincts. Over time, the plaza area was filled with new structures, many of which had relatively high wall post densities, suggesting a more lengthy occupation. Some were added and others removed in such a way that the original village plan appears to have been discarded entirely.

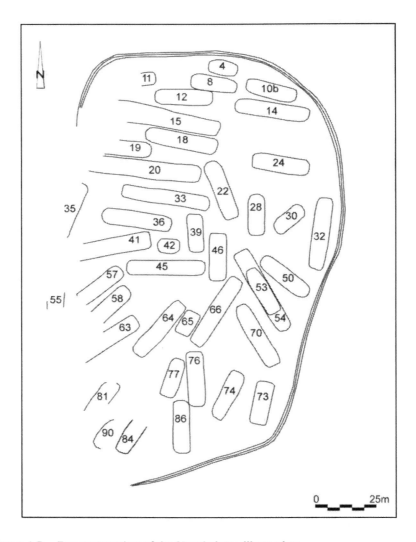

Figure 4.7.   Reconstruction of the Mantle late village plan

However, certain structures including the large Houses 15 and 20, as well as other houses in their immediate vicinity (Houses 12, 18, and 19) retained their position on the highest ground. Unlike these well-situated and enduring households, other longhouses were dismantled and possibly relocated or re-positioned. Many of the houses along the western side of the site were dismantled and rebuilt entirely. Some of these, such as Houses 33 and 34 or Houses 52 and 53, only shifted their footprint slightly, whereas others were completely dismantled (Houses 37, 40, and 44) and new houses with very different orientations built in their place (Houses 57, 58, and 63). This nod to expediency as opposed to maintaining a strict plan is perhaps in keeping with a relatively egalitarian society; this was not a formal plaza that was necessary to legitimize cosmological or chiefly power, but rather an integrative structure for the community. If the needs of the community changed, for whatever reason, so did the configuration of the village plan.

COMPARING THE DRAPER AND MANTLE SITES

By comparing features of the settlement plans of these communities over time, including population estimates, village layout, fortifications, and refuse disposal practices, changes in the materiality and spatiality of practices can be identified that directly address processes of cultural change in the context of coalescence.

Population Estimates

Constructing population estimates based on settlement remains can be challenging, since fundamental problems arise when attempting to calculate the momentary population of sites that had dynamic histories of occupation. Warrick thoroughly reviewed the strengths and weaknesses of a variety of approaches and concluded that settlement remains should display a high correlation with momentary population (2008:52–72).

We have adopted a formula based on multiple cross-cultural studies that suggest that the average value of roofed floor space per person in multifamily dwellings is 6 m^2 (Casselberry 1974). Because of the large degree of flexibility in human population densities, due in part to various human proxemic systems, any formula is still far from a reliable predictor of population size. Ethnographic descriptions of life in Wendat longhouses suggest that these structures were quite crowded (Tooker 1964:40). As such, we might assume that the proxemic systems of the Wendat and their ancestors were amenable to densely populated dwellings.

Our population estimates for the Draper and Mantle villages are presented in table 4.4. They indicate that the Draper village began with a population of approximately 458. As the village expanded, each additional group of longhouses increased the village's population by between 144 and 298 persons until the Draper site, including the main village and south field, reached a maximum estimated population of 1831 including the core before its abandonment. This population growth would have no doubt led to increasing scalar stresses (G. Johnson 1982), which appear to have been managed initially by retaining the previous social group divisions.

We have no way of estimating the population of the Spang site. The estimated maximal population of the Draper site is relatively close to our estimate of the population of the earliest phase of the Mantle site, which is 1730 individuals. However, if we assume that House 26—the long, north-south-oriented house on the northeastern edge of the site with little evidence of sustained habitation—was not permanently occupied, this figure drops to 1667. The population estimate for the late phase of the Mantle site is 1338 individuals. There are two explanations for this possible population loss. The decrease in roofed area may not reflect actual population loss but rather an increase in settlement "packing," in which more people are living in the remaining structures (between the early and late phases the momentary number of houses and total roofed area decreases from fifty-one houses and 10,382 m^2 to forty-one houses and 8,031 m^2). Alternatively, the decrease in population might reflect a loss of 392 community members. Interestingly, this figure corresponds relatively closely to the assumed populations of some of the smaller villages that initially aggregated to form the Draper community. Indeed, sites that are 0.8 to 1.0 ha in area, the average size for early-fifteenth-century Iroquoian sites, are inferred to have had a population of approximately 300 to 400 persons (Warrick 2008:175). If a social segment of the Mantle community decided to relocate elsewhere, we might expect the

Table 4.4. Estimated Populations of Various Phases of the Draper and Mantle Sites

Village and Phase	Estimated Population
Draper core (A)	458
Draper after expansion 1 (A,C)	602
Draper after expansion 2 (A, C, D)	900
Draper after expansion 3 (A, C, D, E)	1330
Draper after expansion 4 (A, C, D, E, B)	1474
Draper after expansion 5 (A, C, D, E, B, F)	1648
Draper main village and south field (Maximum)	1831
Mantle Early Village	1730
Mantle Late Village	1338

size of that group to be in this range. Houses 1, 3, 5, and 6 were dismantled in order to facilitate the contraction of the palisade in the northern portion of the village; perhaps it was these households that left the community.

The cause(s) or decision process leading to settlement packing or a group leaving is unknown. Packing of that nature may be a reflection of planning for the better use of space in a decade-old community, although it is not immediately apparent why that might be the case. In terms of a group's departure, while there is no evidence of inability for the community to meet its needs in relation to agricultural production, it may have been difficult to obtain the required hides for clothing and other uses (see chapter 5) for such a large population, and a group may have decided to relocate in the hope of better opportunities for procuring deer. Of course it is also possible that factionalism developed in the community for some reason and with a decreasing threat of conflict, they decided it would be preferable to "go it alone."

Village Layout and Social Integration

Built forms and their spatial organization both reflect and structure the social relations that go on in and around them (cf. Bourdieu 1970; Kent 1990; Parker Pearson and Richards 1994; Rapoport 1994). In small-scale societies, the discordant or concordant organization of structures, the presence or absence of public spaces, and the relative size and placement of built forms can reveal a great deal about a community and the relationships between its inhabitants. As such, changes in the built environment of the Draper and Mantle sites represent changes in the sociopolitical organization and integration of this community as it underwent the process of coalescence.

A recurring problem in Iroquoian archaeology is that aligned groups of longhouses have been interpreted both as households belonging to the same clan segment and as previously distinct communities that have merged into one settlement (Finlayson 1985:172; Pearce 1996; Trigger 1985:92; Tuck 1971; Warrick 1984:35; 2008:136–37; see Birch 2008). While both interpretations may be equally valid, they have been used interchangeably to explain the sociopolitical organization of Late Woodland villages. It is nearly impossible to archaeologically link longhouses to a particular clan affiliation, although we can reason that, when added to an already existing village, groups of aligned houses may represent an influx of people with closer social ties to one another, likely established through previous coresidence. In this way, Draper is essentially a village composed of a number of distinct groups, each of which retained a separate spatiality, and potentially distinct identities, within the larger community. The physical aggregation of these previously independent groups preceded their social and political integration.

Mechanisms to deal with social protocols, communication, and political organization in a coresidential community of Draper's size had not yet been developed. The means of coordinating decision making functions related to domestic affairs (e.g., land tenure, resolving internal disputes) and external affairs (e.g., trading route rights, raiding, and warfare) were likely still evolving. Structures do not exist outside of their continuous repetition through practice (D. Braun 1995; Pauketat 2003:43; Shennan 1993), and at the Draper site, social and political structures were in a state of becoming. Individuals were making choices, deciding how to make this new larger social group function. They would have used remembered traditions and existing social structures to develop these mechanisms, but they would also have been responding to novel social, political, and economic circumstances.

Compared to the Draper site, the early phase of the Mantle village is characterized by a highly organized and clearly preplanned layout. The social and cultural significance of structural changes in the built environment of successive villages occupied by the same community group is made clear when one considers the fact that the organization of space cognitively precedes its material expression (Ingold 2000:179; Rapoport 1994:488). In this way, the concept of the settlement plan of the early Mantle village must have been envisioned prior to its construction; the community began seeing themselves as more of an intergated whole than they did previously. House clusters are no longer evident, replaced instead with a consolidated village plan that favored the parallel and radial alignment of houses around a single plaza. The plaza itself can be interpreted as a symbol of the integration of the community. Functionally, it would have provided a space where villagers could gather for events and ceremonies, or perform more mundane tasks such as tool-making or the preparation of hides, consolidating their new larger sense of community.

Longhouse Length, Social Units, and Political Organization

It has been established that longhouse length in south-central Ontario reached a maximum in the fifteenth century and declined thereafter (Dodd 1984; Warrick 1996). Attempts to explain these patterns have included economic competition (Hayden and Cannon 1982; Varley and Cannon 1994), defense (Finlayson 1985:407; 1998:20), and overcrowding, both perceived and real (Warrick 1996:18; 2000:449).

Thirty-two percent of houses at Draper exceed 40 m, as opposed to only 20% at the Mantle site. When the overall lengths of houses in the two villages are compared, it is apparent that there is a general tendency toward shorter structures in the Mantle village. While the economy of space was likely a factor in limiting longhouse size at Mantle, this pattern may also be related to changes in sociopolitical organization.

The coresidential longhouse, particularly in its maximal form, may have been the most important decision making unit in precoalescent villages. Large lineage-based households may have been important in formative village aggregates, as individuals and kin groups struggled to position themselves in relation to one another. Decreasing longhouse length may then be related to a shift in village government, whereby supra-household identities emerge as more important in structuring local political organization, with clan segments taking over some of the functions once vested in the coresidential longhouse (Engelbrecht 1985: 174; Trigger 1990: 128; Warrick 1996: 20, 2000:449).

Increasing degrees of social integration by implication results in fewer communal facilities (Adler and Wilshusen 1990; Hegmon 1989; Rautman 2000). Seventeenth-century observers noted that community leaders resided in the largest longhouses, which also served as venues for events such as feasts, community discussions, and meetings of the village council (Thwaites 1896–1901, 10:181, 229–31, 261–63; 13:59). If this was also the case in precontact villages, certain large longhouses encountered archaeologically can be viewed as socially integrative structures.

At the Draper site, every longhouse cluster contains one or more "long" longhouses, greater than 40 m in length (Finlayson 1985). If these long longhouses are interpreted as communal facilities that may have been used to host political meetings, we might infer that every house cluster included at least one, and in some cases two, structures that perhaps hosted meetings of that segment. This is not to say that later in the site's occupation, one or more of the long longhouses did not emerge as the major place for village council meetings, yet there were no central places built into the physical structure of the Draper village.

Conversely, at the Mantle site, Houses 15 and 20 are among the longest buildings and were constructed on the highest ground in a commanding, desirable location. This suggests that these two structures played a significant and persistent purpose in the community and were probably residences of high-ranking lineages or of village leaders, whose dwellings also served as council houses. The fact that there were only two of these enduring, long longhouses supports the inference that the Mantle village was more politically integrated than its predecessors.

In Iroquoian societies, domestic and public activities occupied the same spaces. Domestic structures can be transformed into public venues by altering the social practices that occur in and around them. For example, if a council meeting was to be held in a longhouse, a particular order of seating according to status or gender could have been adopted (cf. Bowser and Patton 2004). When the meeting was over, less formal rules may have resumed about who could sit, move, and speak, and in what ways. Similarly, the plaza at Mantle could have been a venue for everyday activities such as making pottery, working hides, children's play, and so on. But the social rules involving its use could change when an important event was planned.

Other changes in social organization may be suggested by the high percentage of small longhouses at Mantle, where more than 50% of houses are less than 30 m in length. While a larger number of small longhouses may have been a function of concern for the economy of space, it may also have resulted from the breakdown of large, lineage-based household groups. This may have been due, in part, to the increasing importance of clans in village affairs, as discussed. Snow (1995b:362–63), on the other hand, has suggested that social disruption may result in the "repackaging" of mixed families, as was the case in the seventeenth century when large numbers of Wendat refugees were adopted into Iroquois villages. It is possible that the geopolitical reorganization that was occurring throughout the Lower Great Lakes in the late precontact period resulted in the fragmentation of lineages into smaller social units (Engelbrecht 2009:186). While households may not have been created ad hoc from scattered social remnants, as occurred during the crises and upheavals of the contact period, the consolidation of social fragments into larger villages may have been an important function of coalescent communities.

Fortifications and Defense

The main village at Draper was originally surrounded by a four-row palisade that enclosed an area of 1.19 ha. Short rows of posts on the western side of the village were interpreted as possible supports for watchtowers or galleries (Finlayson 1985:110). This original palisade was expanded five times to accommodate new houses. For the second, third, and fourth expansions, the number of rows of palisade posts was reduced to three, except for the fifth and final expansion, which was constructed with four rows of palisade posts. The final size of the palisaded enclosure was 3.42 ha—nearly a kilometer (880 m) of palisade.

Fortification of the Mantle community was still a fundamental concern with regard to village planning and ultimately involved three separate phases of palisade construction. The first palisade phase comprised 640 linear meters and enclosed an area of 2.9 ha. This area was then contracted to 2.5 ha and 554 linear meters of palisade, a significant reduction in the size of the defenses that would have been maintained and monitored. The addition of an earthen embankment, however, represented a significant additional investment in labor.

In his interpretations of the Draper settlement plan, Finlayson (1985:407) argued that long longhouses were placed parallel to one another and to the palisade in order to create long, narrow corridors that could be easily defended should enemies gain access to the village. While houses may have been placed with defense in mind, the entrances to the village identified in the Draper palisade do not seem to have been placed according to a defensive strategy (Finlayson 1985). When one examines the placement of entrances to the Mantle village, it appears that they may have been positioned so that the doorways of Houses 26, 32, 35, and 55 were directly adjacent to palisade entrances (ASI 2012a). All of these houses were constructed at right angles to the dominant orientation of other houses in the immediate area. Engelbrecht (2009:186) reminds us of the importance of ancient metaphors and the function of "doorkeepers" who occupied and protected the ends of longhouses. The League of the Iroquois was described as a longhouse, with the Seneca and Mohawk being the keepers of the western and eastern doors, respectively. If the presence of only two longhouse doors was related to defensive concerns, then the title of doorkeeper takes on a military dimension that is generally overlooked.

It is interesting that these innovations in defensive technology occur at Mantle as other evidence for warfare is limited, suggesting that in the sixteenth century, fortifications may have become part of the architectural habitus of this community and the investment in labor may not be directly proportional to the actual levels of conflict.

Refuse Disposal Practices

Different refuse disposal practices are evident at the Draper and Mantle sites, which provide additional insights into collective decision making and changes in the most mundane of practices during this process of community consolidation.

A total of twenty-two middens were recorded and excavated in the main village at the Draper site (Finlayson 1985). Some middens were located on the base of, or adjacent to, palisades. Middens located at the ends of houses appear to have been contributed to by more than one house (Finlayson 1985:398). In some cases, new houses were constructed over middens (e.g., Midden 57 and House 5); in others, middens were deposited where portions of houses had previously been occupied (e.g., Midden 66 over House 6; Midden 52 over House 10). These latter cases were both in the village core, which suggests that the central, longest-lived portion of the site was abandoned first, and refuse accumulated in those areas, while other areas of the site continued to be occupied. It also suggests that houses were dismantled, perhaps in order to reuse building materials in the new village.

Compared to Draper, the refuse disposal patterns at the Mantle site were uniform, to such a degree that it appears that there was an organized waste management strategy in place. Prior to the stripping of topsoil from the site, a series of one-meter units was excavated on a five-meter grid across the entire village area. These excavations did not reveal midden deposits within plow-disturbed areas within the village precincts. Midden 1 was located on the slope immediately west of the village, at the base of the palisade. The full extent of Midden 1 was difficult to estimate, as large sections were impacted by historic and modern disturbances. The nineteenth-century mill and farmhouse obscured the eastern and northern limits of the midden, and the southern limit was impacted by a gully that led down to the associated mill race. Photos of the farm taken in the 1950s and 1960s suggest that other midden deposits may have been present along the western edge of the site but were lost to modern landscaping. That midden deposits were lost is further suggested by the quantities of artifacts recovered from the Mantle site compared to the Draper site. For example, whereas the Draper site assemblage contained 12,969 analyzable rim sherds (Pihl 1984), the Mantle site assemblage contains not quite 2,000 vessels, which consist of considerably fewer rim sherds than recovered from Draper.

The remaining deposit, Midden 1, covers approximately fifteen meters from east to west and was only partially excavated, as this portion of the slope was not to be impacted. Thirty-seven one-meter units were excavated in Midden 1, the depth of which ranged between 30 and 120 cm, mainly due to the slope. In the late phase of the village's occupation, the borrow trench that surrounded the third phase of palisade construction became filled in with refuse, creating a "trench midden." The palisade trench may have offered an alternate, expedient place to dispose of refuse, as it surrounded the community and was therefore easily accessible. Its use came with a radical reorganization of the community that may have included a shift in decision making and collective or household waste management strategies.

Refuse disposal patterns and practices help inform us about the political organization of this community. The residents of the Draper village disposed of their waste within the village precincts, and often only a few steps from their hearths, whereas residents of the Mantle site adopted an organized system of refuse disposal that channeled waste outside of the palisaded enclosure. While hillside middens are not unique in the Ontario Iroquoian archaeological record, the scale of the decision making process that resulted in this waste management plan to the exclusion of large-scale disposal of waste within the village precinct speaks to the strength of collective decision making in the Mantle community.

There are a number of practical explanations for the development of waste management strategies in a village of Mantle's size, including potential threats to human health (Armelagos, Goodman, and Jacobs 1991) as a result of infectious diseases, pests, and environmental contamination. We must be mindful, however, that such concerns may derive from our own ethnocentric biases, as there are many ethnographic and archaeological examples of similar conditions in other cultures (cf. Lightfoot, Martinez, and

Schiff 1998; Staski and Sutro 1991) and ethnohistoric accounts are heavily influenced by European attitudes about cleanliness (cf. Robb 2008). Changes in waste management practices may be explained by the fact that people will change their behavior when their physical environment changes or presents limitations (Lawrence and Low 1990:460). It may have been that the Mantle village plan and the premium that it placed on space, with more houses in a smaller palisaded area and limited paths for moving through the community, did not permit waste disposal within the village. Ultimately, what is striking about the refuse disposal practices at the Mantle site is the fact that they were adopted by the village as a whole, and not on the basis of individual house-holds or household groups, which implies coordinated decision making based on a plan with which everyone agreed.

SUMMARY OF COMMUNITY HISTORY

This chapter has shown that by examining the occupational history of two sequential villages occupied during a pivotal time in the history of Iroquoian societies, many specific insights can be gained into the social and cultural changes that accompanied historical processes of coalescence at the community level. When changes in practice are identified, patterns emerge that directly identify social and political transformations that accompanied coalescence in this local community group.

In practice, coalescence involved negotiations between the multiple social segments involved. Initially these negotiations must have concerned the relocation of local groups into a single village, and later, how these groups were going to manage the challenges and opportunities that came from living together in a group larger than any would have experienced before. This site sequence demonstrates that coalescence is not an event but rather an ongoing process. Physical aggregation does not immediately equate with social integration. Rather, the negotiations and shifts in community-based identities play out over multiple generations, and in this sequence, through the occupation of three villages and multiple phases of construction.

Chapter Five

The Necessities of Life

This chapter examines the economic organization of the Mantle community in terms of the construction and maintenance of infrastructure and the production and consumption of the necessities of life such as food and clothing. Numerous logistical concerns resulted in the design and implementation of complex planning processes before, during, and after the occupation of the village.

Well before the abandonment of the Spang site, the village that preceded Mantle, the community would have needed to plan for its relocation. This would have involved the felling of thousands of trees for construction, as well as the preparation of thousands of sheets of elm and cedar bark for covering houses, all of this in addition to dealing with the community's regular maintenance needs. The village infrastructure would have required constant maintenance, as has been demonstrated through experimental construction of longhouses and palisades. Also, ever decreasing soil fertility in the absence of fertilizing methods would have required ever expanding fields. Hundreds of acres of new agricultural fields would have been cleared, planted, tended, and harvested in order to provide the more than fifteen hundred pounds of maize required daily to feed the population. Isotopic and macrobotanical data, together with insights gleaned from the ethnohistoric record, are presented in this chapter to trace the community's reliance on maize and other cultigens.

Substantial quantities of nonagricultural food were also obtained through hunting, fishing, and gathering activities. Nitrogen isotope data will be presented to explore the importance of lake fish in the diet, since the fish remains in the faunal sample are dominated by those species. Ongoing material culture requirements will also be discussed, including the use of bone for tool production and ornamentation.

A primary ongoing subsistence need was hides for clothing the population. Detailed and comprehensive analyses of the faunal remains of the site, in comparison with samples from other villages, reveal that strategies for clothing populations had to have involved the procurement of hides through exchange. This suggests that Iroquoian researchers have perhaps seriously underestimated previously the role of northern Algonquians and other Iroquoian groups in late ancestral Wendat community subsistence patterns, although some may have been correct in attributing increases in conflict to competition over hunting territories.

PLANT RESOURCES: BUILDING, GATHERING, AND FARMING

The plants used on the site were collected or harvested from the site environs and, once processed, found their way into the archaeological record of the village. While some macrobotanical remains of plants such as maize kernels and cob fragments were found while screening the contents of refuse deposits and various features within the houses, much of it was found through the process of flotation. Samples were taken from interior and exterior house features and posts from across the site, as well as from Midden 1 and the borrow trench surrounding the third phase of palisade construction (Monckton and Forrest 2012).

These and a number of macrobotanical samples from Midden 1 yielded 558 g of maize (*Zea mays*) in the form of kernels and 69 g in cob fragments. Maize represents 28.8% of the total number of identified plant remains. Negligible quantities (<1 g) of bean (*Phaseolus vulgaris*), cucurbit/squash (*Cucurbita pepo*), and tobacco (*Nicotiana rustica*) were recovered, along with 3 g of sunflower (*Helianthus annuus*). These results are consistent with accounts by the first European visitors to reach the Wendat a century after the occupation of Mantle. They commented on the primary importance of maize (Biggar 1922–1936, vol. 3, 3:125; Thwaites 1896–1901, 10:101; 11:7; 15:153, 159; 33:77; Wrong 1939:80, 104–8), mentioning also that beans, squash, and tobacco were grown. Sunflower was used for hair and body oil (Biggar 1922–1936, vol. 3, 3:50) although it probably also made up part of the diet as it is commonly found with other food remains (Monckton 1992:82).

Collected plants included the common fruits of bramble (*Rubus* sp.), strawberry (*Fragaria* sp.), cattail (*Typha latifolia*), seeds of sumac (*Rhus typhina*), chenopod (*Chenopodium* sp.), spikenard (*Aralia* sp.), a small grass (cf. *Echinochloa*), purslane (*Portulaca oleracea*), black nightshade (*Solanum americanum*), hawthorn (*Crataegus* sp.), plum (*Prunus* sp.), ironwood (*Carpinus caroliniana*), erect knotweed (*Polygonum erectum*), elderberry (*Sambucus* sp.), pincherry (*Prunus pensylvanica*), cleavers (*Galium aparine*), delta seed (*Leucadendron* sp.), grape (*Vitus labrusca*), peppergrass (*Lepidium virginicum*), knotweed/sedge (*Carex* sp.), amaranth (*Amaranthus retroflexus*), barnyard grass (*Echinochloa crus-galli*), pokeweed (*Phytolacca americana*), and serviceberry (*Amelanchier arborea*).

The most abundant category of plant remains apart from wood charcoal came from fleshy fruits. Bramble and strawberry were the most frequent, and they were found often and in large numbers in longhouse samples. This is contrary to a number of earlier Iroquoian settlements in southern Ontario. For example, the early-fourteenth-century ancestral Neutral Myers Road site yielded comparative quantities of fruit (40%) to that of maize (39.6%) (Monckton 1998), but they were concentrated in exterior longhouse fruit-rich deposits, suggesting the use of these locales in the spring or summer. A preponderance of strawberry seeds might be representative of early summer activities, such as first fruit festivals (Waugh 1916:125–28). In the case of the Mantle site, processing activities certainly seem to have occurred outdoors, since large quantities of fruit seeds were encountered outside of longhouses; a far greater quantity of such seeds were recovered from within longhouses, perhaps reflective of their being dried and stored for winter use. With greater numbers of people aggregating in a single planned and integrated village than previously, the need to prepare foods for winter may have resulted in an intensification of seasonal gathering activities. Monckton has suggested that areas around villages like Mantle were managed to encourage the growth and eventual collection of wild, anthropogenic foodstuffs (1992:93–94).

Small numbers of other plant taxa were also found, as they are on other Iroquoian settlements. The most common ones are cattail and sumac. Cattail is not mentioned in historical accounts but may represent what the Jesuits referred to as rushes, used to cover the longhouse floors and roofs (Thwaites 1896–1901, 42:205; 58:209; 59:129, 133, 155). While these are mainly found in longhouse contexts, they are also fairly well represented in the external features. One feature in House 12 contained over four hundred cattail seed specimens; House 12 was the only house with an intact living floor, suggesting that this otherwise anomalous number of cattail seeds is an effect of preservation. Sumac commonly grows in disturbed areas, and Ojibwa, Menomini, and Potawatomi people are known to have used the plant in beverages, medicines, and for smoking (H. Smith 1933:38). The majority of sumac seeds at Mantle were recovered from within longhouse features.

Firewood and Building Materials

The recovered wood charcoal is dominated by maple (*Acer saccharum*) and beech (*Fagus grandifolia*), followed by ash (*Fraxinus* sp.), elm (*Ulmus americana*), ironwood (*Ostrya virginiana*), white pine (*Pinus strobus*), cedar

(*Thuja occidentalis*), and red and white oak (*Quercus rubra* and *Q. alba*). Significant numbers of the unidentifiable fragments were designated as deciduous tree wood. These data indicate that the most abundant tree species present are a reflection of the typical forest community of the region and the fact that deadfall would most probably have been collected for firewood.

In the case of building materials, Mantle required tens of thousands of trees for a single phase of construction. Once an appropriate location was chosen and planning to relocate was started, possibly years in advance of actual relocation, work would have begun to clear the site and surrounding fields of trees and gathering the supplies for construction of houses and palisades. Trees and saplings being cleared from future maize fields were likely stockpiled for building purposes, perhaps in water to maintain their suppleness. Other necessary building materials would have included bark for covering houses, and cord and roots (such as spruce) for lashing. It is likely that advance work parties spent considerable amounts of time at the site in advance of households actually moving to the village. Ethnohistoric accounts indicate that men were responsible for constructing houses and palisades (Biggar 1922–1936, vol. 3, 3:137; Wrong 1939:101), although it is possible that women may have assisted or accompanied them to the site of the new village at times. The work would have been undertaken at the time of year when men's other duties (hunting, fishing, trading, or warfare) permitted.

Eric Jones has recently produced a model that suggests the location of stands of maple-beech hardwood may be a significant index of village location for the Iroquois (2010b:10). This appears to be at odds with the identification of softwoods as the preferred construction choice for Wendat builders, based on a Jesuit description of a palisade made of pine (Thwaites 1896–1901, 34:123) and on the identification of eastern white cedar in building features of Neutral sites in southwestern Ontario (Lennox 1984:17; see also Warrick 1988). One of the few environments in which one could find sufficient softwood building materials of an even age, and therefore size, was that of even-aged cedar swamps or cedar pole stands.

It is difficult in the absence of an entire charred post to know whether the charcoal sampled from a post is derived from background charred material reflective of firewood and incorporated into the post fill or from actual construction material. Charcoal from support and wall posts at the site was identified as mainly maple, beech, and ash with some cedar. Samples from House 53, which burned down and therefore contained a sizable amount of wood charcoal in posts, presumably from construction material, are consistent with the general pattern at Mantle in which maple, beech, and ash were used preferentially.

The Forest Region in which the Mantle site is situated constitutes a mosaic of hardwood, mixed hardwood, and conifer that reflects a transition between the more southerly deciduous forest, which extends along the north shore of Lake Ontario almost to the site itself, and northern shield boreal forest (MacDonald 2002:196–235). The principal taxa in this region are sugar and red maple, beech, hemlock, white pine basswood, white ash, and red oak. Wetland communities featuring eastern white cedar, tamarack, and black spruce are also common. Some understanding of the original state of forest growth at the time of the occupation of the site can be gleaned from historic vegetation records. These records are derived from the late-eighteenth- and early-nineteenth-century land surveyors who laid out township lots in southern Ontario. While marking boundaries, they also recorded vegetation cover and other natural and cultural environmental features on the land.

The presettlement vegetation has been mapped onto a GIS platform for the lands surrounding the site, although data are missing for the east side of the site beyond 1.5 km (Puric-Mladenovic 2003). Within 500 m of Mantle, the majority of land was covered with maple-beech forest with a secondary presence of maple-mixed and elm-mixed patches. Cedar-mixed forest lined the valley of Stouffville Creek adjacent to the site. Within 1 km of the site, the majority of the vegetation to the east, north, and west was maple-beech forest, while to the south there was more variety, which included elm-mixed, maple-mixed, and a few pockets of cedar forest. Within 2–5 km of the site, maple-beech predominates along with small pockets of cedar-mixed forest extending along the local waterways.

The use of nonexhausted wood and bark supplies from the previously occupied village would have been essential, and at the time of a village's relocation there would have been a planned deconstruction event to claim any usable posts, bark, and firewood. It also seems clear that when hundreds of acres were required for field systems as well as thousands of small saplings for construction, secondary growth forest of small hardwoods along with pole stands of small cedars would have been the most cost-effective choices for wall posts. It would appear that these building materials were within easy access of the site.

Agricultural Production System

Maize was the most important component in the diet of the site inhabitants. It was prepared in a soup (*sagamité*) or baked into bread. There would have been considerable concern over crop failure, leading to the regular production of surpluses, which might also have been used to trade with northern Algonquians or other Iroquoian groups.

Bean, cucurbit (squash), and sunflower would also have been cultivated by the community and may have been a significant part of the subsistence system. The processing of bean renders it largely invisible in the record at this and many other Iroquoian sites. Cucurbit is also archaeologically elusive, although seven charred specimens were recovered at the site. Preparation for consumption often involved cooking them whole in ashes (Thwaites 1896–1901, 10:103; 15:161–62) or cutting them into small pieces for adding to the *sagamité* (Wrong 1939:107). At most Iroquoian sites, cucurbit remains recovered are in the form of seeds rather than rind, while at Mantle charred peduncles were found in midden deposits. Remains of sunflower, on the other hand, are fairly common in Iroquoian village deposits perhaps due to its distinctive micromorphology and durability (Monckton 1992); small fragments of achenes or shell were found in large quantities at the site.

Unlike the other cultigens, tobacco is represented by extremely small and delicate seeds. When one considers the prodigious quantities of seeds this plant produces (up to a million seeds per plant) and the regular use of smoking pipes by men on a day-to-day basis (e.g., Thwaites 1896–1901, 7:137, 139; 17:81, 127; 20:187), it is surprising that more remains are not found in the archaeological deposits of villages. Given their delicate and hollow nature, however, and the fact that tobacco was often thrown directly onto the fire (Thwaites 1896–1901, 10:159; 23:55), the direct flame would have incinerated most of the seeds. Charring without their complete destruction requires indirect heat by fire; perhaps while smoking too tightly packed pipes resulting in incompletely burned material. While the record of the ceramic smoking pipe complex at Mantle is rich, there are few recovered tobacco seeds.

The first researcher to investigate the Wendat subsistence economy in any significant detail was the cultural geographer Conrad Heidenreich (1971). Citing early anthropologists who argued that maize formed between 50% (Kroeber 1939:146) and 75% of the diet of early agriculturalists (Popham 1950:88), Heidenreich suggested maize contributed about 65% of the diet for the historic Wendat. The results of initial isotope research suggested that although gradually adopted as a main staple, by AD 1300 the diet of most southern Ontario Iroquoians consisted of about 50% maize reliance (Schwarcz et al. 1985). The degree to which maize contributed to diet would of course differ among various communities at different times depending on the pressures for intensification of production brought about by amalgamating populations. At the late-thirteenth-century ancestral Wendat Moatfield village, maize appears to have contributed 70% of the diet for one generation (for those between twenty and thirty years of age), perhaps during the formation of the village when there was an intensification of population, and then stabilized for later generations at about 55%–60% of the diet (van der Merwe et al. 2003).

This general depiction of maize consumption was confirmed by isotope data recovered from testing loose teeth recovered from within the Mantle village and from a sample of teeth recovered from those who were interred in the village cemetery (see chapter 6), who while perhaps "others" nevertheless shared a similar diet to other site occupants. Ten loose teeth from various contexts within the village as well as five teeth from various adult individuals in the village cemetery were evaluated for $d^{13}C$ enamel and $d^{13}C$ dentin collagen (Pfeiffer et al. 2013). The relative contributions of these isotopes to the diet were evaluated in the context of the established estimated foodweb fractionation of 13C (Lee-Thorp, Sealy, and van der Merwe 1989; Tieszen and Fagre 1993) and 15N (Schoeninger and DeNiro 1984; Schoeninger, DeNiro, and Tauber 1983) in human tissues based on established standards (Pee Dee Belemnite). More recently, similar techniques have been used to examine the dietary composition for peoples from a variety of different sites (Bourbou et al. 2011; Katzenberg, Goriunova, and Weber 2009).

Using this model, also applied previously at Moatfield (van der Merwe et al. 2003), it can be estimated that based on enamel, 60% of the Mantle diet was maize (66% based on dentin). The apparent absence of correlation between enamel and dentin values may be based on the fact that enamel forms before dentin and use may have been heavier during initial weaning, although the model employed is approximate only and lacks any kind of error term. What is significant is that the values recorded for Mantle and other regional early-sixteenth-century Iroquoian sites are higher than earlier or historic sites (table 5.1).

So what does this mean for the Mantle site occupants? Heidenreich (1971:162–64), using observations of the early ethnographers of two meals a day for the Wendat and an estimated requirement of approximately three thousand calories a day, suggested the Wendat were consuming about 1.3 pounds of maize per day per person at 65% of the diet, an estimate that compares favorably with other Neolithic societies (Cowgill 1962:277). The Mantle isotope data, together with data from other, slightly earlier fifteenth-century villages seem to be consistent with such an estimate of maize contribution, and there is no reason not to use the values provided by the isotope study. We will therefore assume the Mantle occupants were on average consuming 1.3 pounds of maize a day.

While the fields appear to have been owned by the individual nuclear family, the extended family seems to have shared in the product and crops were available to the families of the village in times of scarcity (Heidenreich 1971:168–71; Trigger 1976:36). Once men had removed trees and brush from the fields (probably early succession forests whenever possible for ease of clearance), Wendat women worked the fields, growing corn in small hills a foot or so high and several feet in diameter in which they planted water-soaked seeds. Based on assessments of still surviving fields in the nineteenth and twentieth centuries, there could have been about two thousand to twenty-five hundred of these hills per acre. Hills functioned to reduce erosion, enhance solar heating, and trap cold air at ground level, thereby reducing the risk of late frost damage (Heidenreich 1971:177; 1974; Mt Pleasant 2006).

Table 5.1.   **Delta 13C Values for Archaeological Sites in Ontario**

Site/ Component	Approx. Date	*n*	Average delta13C	STDV	Sources
Morrison's Is.	2300 ± 400 BC	3	-20.8	1.4	Schwartz et al. 1985
Donaldson site/ Cemetery 1	530 BC (555 ± 25 BC)	1	-19.2	0.3	Schwartz et al. 1985
Donaldson site/ Cemetery 2	AD 5 ± 75	3	-19	0.9	Schwartz et al. 1985
Levesconte mound	AD 174 ± 55	4	-21.9	0.4	Schwartz et al. 1985
Serpent mounds/ Mound E	AD 205 ± 90	3	-21.1	0.7	Schwartz et al. 1985
Serpent mounds/ Mound G and I	AD 400 ± 100	4	-21.1	0.4	Schwartz et al. 1985
Monarch Knoll	AD 500	1	-20.5	0	Katzenberg et al. 1995
Surma	AD 700	4	-17.7	1.4	Katzenberg et al. 1995
Varden	AD 920	11	-19.4	0.2	Katzenberg et al. 1995
Miller	AD 1152	5	-13.9	0.9	Katzenberg et al. 1995
Serpent mounds/Pit 2	AD 1170 ± 120	3	-15.3	0.8	Schwartz et al. 1985
Bennett	AD 1275	1	-11.5	0	Katzenberg et al. 1995
Serpent mounds/Pit 3	AD 1290	2	-15.8	2.9	Schwartz et al. 1985
Force site	AD 1240 ± ?	2	-12.6	0.7	Schwartz et al. 1985
Moatfield ossuary	AD 1300	11	-12.3	1.3	van der Merwe et al. 2003
Fairty ossuary	AD 1350 ± 50	4	-11.3	1.1	Schwartz et al. 1985

Hidden Spring	AD 1430-1480	7	-12	0.5	Bower 2011
Uxbridge	AD 1450-1500	9	-10.8	0.5	Harrison and Katzenberg 2003
Mantle	AD 1500-1530	15	-10.6	1.2	Pfeiffer et al. 2013
Mackenzie-Woodbridge	AD 1500	3	-11.6	1.1	Katzenberg et al. 1995
MacPherson	AD 1550	29	-10	1.3	Katzenberg Saunders and Fitzgerald 1993
Ball site	AD 1600	5	-12.6	0.9	Schwartz et al. 1985
Kleinburg ossuary	AD 1600	4	-12.2	0.4	Schwartz et al. 1985
Ossossané ossuary	AD 1636	4	-12.2	1	Schwartz et al. 1985
Cooper ossuary	AD 1645	3	-13.6	1.4	Schwartz et al. 1985

No fertilizer was used on the fields, although it has been argued that the burning of fields to remove extraneous vegetation and the planting of beans in a variety of the hills with the maize may have replenished nitrogen and increased soil fertility in certain circumstances (Heidenreich 1971:182–84); more recent studies have concluded that these practices did not ameliorate fertility depletion (Baden and Beekman 2001:510). The practice of using small mounds in the fields, however, may have improved soil structure, as the integration of the previous season's crop residue and the concentration of activity on the mounds alone would have constituted a slower, more focused decomposition of organic material, resulting in more effective nutrient and mineral delivery to the plants (Mt Pleasant 2006; Mt Pleasant and Burt 2010).

The best description of the actual variety of corn grown is that provided by Sagard (Wrong 1939:104), who observed that one stalk bore "two or three ears, each ear yielding a hundred, two hundred, sometimes four hundred grains, and there are some that yield more. The stalk grows as high as a man and higher . . . and the grain ripens in four months, or in three in some places." Sagard went on to observe that he had even lost his way in the agricultural fields surrounding communities. The variety of maize found at Mantle was the Eastern Eight Row variety, commonly found on Wendat sites (Monckton 1992:52).

Heidenreich (1971:189–95) explored crop yield estimates in bushels of corn per acre based on early ethnographic and anthropological accounts, nineteenth-century yields in southern Ontario, and comparable ethnographic accounts from elsewhere. He concluded that an average of twenty-four bushels per acre, with a low of nine and a maximum of thirty-three, would be reasonable and assumed that once field fertility had decreased by 60%–75% of their best yields, they would have been abandoned. While Heidenreich suggested that a four-inch cob of this variety would yield about 200 kernels per cob (an average in line with Sagard's observation), Stephen Monckton has argued, based on counting kernels from complete archaeological cobs from three Wendat sites (Monckton 1992:33), that a more appropriate estimate would be about 165 kernels per cob. Using Monckton's figure and two ears per plant, the average yield per plant would be approximately 330 kernels. At an average of three stalks per hill, the yield per acre (using twenty-five hundred hills per acre) would be 27.6 bushels per acre (56 pounds per bushel) (see also Heidenreich 1974). Using an estimate of 20% loss before harvest, as did Heidenreich (1971:192), this would bring the average yield to 22.4 bushels per acre. Once this yield dropped to 6 bushels (25% of average yield), the field would be abandoned.

The Jesuits claimed that Wendat fields became exhausted after twelve years at the most and usually after eight to ten years (Thwaites 1896–1901, 15:153; 19:133). Heidenreich (1971:180–87), accounting for historic Wendat agricultural practice and comparing the observed yields with the practice of modern farmers in Simcoe County and comparable slash-and-burn agriculturalists elsewhere in the world, concluded that sandy fields may have been cultivated for five to six years, loamy sands for six to eight, and sandy loams for eight to twelve years. It may have taken at least thirty-five to sixty years for the fields to regain their fertility, depending on soil type.

While loams are recognized as having excellent productivity for plants generally, modern corn reaches maximum yields in sandy clay loams with sufficient soil depth, a balanced pH, sufficient temperatures, and weeded fields. Mt Pleasant and Burt (2010) have argued that maize grew well in well-drained sandy loam soils with a high organic content, median growing season temperature of 25°C or warmer, sufficient frost-free days, a suitable amount of sunlight, and 30 to 36 cm of precipitation during the growing season.

Loams constitute 100% of the soils within three kilometers of the Mantle site and 40% of the three-kilometer Draper site catchment soils, along with 40% sandy loams and 20% clay loams. While it is clear that the Draper and Mantle site occupants chose their site locations for a multitude of reasons, if one assumes favorable climatic conditions and that careful attention was paid to weeding fields, the soils surrounding these sites would certainly have been equally as, if not more fertile than, Simcoe County fields. Average yields of 22.4 bushels per acre are therefore not unreasonable, and the fact that it would take ten years to reach a yield of 6 bushels at a steadily decreasing rate suggests a maximum yield of 38.8 on the first use of fields at Mantle.

Alternatively, Sissel Schroeder (1999) has argued that estimates of maize productivity such as those of Heidenreich have been overestimated. She considers the productivity estimate from the Jesuit Relations of "one hundred grains for one" (Thwaites 1896–1901, 15:157), to be unreliable, although Heidenreich had reasoned that depending on interpretation it was not far off his own estimates. Using instead yields compiled from government administrative accounts of nineteenth-century Native American and nineteenth- and early-twentieth-century Euro-American farmers in Illinois and Missouri, she concluded that the average yield for Native Americans who lacked plows was 18.9 bushels per acre; she then reduced this by half to account for intercropping and "confounding" variables, thereby suggesting that precontact farmers would only have averaged about 9 to 10 bushels per acre. She then constructed a model of field production requirements for annual needs on the part of a nuclear family with two adults (2,500 calories/day) and three children (1,910 calories per day) at a variety of percentage maize contributions to the diet. For a 55% reliance on maize, she calculated that at 18.9 bushels per acre the family would need to tend 1.25 acres, and at 10 bushels per acre, 2.36 acres. This would mean between 375 and 708 acres of field in production (at those yields) in any given year for a community population of 1,500, without accounting for fields within the system that had various levels of fertility from abandoned to new.

Schroeder's methods of analysis and estimates came under criticism by William Baden and Christopher Beekman (2001), the former having modeled stability and change in Mississippian agricultural systems in his PhD dissertation (Baden 1987). They prefer a modeling approach that considers behavioral, climatic, environmental, and varietal data to recreate the indigenous agricultural complex.

While such an approach is adopted here, we nevertheless modeled using Schroeder's values for the Rouge-Duffins precoalescent and coalesced populations. Estimated populations for the sites were generated as was done for Mantle, using available settlement pattern data where sites had been partially or completely excavated or site size based on surface collections and the durations on the basis of the hypothetical sequence of sites joining Draper. Schroeder's model resulted in catchments for community field systems that would have been completely untenable—they are simply too large and overlap by more than half their areas (table 5.2).

Moreover, Schroeder's approach failed to account for the need to grow a surplus of maize for scarcity or for trade, which was thought by Sagard to be as much as two to three years' supply (Wrong 1939:103). The Jesuit Jean de Brébeuf claimed Huronia was the granary of their Algonquian neighbors (Thwaites 1896–1901, 8:115), and at the time, Champlain thought the population of the Nippissing was 700–800 souls (Biggar 1922–1936, vol. 3, 3:40).

The concerns about scarcity were rooted in episodic drought and pluvial events as well as early frosts (Thwaites 1896–1901, 8:99; 10:37, 43). In 1624, Sagard (Wrong 1939:178) noted that "about the months of April and May the rains were very heavy and almost without cessation (in contrast to France which was very dry that year), so that the savages were convinced that all their corn would be ruined and rotted, and in this calamity they did not know where to turn except to us; for they had already performed all their superstitious rites to no advantage." Thus in addition to drought, sustained or severe pluvial events had dramatic impacts on horticultural productivity, as a result of mould and spores, crop rot, and root damage to the plant. The risk of spoiling dried surpluses also increased. The mound system may have helped in times of heavy precipitation to encourage pooling at the lower sides of the mounds in the interstices, where any water is far enough from the plant to avoid damage yet remains accessible to the root system of the plant (Mt Pleasant and Burt 2010).

Understanding the frequency of these climatic threats is difficult. The global climatic event known as the Little Ice Age, consisting of climatic cooling and instability, lasted from the early to mid-sixteenth century to the mid- to late nineteenth century (Free and Robock 1999; Stahle and Cleaveland 1994). Recent data, collected primarily from tree-ring sampling, allow for reconstruction of precipitation, temperature, amount of solar radiation, and regional vegetation with some precision (Diaz and Stahle 2007). Tree-ring data in Buckley et al. (2004) and Cook and Krusic (2004) indicate mild drought conditions between AD 1450 and AD 1480, followed by a more severe, multidecadal drought around AD 1480 to AD 1500. This in turn was followed by a moderate pluvial period after AD 1500. While complete crop failures may not have occurred during these periods, it is likely that surpluses helped to deal with climatic uncertainty.

Using Heidenreich's basic model and adjusting for the considerations delineated above, the field systems for the precoalescent, Draper, Spang and Mantle villages were modeled on a GIS platform (see table 5.2; figure 5.1). The model assumed a 1.3 pound per person daily requirement (8.4 bushels per year) and an average yield of 22.4 bushels per acre (based on sandy loams).

It was also assumed that it would take ten years to reach a yield of 6 bushels. While the actual rate of loss of field fertility is unknown, if one assumes a steadily decreasing linear rate of 10%–15%, the initial field yield

Table 5.2. Models of Agricultural Field Systems

Agricultural field systems modeled as per Schroeder (1999)

Site	Population (est.)	Dates	Years Occupied (est.)	Bushels Required[a]	Acres Required[b]	Distance to Edge of Field System (m)[c]
Pugh	400	1430-1450	20	4032	2267.50	1709.06
Robin Hood	150	1430-1455	25	1512	929.66	1094.32
Wilson Park	300	1430-1450	25	3024	1859.31	1547.60
Dent Brown	300	1440-1460	20	3024	1700.62	1480.08
Carruthers	200	1440-1465	25	2016	1239.54	1263.61
Gostick	250	1440-1465	25	2520	1549.43	1412.76
White[d]	200	1450-1465	15	2016	1048.53	1162.18
Best	300	1450-1470	20	3024	1700.62	1480.08
Draper	1831	1450-1475	25	18456	11348.00	3823.34
Spang	1800	1475-1500	25	18144	11155.87	3790.84
Mantle	1523	1500-1520	20	15352	8633.50	3334.85

Agricultural field systems as per our model

Site	Population (est.)	Dates	Years Occupied (est.)	Bushels Required[a]	Acres Required[b]	Distance to Edge of Field System (m)[c]
Pugh	400	1430-1450	20	4032	521.15	819.34
Robin Hood	150	1430-1455	25	1512	194.42	500.44
Wilson Park	300	1430-1470	25	3024	390.46	709.20
Dent Brown	300	1440-1460	20	3024	390.46	709.20
Carruthers	200	1440-1465	25	2016	259.77	578.46

Gostick	250	1440-1465	25	2520	325.11	647.14
White[d]	200	1450-1465	15	2016	259.77	578.46
Best	300	1450-1470	20	3024	390.46	709.20
Draper	1831	1450-1475	25	18456	2395.17	1756.51
Spang	1800	1475-1500	25	18144	2070.13	1632.98
Mantle	1523	1500-1520	20	15352	1991.03	1601.48

[a] over the period of occupation.
[b] by the end of occupation.
[c] at end of occupation based on idealized radius.
[d] lower terrace.

would have been 38.8 bushels per acre. More acres would have to have been added annually in order to maintain the levels of production to feed the population. For each year, existing field production was recalculated based on the lower production levels. The difference between the population requirements and the lower production was then compensated with additional fields. These calculations were then made for the lifespan of each site, ranging from a fifteen-year cycle to a twenty-five-year cycle. The final number of acres required represents the total area that was used during the entire life cycle of the site, including abandoned fields.

To model for surplus retention, we assumed that an additional two years of crop would have been grown early in the occupation of the village, which was then replaced on an annual basis due to loss resulting from trade, scarcity, and predation, using an annual growth surplus of 20%.

In terms of soils, we assumed that sandy loams, loams, and clay loams were employed while certain areas were excluded. Soil data from Agriculture and AgriFood Canada (2012) were used to identify areas that are classified as being poorly drained, bottom lands, sufficient for natural grazing only, having no capability for agriculture, or having the presence of adverse topography or a slope greater than twenty degrees. These identified zones were removed from the total areas of each site. In order to compensate for the removed areas, the buffers were increased until the requirements were fulfilled.

It was assumed that directionality was not a concern, in that their nearest neighbors were at least thirty kilometers distant. This assumption allowed for the use of a simple buffer to create polygons that represented the total areas

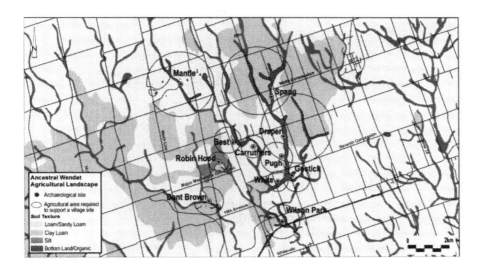

Figure 5.1. Modeled pre-contact agricultural field systems for village sites in the Duffins Creek drainage

required for corn production for each site. Some minimal adjustments to field directionality were made, however, to ensure that any overlap in the fields of the communities represented those fields initiated in the final years of occupation, in an assumption that as populations moved from village to village, some of the agricultural lands from the previous village were still being used as the new village was being established.

This model demonstrates that given the assumptions employed, the natural environment of the middle range of the West Duffins Creek system could certainly have supported the agricultural requirements associated with the community sequence that led to the occupation of the Mantle site. Modeling even with thirty-year site occupation duration estimates of Warrick (2008:119) for the sixteenth century shows that at least in the case of the coalescent and postcoalescent sites, those occupation durations are plausible in the context of sustainable field systems. Indeed, it would seem that the Mantle site was positioned to allow for such an occupation length without requiring use of abandoned fields from the Draper and Spang systems. Of course, with a sustained population of well over a thousand people, other resource requirements may have necessitated village relocation, such as the absence of easily gathered firewood close to the village or accumulations of organic refuse that led to unpleasant environments.

ANIMAL RESOURCES: HUNTING, FISHING, AND CLOTHING

While the agricultural field systems would have required the expenditure of significant effort at clearing forested areas by men and planting, tending, and harvesting crops by women and children in addition to gathering wild plant stuffs, the subsistence system of the site inhabitants also included the exploitation of animal resources for meat protein, hides for the manufacture of clothing, and bone for making tools. The faunal sample consisted of 37,542 specimens, most of which were recovered by manual soil screening with 6 mm mesh (95%) while the remainder was found through flotation using 3 mm mesh (5%). It should be noted that the sample examined, while constituting all of the bone recovered from our excavations, does not represent the entire village sample due to previous destruction of hillside midden deposits along the west side of the village and the fact that portions of the middens on the slope have been preserved in situ.

The sample includes a few shells of bivalves and gastropods, the exoskeleton of a crustacean, the bones of fish, amphibians, reptiles, and birds, and the bones, teeth, and antlers of mammals. From among these, sixty-seven separate taxa were identified. Bone identified to species represents 16% of the assemblage. A full description of the analysis of the assemblage, including recovery techniques, site taphonomy, and species habitat and habit descriptions, can be found in Needs-Howarth (2012), from which much of this summary is drawn.

Both number of identified species and minimum number of individuals (MNI) estimates were determined and are reported below in some cases; MNI was calculated conservatively using element duplication, side, size, and age. Moreover, in the case of Mantle, for small-sized taxa, it is unlikely that bones from the same individual animal would have been distributed among multiple refuse contexts or houses. Alternatively, for large animals or animals used during feasting, sharing of the carcass might have occurred between individuals and houses; since this is difficult to define, Needs-Howarth chose to aggregate the assemblage at the site level. While the faunal assemblage is a sample of the animals taken over time and the MNI is only a fraction of the number of animals that must have been consumed, all bone recovered from the excavation was examined and the assemblage from the site is thought to be generally representative of the hunting and fishing pursuits of the site inhabitants.

Mammal bones dominate the assemblage (87%) with fish making up 6%, birds 2%, and all other classes making up 1% or less each. The minor categories included 167 frog and toad elements, one burnt and one unaltered piece of a probable crayfish recovered from the midden, a few shell fragments from locally available freshwater taxa, and both thin-shelled terrestrial and thick-shelled aquatic snails, a few of which appear to have been modified, suggesting that they were not intrusive. Reptilia remains also constituted less than 1% (n=174) of the identified specimens and include snapping turtle (*Chelydra serpentina*) and painted turtle (*Chrysemis picta*); a few carapace and plastron fragments were beveled or modified.

Birds

Birds, which could be procured with bows and arrows and nets, represent fourteen unique taxa and make up 2% (n=817) of the identified specimens. Less than 20% of the bird remains could be classified to a level below class due to excessive fragmentation and the relatively high proportion of worked bone (14%); by way of comparison, only 3% of mammal bone was worked. Needs-Howarth (2012) noted that curated artifacts such as bird bone beads are notoriously difficult to identify beyond size class, especially if they had been manufactured at an earlier village where the identifiable longbone end waste material was deposited. Beads are known to have been made from the long, straight wing bones of Canada goose, turkey, and sandhill crane. Some species, like colorful woodpeckers or eagles, may have been caught for their feathers for fletching arrows or adornment (e.g., Wrong 1939:98; 117), while raven and other birds of prey may have been collected for ornamental and/or ideological reasons related to war (Steckley 2007: 201–5; Thwaites 1896–1901, 26: 267; 10: 325n17; see also C. Ramsden et al. 1998a: 73).

Migratory waterfowl are represented by a distal radius fragment of the common loon (*Gavia immer*), a tentative identification of the distal ulna of a male tundra or female trumpeter swan (cf. *Cygnus* sp.), probably caught in their migration through southern Ontario, and twelve fragments of Canada goose (*Branta canadensis*), which at the time of the occupation of the site did not typically winter or breed in the area. All of the duck material was fragmentary, and none of it could be identified below family.

At least three species of raptor were identified, including red-shouldered or red-tailed hawk (*Buteo* sp.; House 71); bald eagle (*Haliaeetus leucocephalus*; Midden 1 and Houses 4, 86/87); and northern goshawk (*Accipiter gentillis*; northern borrow trench). The goshawk element was a coracoid but the remaining specimens appear to have been from distal hind limbs and may represent curated feet. Two owl identifications, including one ulna fashioned into a bead (House 71/73), both match the size of great horned owl (*Bubo virginianus*). It is interesting to note that House 71 yielded two raptor elements, which may signal that special activities occurred in the house.

The upland game birds included ruffed grouse (*Bonasa umbellus*, n=21), wild turkey (*Meleagris gallopavo*, n=16), and passenger pigeon (*Ectopistes migratorius*, n=66). The latter comprise 13% of the bird remains and 67% of the identified bird specimens. Passenger pigeons are now extinct, but their remains are ubiquitous on Iroquoian sites as they were once so numerous that one in four birds in North America was a passenger pigeon, with nesting colonies in oak or beech forest occupying "hundreds of square miles" (Godfrey 1966:208).

Common crow (*C. brachyrhynchos*) was found at the site, and a common raven (*Corvus corax*) tibiotarsus was tentatively identified in Midden 1. This specimen could represent a very large crow or raven, which was once common in southern Ontario (Cadman et al. 2007:384). According to Sagard (Wrong 1939:221), crow was not eaten, and raven remains have been linked with Wendat war bundles (Steckley 2007:204–5). Four small woodpecker (northern flicker or yellow-bellied sapsucker) ulnae were found, perhaps indicating that these elements had been processed for their bright-colored feathers.

Fish

Fish accounted for 6% of identified animal specimens. Fish represented 8% of the animal bone from Draper (Burns 1979) and 14% from Parsons (Thomas 1998). Where data are available for precoalescent sites in the Rouge-Duffins drainage, they have far higher percentages of fish bone. For example, the faunal assemblage from the White site consisted of 44% fish remains (Tripp 1978), from Burkholder 2 33% (ASI 2005a), and from the Robin Hood site 50% (Williamson 1983). Similar aged sites in the Don River drainage system to the west have 50%–60% representation of fish, and even the Keffer site, a coalescent village, has 61% fish in the animal bone (Stewart 1991). The fourteenth-century Robb site in the Rouge River system had an even higher 70% fish (ASI 2010a). While there are many taphonomic factors that might affect the survival and recovery of fish bone, the percentages for Draper and Mantle compared to earlier sites indicate that fishing was not as important an activity as it had been in precoalescent villages. The Don River data also suggest that significant effort was expended on fishing until the end of the fifteenth century, unlike at Draper and Mantle in the Rouge-Duffins system or at Parsons and Damiani (ASI 2012d) on the Humber River.

While fishing strategies no doubt varied through time and among communities adapted to differing natural environments, ethnographic descriptions of contact-period Wendat fishing clearly situates the activity in the context of their worldview that attributes a spirit/soul to all plants and animals as well as inanimate objects. These narratives also enumerate human responsibilities for the careful maintenance of the relationships with those spirits (see also Engelbrecht 2003:4–6; Sioui 1999). Sagard noted, for example, that fish bone could not be thrown into a fire as the spirits of the bone would warn other fish not to be caught (Wrong 1939:186–87).

Almost 55% of the fish from Mantle could be classified to a taxonomic level below class, and 47% could be classified to family or lower. The site yielded twenty unique fish taxa. A number of different fish habitats would have been available within a day's travel of the site. Duffins Creek is dominated by cold-water aquatic communities and currently features forty-five riverine species of fish; the lower watershed is a natural warm-water reach that, with its associated marsh, provides good habitat for a number of warm-water species such as smallmouth bass, northern pike, and pumpkinseed (TRCA 2002:3–4). Ten of the taxa known from Duffins Creek were identified in the archaeological assemblage, namely Atlantic salmon (*Salmo salar*), white sucker (*Catostomus commersonii*), brown bullhead (*Ameirus nebulosus*), channel catfish (*Ictalurus punctatus*), American eel (*Anguilla rostrata*), rock bass (*Ambloplites rupestris*), pumpkinseed (*Lepomis gibbosus*), smallmouth bass (*Micropterus dolomieu*), largemouth bass (*Micropterus salmoides*), and yellow perch (*Perca flavescens*). Today, eel and channel catfish are found only in the creek estuary.

The distance from the site to Lake Ontario, whose coastal wetlands and estuaries were attractive environments due to their high biotic productivity, is about thirty kilometers to the south of the site. Similar environments on the shores of Lake Simcoe are about forty kilometers to the north. Not all of the waterways leading to these lakes would have been navigable by canoe. In the absence of a carefully constructed hydrographic model to estimate preclearance water levels, it can only confidently be stated that the lower few kilometers of waterways would have been navigable. A series of well-established trails called the Humber and Rouge Carrying Places were historically documented, and their correlation with ancestral Wendat sites suggests their long-standing use to travel between Lake Ontario and Lake Simcoe (Veilleux 2011). That they were not navigable above a few kilometers inland is evident in the historic record of René-Robert Cavelier, Sieur de La Salle, for example, who had to portage his supplies on a number of occasions in the early 1680s from Teiaiagon, a Seneca village located on the Humber River, to the Holland River (Robinson 1933:36–41).

It is also not possible to determine how far spawning lake fish could have ascended the rivers of the area, because precontact groundwater levels are unknown and there may have been obstructions such as beaver dams hindering movement of fish in the upper reaches. This suggests that fish extracted from the lower reaches of the creek and Rouge River and offshore shoals would likely have been processed there rather than transported back whole.

Two seasonal fisheries have been postulated for ancestral Wendat communities along the north shore of Lake Ontario, including a generalized warm-weather fishery of the low-gradient lower reaches and estuaries of the streams and shallow inlets along the north Lake Ontario shoreline for resident taxa such as sucker, brown bullhead, rock bass, or immature, non-spawning yellow perch; a fall lake fishery focused on the nearshore streams and inshore shoals targeting autumn-spawning Salmonidae (e.g., Williamson, Thomas, and MacDonald 2003).

Of these, the fall lake fishery seems to have been a major focus for the Mantle site occupants. Salmonidae (Atlantic salmon, lake trout, whitefish), identified mainly from their vertebrae, comprise about 50% of the identified fish remains. Needs-Howarth (2012) noted that although the fragility of cranial bone no doubt affects its survival in the archaeological record, the relative lack of cranial bone may evidence off-site processing, whereby the heads were removed and (part of) the vertebral column was left in the dried or smoked fish, a processing pattern described by Sagard for historic Wendat (Wrong 1939:186). A similar pattern was documented at the early-fourteenth-century Moatfield site on the Don River (Williamson, Thomas, and MacDonald 2003), where it was hypothesized that people may have processed and dried (or smoked) salmon caught at camps located at the Lake Ontario shore for ease of transport back to their village upstream. There are numerous early historic reports of exceedingly rich salmon fisheries in the streams draining into the north shore of Lake Ontario (MacKay 1963:57) involving the taking of over a thousand fish in a single fall evening. The presence of a few cranial bones suggests that at least some whole salmonids were transported to the site.

Twenty bones of American eel (*Anguilla rostrata*) were also identified, including fragments of three crania and seventeen vertebrae. Since eel cranial bones are very fragile and the caudal vertebrae are small enough to fall through 6 mm mesh, eel may be underrepresented in the assemblage. Like Salmonidae, eel can be stored after smoking, and their skins were said by Champlain to have been used for tying women's hair (Biggar 1922–1936, 3:134). Catching eels would have necessitated a trip to the mouth of the creek at Lake Ontario; they too would have been taken during the fall lake fishery (see also Williamson, Thomas, and MacDonald 2003:56).

Those fish that could be caught closer to the site in nearby rivers or streams include perch (*Perca flavescens*); brook trout (*Salvelinus fontinalis*); suckers (*Catostomidae*), which account for 16% of fish identified below class; channel catfish (*Ictalurus punctatus*); brown bullhead (*Ameiurus cf. nebulosus*); walleye or sauger (*Sander* sp.); northern pike (*Esox lucius*); and muskellunge (*Esox masquinongy*). Forty-four Ameiurus identifications were all very similar to brown bullhead, and an additional forty-three bones were identified to the catfish family and could conceivably include stonecat (*Noturus flavus*), which is known from Duffins Creek today. Many of these fish were likely exploited incidentally throughout the warm weather, perhaps using basket traps or pound nets (Williamson, Thomas, and MacDonald 2003:68–69).

In summary, there seems to have been an emphasis on the mass capture of fall-spawning fish that are amenable to storage, namely lake trout, whitefish, Atlantic salmon, and eel. Another focus was on suckers, which are most readily caught during their spawning run in spring, but which can be caught at other times with little effort. The fall fishery would have gone on for about two months, and gillnets would have to have been tended regularly to extract those fish that became entangled and died.

Despite the emphasis on the fall fishery reflected in the faunal assemblage, the mean nitrogen isotopic value of 10.5 taken on a sample of fourteen teeth from Mantle indicates that the contribution of lake fish to the diet of the Mantle inhabitants was minimal by comparison with Middle Woodland populations and earlier precoalescent north shore sites (e.g., Moatfield) (table 5.3). Even values for the late-sixteenth-century terminal Humber River population (e.g., Skandatut/Kleinburg) display relatively low values in comparison with later contact-period Wendat populations (e.g., Ossossané), which yield significantly higher values reflecting their historically recorded reliance on lake fish for protein. In light of the scarcity of large game in the Simcoe County environment (Robertson, Monckton, and Williamson 1995:77–80), the Wendat, while still undertaking fall deer hunts along the north shore of Lake Ontario, traded for large numbers of hides for clothing and the fall lacustrine fishery resumed its crucial importance in the economic strategies of certain Wendat tribal systems, as it had been for their ancestors on the Iroquois Plain three hundred years previously.

Mammals

The mammal portion of the assemblage contains twenty-three unique taxa, although it is overwhelmingly dominated by deer (61%). On the other hand, small mammals were documented and, while fairly costly and difficult to exploit for hunters, represented an easily accessible food source in the context of Iroquoian villages, where these kinds of animals would have fed on village refuse or corn in the surrounding fields (Thomas, Carscallen, and Needs-Howarth 1998; Williamson, Thomas, and MacDonald 2003:77).

Stephen Cox Thomas (Williamson, Thomas, and MacDonald 2003:77) calls these "garden-hunted species" and includes the following animals in the category: snowshoe hare (*Lepus americanus*), eastern cottontail (*Sylvilagus floridanus*), gray squirrel (*Sciurus carolinensis*), red squirrel (*Tamiasciurus hudsonicus*), chipmunk (*Tamias striatus*), and woodchuck (*Marmota monax*). All of these animals have pelts, which were desired; the Neutral, for example, made highly prized robes of squirrel skins (Thwaites 1896–1901, 17:243n8; 33:193–95). Gray squirrel (n=30), American red squirrel (n=31), and twenty-six Sciuridae fragments not identified to species were recovered. Only a few fragments of snowshoe hare or rabbit family were recovered.

Chapter 5

Table 5.3. Delta 13N Values for Archaeological Sites in Ontario

Site/Component	Approx. Date	n	Average Delta15N	STDV	Source
Morrison's Is.	2300 ± 400 BC	3	12.3	0.4	Schwartz et al. 1985
Donaldson site/ Cemetery 1	530 BC (555 ± 25 BC)	1	13.7	0.2	Schwartz et al. 1985
Donaldson site/ Cemetery 2	AD 5 ± 75	2	12.6	1.1	Schwartz et al. 1985
Levesconte mound	AD 174 ± 55	4	13.4	0.2	Schwartz et al. 1985
Serpent mounds/Mound E	AD 205 ± 90	3	12.7	0.6	Schwartz et al. 1985
Serpent mounds/Mound G and I	AD 400 ± 100	4	12.5	1.1	Schwartz et al. 1985
Monarch Knoll	AD 500	1	11.2	0	Katzenberg et al. 1995
Surma	AD 700	4	12.8	0.7	Katzenberg et al. 1995
Varden	AD 920	11	11.2	0.4	Katzenberg et al. 1995
Miller	AD 1152	5	13.4	0.9	Katzenberg et al. 1995
Serpent mounds/Pit 2	AD 1170 ± 120	3	12.3	0.8	Schwartz et al. 1985
Bennett	AD 1275	1	12.1	0	Katzenberg et al. 1995
Serpent mounds/Pit 3	AD 1290	2	12.5	0	Schwartz et al. 1985
Force site	AD 1240	2	11.8	0.1	Schwartz et al. 1985
Moatfield ossuary	AD 1300	11	12.4	0.7	van der Merwe et al. 2003
Fairty ossuary	AD 1350 ± 50	4	11.8	0.4	Schwartz et al. 1985
Hidden Spring	AD 1430-1480	7	10.7	0.7	Bower 2011
Uxbridge	AD 1490	9	11.1	0.7	Harrison and Katzenberg 2003
Mackenzie-Woodbridge	AD 1500	3	10.8	0.7	Katzenberg et al. 1995

Mantle	AD 1500-1530	14	10.5	0.5	Pfeiffer et al. 2013
MacPherson	AD 1550	29	12.4	1.3	Katzenberg et al. 1993
Ball site	AD 1600	5	11.8	0.7	Schwartz et al. 1985
Kleinburg ossuary	AD 1600	4	12.2	0.1	Schwartz et al. 1985
Ossossané ossuary	AD 1636	4	13.2	0.6	Schwartz et al. 1985
Cooper ossuary	AD 1645	3	11.2	0.6	Schwartz et al. 1985

Woodchucks (n=137; 3%) and chipmunks (n=23) would have been particularly attracted to corn and are known garden pests. Some of these fur-bearing species may also have contributed meat to the diet.

Larger fur-bearing species would have been especially targeted. Beaver (*Castor canadensis*) were certainly hunted in the summer and early fall for their furs, incisors, and possibly meat. The basic garment of the historic Wendat was described as a single beaver skin worn over the shoulders or back (e.g., Thwaites 1896–1901, 15:155). The 107 beaver bones in the assemblage, however, constitute only 2% of the mammal identifications. The relative dearth of beaver in the assemblage suggest they may not have been available in the immediate environment at this time, or perhaps that larger mammal pelts were preferred for the manufacture of clothing by these ancestral Wendat. Similarly, only seven muskrat (*Ondatra zibethicus*) specimens were recovered, all of which could have come from a single individual, and a few bones of both red fox (*Vulpes vulpes*) and gray fox (*Urocyon cinereoargenteus*) were also identified.

Black bears (*Ursus americanus*) are best caught just before they go into hibernation in the late fall or early winter, when they are fat and sluggish from eating and their pelts are in prime condition. Just over eighty fragments (MNI of 3) of adult bear were found, suggesting hunting of the species. Heidenreich (1971:204–5) has argued that the historic Wendat did not engage in systematic bear hunting because their wide ranges and low population densities would have resulted in high search costs. The presence among the remains of a number of bear canines and phalanges suggest these were curated and used in ornamentation or came with hides. The Jesuits and Champlain did, however, document the practice among the Wendat of raising young bears in enclosures within longhouses and killing them after two or three years for a feast (Biggar 1922–1936, vol. 3, 3:130); there was no obvious evidence of this practice in the settlement patterns of Mantle, although one canine, one mandibular fragment, and one tibial fragment of young bear were recovered from Midden 1.

Raccoons (*Procyon lotor*) are omnivorous, and corn is a preferred food when available (Banfield 1981). Raccoons would also be in prime condition in terms of meat and pelts in fall. The seventeen raccoon specimens include three bacula or penis bones, which on the basis of their polish, are likely to have been curated, perhaps as pendants. No bacula of other animals were identified.

It is unlikely that Iroquoians would have eaten mink or marten on a regular basis as their meat would have been largely unpalatable. They too were valued for their fur, as occasional skinning marks demonstrate. Sixteen Mustelidae identifications, including marten (*Martes americana*), tentative fisher (cf. *Martes pennanti*), and mink (*Mustella vison*), came from a variety of midden, feature, and post contexts. Two probable otter (*Lontra canadensis)* phalanges were also found and were likely attached to a pelt.

Lynx and bobcat are similarly boned but differ in size. The *Lynx* sp. is represented by two teeth and two left ulnae, while a tentatively identified bobcat (*Lynx rufus*) proximal phalanx was also found. While these felids are very shy of humans and would have been difficult to procure, Sagard (Wrong 1939:224) noted that the Wendat hunted a kind of wildcat; the Erie, another Iroquoian-speaking group situated south of the Neutral, made robes or blankets of the skins of a "leopard." Sagard once confused such a robe as having been made with wolf hides, suggesting it might have indeed been bobcat given their similarity in appearance.

While 325 domestic dog (*Canis lupus familiaris*) elements were recovered, an additional 182 were identified as either wolf or dog. Eastern wolf (*C. lycaon*) is present at the site, but only five elements were identified. Verification of the species of wolf is uncertain due to the recent identification in southwestern Ontario of "an eastern wolf that evolved in North America (New World), rather than a subspecies of grey wolf (*C. lupus*) that evolved in Eurasia" (Rutledge et al. 2010:1278) and any possible hybridization among gray wolves and eastern wolves. Indeed, genetically pure *C. lycaon* populations no longer exist.

The incomplete remains of a subadult dog were found in an interior shallow pit situated adjacent to a wall of House 31 and were analyzed by Peter Popkin and Thanos Webb. The remains seem to represent food refuse, given the presence of a cut mark on the coracoid process of the scapula, its location perhaps intended to help with the removal of the humerus during disarticulation of the animal in the course of a meal. In that fragile immature bones of the dog were recovered from within the feature, the missing elements, including for example hip bones and vertebrae, suggest initial processing of the animal may have occurred elsewhere. Dogs were raised for hunting but were also eaten at special feasts and during times of famine (Thwaites 1896–1901, 7:223; Wrong 1939:226).

This does not mean, however, that the Wendat or their ancestors did not form close attachments to some of their animals. Georges Sioui (1999:107) has noted that "much-loved dogs were 'reincarnated' by having their names transmitted to one of their 'kin'" and also that the souls of dogs go to the "Village of Souls" by the way of certain stars that are near neighbors of the human soul's path "the Milky Way," and which the Wendat called "Gagnen-onandahatey the dog's path" (Wrong 1939:172). Joyce Wright (2004: 305–19) has detailed the ways in which dogs were part of the cosmological world of the Wendat as messengers to the spiritual realm, especially in the contexts of causing or curing illnesses and war and sacrifice.

The hunting of white-tailed deer (*Odocoileus virginianus*) and wapiti or elk (*Cervus canadensis*) by the site inhabitants for hides, meat, and bone for making tools must have been one of the most important economic considerations and planned seasonal activities. Deer account for 61% of the mammal bone classified to a taxonomic level below class (n=2,654). In addition, there are confirmed remains of wapiti (n=67), moose (*Alces alces*) (n=1), Cervidae "deer/wapiti sized" (n=112), Cervidae "wapiti/moose sized" (n=26), and antler (probably mostly deer by size) (n=141). *Artiodactyla* remains were also found that could not be identified to family (n=209). Some of these identifications could be sheep, goat, or cow, given the limited presence of those species in the area of the nineteenth-century mill and farm buildings, but most are probably deer.

According to Sagard (Wrong 1939:225), wapiti were present in southern Ontario and were reported in the southern shield in the nineteenth century (Peterson 1966). Wapiti remains were found in a variety of feature, post, and midden contexts, and while teeth, vertebrae, and longbones are present, most are tarsals, metatarsals, and phalanges. Only one worked moose metatarsal was recovered; it features considerable polish, suggesting that it had been curated for some time. As moose were not present in southern Ontario at the time of the site's occupation (Wrong 1939:224–25), it was most likely introduced by an Algonquian visitor to the site.

The 2,654 deer bones present at the Mantle site as a whole provide an MNI for white-tailed deer of 30, clearly an insignificant number in the context of the need for substantial numbers of deer hides on the part of the community. In terms of the caloric contribution of deer meat to the diet, Heidenreich (1971:163) estimated that deer represented about 6% of the caloric requirements of the historic Wendat compared to about 9% subsequently estimated by E. Randolph Turner and Robert Santley (1979). The ethnographic record for the historic Wendat indicates that meat of any nature was rare in times other than during the fall seasonal hunt (e.g., Biggar

1922–1936, 3:126; Thwaites 1896–1901, 17:142; Wrong 1939:82, 106–7), which may have been true for ancestral Wendat populations on the north shore as well, given their annual requirements for hides and the likely competition for deer among neighboring communities. On the basis of the faunal assemblage, it would seem that other fur-bearing mammals were not of major consequence in either the diet or clothing of the community's occupants.

All parts of the deer body are represented in the assemblage, although not in equal numbers. Needs-Howarth (2012) notes that an overrepresentation of lower limb bones in the assemblage may not be due to differential transportation of body parts back to the site because metapodia were regularly altered to produce awls, needles, and projectile points, and phalanges were modified and curated. These elements would have been retained regardless of where the carcass was initially butchered (Burns 1979; Thomas, Carscallen, and Needs-Howarth 1998:95). The recovery of 160 mostly unmodified cranial elements as well as 292 loose teeth or fragments indicates that at least some deer were taken locally, in that their presence at the site represents a proportionately heavy part of the animal with relatively little meat.

Young and adults of all ages were being hunted, as evidenced by epiphyseal fusion and tooth eruption and wear. The presence of unshed antler indicates fall or early winter deposition, a preferable time for the taking of dense antler intended for the manufacture of tools. One cranium with part of the pedicle was found, as well as another where cut marks showed that the antler had been removed by hacking. Six portions of adhering pedicle were also found at the Draper site (Burns 1979:143), suggesting that whole deer were being hunted nearby and brought back to that site.

Most deer would have been taken at places far enough from the village that at least initial processing would have occurred at the kill site or hunt camp and meat and hides returned to the base settlement. While for most of the year deer are solitary, they are found in small groups in mast-producing forest in the autumn and in larger herds in winter when they may congregate ("yard") in stands of white cedar that provide shelter and are free of deep snow. Frances Stewart (1991:25) has outlined the major reasons why deer would be best taken in the fall or early winter, including higher densities of deer in known feeding spots rendering them easier to hunt than in other seasons when they are solitary; better size and quality of antlers that remain on the animals; maximum meat yield by weight (Severinghaus and Cheatum 1956:83); and the best quality of hides since the deer winter coat is longer and stiffer than the summer coat and has an undercoat, which the summer coat does not (Banfield 1981:392). Deer meat obtained in fall could be dried for future use and frozen if taken in the winter. In warmer seasons, the meat was probably smoked.

The historic Wendat certainly participated in fall deer drives or group hunts, resulting in one case in the capture of 120 deer (Biggar 1922–1936, vol. 3, 3:85). Archaeological evidence of such a drive and camp was found at the Early Iroquoian Little site in southwestern Ontario, where a seventeen-meter-wide surround (with blind) was documented within which was found a single feature containing ten thousand bones of at least eight deer (Williamson 1990:314–16).

Investigating the ways in which members of the Mantle community clothed themselves requires consideration of its population, the estimated annual requirement on the part of a family for hides, the regional habitat for deer at the time of the site's occupation, estimates of their densities, and the availability of other animal hides through hunting and/or trade to meet the requirements.

The first detailed attempt of this kind was that of Gramly (1977), who produced an estimate of the requirements of the historic Wendat for hides, arguing that competition over hunting territories may have led to the abandonment of the north shore and that the creation of the Wendat Confederacy was in response to increasing population and rising demands for hides. He argued that by historic times their hunting territory, covering the entire north shore between Toronto and Kingston south of the Canadian Shield, was unable to meet their needs, necessitating trade for hides with their Algonquian neighbors. Webster (1979) criticized Gramly's approach and numbers, arguing that mass fall deer hunts were a successful strategy for the Wendat although costly in terms of effort (see also Trigger 1981b), while Turner and Santley (1979) argued that no single factor could have necessitated the abandonment of the north shore and the formation of the confederacy, noting other sources of ecological stress including increasing requirements for arable land for agriculture and deer meat. These arguments, however, were focused on the historic Wendat and their overall requirements and not that of the north shore communities. The data available now regarding those communities, while far from complete, allow for the modeling of hunting territories just prior to the formation of the Wendat Confederacy.

An initial attempt at modeling hunting territories for the Mantle site used two scenarios based on population estimates of 1,500 and 2,000 people, community requirements of 3,000 or 6,800 hides annually, and deer densities of 2.4 or 1.75 deer/km^2 (Needs-Howarth and Williamson 2010). This resulted in hunting territories of 1,250 or 3,885 km^2. To remodel the hunting territories of Mantle and other regional communities, we have used the methods for estimating populations presented in chapter 4 for Mantle, Keffer, and Seed-Barker and reexamined both hide requirements and deer densities, resulting in different-sized territories.

Evidence permitting an accurate estimate for the number of deerskins necessary to clothe a Wendat person is sparse. The best description comes from Champlain (Biggar 1922–1936, vol. 3, 3:132) in which he describes their breeches as having been made of a moderately large deerskin and their leggings reaching as high as the waist, with many folds of another. He suggests their moccasins are made of the skins of deer, bear, and beaver, which they use in great numbers. The other garment mentioned by Champlain is a cloak with sleeves that tie in the back with a cord. The cloak was later described in 1639 by the Jesuit François du Peron as a single beaver skin worn over the shoulders or back (Thwaites 1896–1901, 15:155), although one beaver skin would not have been of sufficient size to manufacture the garment he describes. Poncho-style cloaks worn by the Blackfeet, Cree, Omaha, Sioux, Crow, Mandan, and Assiniboine were made from two elk hides (McCabe 2002:158). Hides were used for other purposes—for example, the spreading of corn, manufacturing of tobacco pouches and game bags, and wrapping of bodies or offerings at death (Thwaites 1896–1901, 10:265–79; Wrong 1939:59; 102). In reference to the latter use, hides may have been scarce at times for clothing, as it was noted by Le Jeune in 1636 that "you will see them often, in the depth of winter, almost entirely naked, while they have handsome and valuable robes in store, that they keep in reserve for the Dead; for this is their point of honor" (Thwaites 1896–1901, 10:265).

In Kathryn Braund's detailed description of Creek clothing, she describes the requirement for two deerskins to manufacture enough breechcloths for a family of four (two adults and two children), each being approximately five feet long and one-and-a-half feet wide (Braund 1993:71n61), and that one large deerskin could be cut in half longitudinally to make two breechcloths. Despite the fact that northeastern deer are somewhat larger than those found in the southeast, Champlain's suggestion that it takes one deerskin to make a pair of leggings seems low. Based on leggings made by reenactors and anthropologists, it appears that two deerskins are needed to make a pair of leggings (Morgan Baillargeon and David Christensen, personal communications). Essential to these estimates is the use-life of the leggings. Métis reenactor David Christensen claims that leggings can wear out in a couple of months during the hunting season, but that on occasion he has had a pair that lasted for two years; longevity is dependent on the thickness of the hide and the amount of use. Morgan Baillargeon, curator of Plains ethnology at the Canadian Museum of Civilization, suggests that depending on the size of the person and the nature of the trimmings, one large moose hide or two deer hides would be required for leggings, whereas for pants, three deer hides would be required. These could be finished with a single large moose hide.

Moccasins require about one square foot of hide per moccasin; five to seven pairs could be manufactured from a single hide, depending on fringes and large cuffs (L. Turner 1894:285). They wear out quickly, however, and historic Naskapi men needed two to three hides per year to maintain footgear (L. Turner 1894:285). Each family member, especially traders or warriors on long-distance excursions, would likely have had multiple pairs in order to change footwear when they got wet. This practice would have been essential during the winter months, since there is little evidence for fur-lined moccasins in Ontario (Morgan Baillargeon, personal communication).

To summarize, for a family of four, and assuming the use of deer hides given the relative dearth of beaver in the faunal assemblage and the absence of moose in the natural environment, it would seem that two hides would be required for the manufacture of breechcloths, four hides for adult leggings, two hides for children's leggings, four hides for cloaks, four hides for moccasins, and four hides for other purposes, suggesting an annual requirement of twenty hides per nuclear family. Gramly (1977) calculated it would take an average of 3.5 hides per person (men, women, and children) annually to provide moccasins and clothing for a historic Wendat family, not accounting for other uses. These provide for relatively similar estimates of 4.5 to 5 hides per person, including an additional hide per person for all potential uses. For a population of 1,500 people, the annual requirement would be approximately 6,750 to 7,500 deer. For the purposes of modeling here, we will assume an annual requirement of 7,000 deer for the Mantle community.

Reconstructing past deer densities for a region requires an understanding of their reproductive ecology, as well as an appreciation of the natural environment at the time of occupation. To some extent, this can be based on the current potential for the landscape to support deer. The *Canada Land Inventory Map: Land Capability for Wildlife—Ungulates* (Agriculture and Agri-Food Canada 1971) rates the region around the site as Class 1 for white-tailed deer. This is based on the predominance of deep, well-drained clay loams along with local topographical variations that provide a variety of habitats for ungulates—the main implication being that the original vegetation would have included the kinds of plants that deer like to eat. On the other hand, the presettlement old-growth, closed-canopy northern hardwood forest with minimal understory would likely have failed to provide adequate browse for deer (see also Hickerson 1965:54–59). Exceptions to this would be forest edge areas and secondary growth occurring in blowdowns, and the previously cleared and then abandoned agricultural fields of the previous half century of community occupations. Such secondary growth, which was important to the encouragement of necessary browse, would have been extensive throughout the South Slope plain from the Credit River to east of the Rouge River (see chapter 3). Indeed, by the time Mantle was occupied, the former fields of fourteenth- and fifteenth-century sites would have provided better deer habitat in the region than there had been two hundred years earlier.

It is difficult, however, to move beyond the general characterization of the early-sixteenth-century ungulate capability of the site environs with any estimate of actual density. Deer studies from twentieth-century Ontario provide relatively low density figures of 1–6 deer/km^2 (Voigt et al. 1992:31). In some high-density areas such as the Peterborough Crown Game Preserve, Long Point National Wildlife Area, Pinery Provincial Park, Point Pelee National Park, and Rondeau Park, deer have reached densities as high as 22.7 deer/km^2 but only for a short period of time before a shortage of vegetation causes the deer numbers to plummet (Voigt et al. 1992:36–40). Even so, Owen Williams, who managed the deer populations at the Rondeau Park in the 1980s for the Ontario Ministry of Natural Resources, estimated a density of 19 deer/km^2 for the environmental reconstruction on the Caradoc Sand Plain in southwestern Ontario (Williamson 1985:133). Other estimates provided by researchers include 13.1 deer/km^2 for Canada (Banfield 1981:393), 15.45 deer/km^2 for an undisturbed eastern deciduous forest (Shelford 1963:26), 8–10 deer/km^2 for forest edge environments in southern Wisconsin (Hickerson 1965:55), and 11.6 deer/km^2 for an upland Mississippi valley habitat or 19.3 deer/km^2 for a lowland Mississippi valley habitat (B. Smith 1975:41). Arthur Keene (1981) provided a projected deer density for the Saginaw Valley in Michigan, arguing that the most important factors determining density are the availability of mast, forage, and the degree of predation (Keene 1981:101). After a close consideration of the reconstructed environment, he provided a conservative figure of 7.72 deer/km^2. The deer densities for the Cherokee Territory during the eighteenth century were estimated to range from 5.6 to 13.2 deer/km^2, with a mean value of 9.4 deer/km^2 (Bolstad and Gragson 2008:567). Using modern wildlife data, Gramly (1977:603) postulated that if the Wendat purposefully rotated their hunting territories, they could maintain a yield of 1.8 deer/km^2 assuming 50% predation, meaning a density of roughly 4 deer/km^2. Turner and Santley's (1979) model resulted in a range of between 1.4 and 2.4 deer/km^2. Current deer populations in the north shore region range from 5 to 12 deer/km^2.

For the purposes of this study, we will use a figure of 15 deer/km^2, reflecting Shelford's density for an undisturbed eastern deciduous forest. In using this figure, we assume that the presence of substantial secondary growth due to the presence of abandoned agricultural fields was a crucial factor in providing for browse but are mindful of modern ecologists' arguments about the sustainability of too-high densities and of our uncertainty around predation rates in precontact times.

Using that density and a requirement of 7,000 deer annually, the Mantle occupants would have required 1428 km² of hunting territory to sustain populations, assuming a 35% predation rate (Bolstad and Gragson 2008) rather than the 50% assumed by Gramly (1977). Visualized as an umland around the community, it would have a radius of 21 km and would certainly have overlapped with the required deer territories of the Keffer and Seed-Barker neighboring villages, had they been occupied concurrently with populations of 600 and 1,000 respectively.

We also modeled using the watersheds within which the communities were located, predicated on the notion that their edges might represent borders or contested lands between site catchments, perhaps minimizing conflict between villages and even helping to sustain animal populations in the transition zones (Hickerson 1965; McCabe 2002:148). For the Mantle site, the Rouge-Duffins watershed was used; for Keffer, the Don River watershed; and for Seed-Barker, the Humber River watershed. Using these watersheds resulted, however, in the realization that the hunting territories of these or their predecessor communities would have overlapped to the extent that it is unlikely that they were coterminous (figure 5.2). In particular, the model demonstrates that the coterminous occupation of Parsons, Keffer, and Draper would have been impossible, especially if warfare was intricately linked with competition for deer as has been postulated for precontact tribal societies based on historically recorded patterns (McCabe 2002:148). Given the recovery of considerable quantities of scattered human bone from all three sites, there seems no doubt that increasing competition over deer-hunting territory may have been the factor that led to the abandonment of the Don drainage around AD 1500, thereby creating a buffer zone between the Humber and Rouge-Duffins communities. Only the upper Humber watershed was large enough to have accommodated the needs of the Parsons and later Seed-Barker community, although if their hunting had been restricted to their watershed, they would have had to travel a considerable distance westward and northward.

Given these models, it is difficult to imagine the Mantle villagers not having mounted numerous mass-capture hunting expeditions each fall at some distance from their village. The labor and time required for providing hides for clothing would only have increased if people had used alternate, non-mass-capture sources such as trapping small fur-bearing mammals. Yet there is no evidence of deer drives or hunting camps yielding large quantities of processed deer bone in the archaeological record of the north shore. They therefore may have traveled some distance, perhaps northward to southern Simcoe County, to undertake these hunts, probably in an effort to avoid encountering hunting parties from other villages. The Mantle occupants no doubt also traded shelled maize for hides with northern Algonquians, as the ethnography of the historic Wendat indicates.

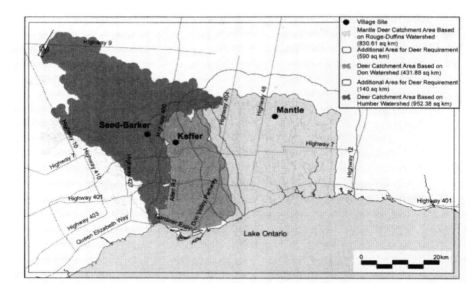

Figure 5.2.   Modeled deer catchments for sites in the Humber, Don and Rouge-Duffins Watersheds

Modified Bone

The hunting of deer, other small mammals, and birds also provided bone for making certain classes of tools. About 3% (n=1,142) of the faunal assemblage had been modified by humans; 82% was mammal, mostly deer, and 10% bird (Needs-Howarth 2012). Many fragments of modified deer longbone and metapodial, for example, were recovered. The metapodial fragments were modified into tools (and some of these were also heat altered), while the longbones had discontinuous polish on the spiral fracture margin, suggesting their use as expedient hide-working tools.

Several formal complete perforating devices, commonly called awls, were recovered. While most of these are thought to have functioned as hide-working implements, a few with styloid-tipped points may have functioned as tattooing needles. One awl, manufactured of deer metatarsal, is ground and polished and decorated with incised chevrons of different sizes and spacing, as well as oblique, vertical, and horizontal lines along its entire length (figure 5.3). Some of these designs perhaps represent lightning energy symbols or journey or snake manifestations (Williamson and Veilleux 2005).

Two complete thin netting needles for manufacturing fishnets or snowshoes were also recovered. One appears to have been fashioned from a piece of dog-sized mammal longbone that has been ground flat and then tapered at both ends and perforated about halfway along its length. The other is likely

Figure 5.3. Awl and Netting Needles

made from deer longbone and is perforated approximately one-third of the way along its length. The fact that these items are largely intact, despite their extreme thinness, is probably due to the small holes, rendering them less susceptible to breakage at the point of perforation (see figure 5.3).

Pendants include mammal teeth, including a dog lower canine that had been perforated transversely through the root. The perforation is intact and there is use wear or polish on the root; the enamel of the tip was worn or removed by spalling (figure 5.4). A number of bear canines were also recovered, one of which had cracked at the point at which the root narrows near the tip, perhaps as a result of attempts at modification to facilitate its attachment to a cord.

As noted, 14% of the bird bone was modified, much of which was likely intended to produce bone beads or tubes. Yet, few complete beads were recovered from Mantle (n=4). One of these is a piece of bird or mammal longbone that had been ground perpendicular on both ends and highly polished on the outer cortex—perhaps intentional polish rather than that resulting from use (Needs-Howarth 2012) (see figure 5.4).

The rarity of finished beads is noteworthy. In a survey of decorated bone beads from Iroquoia, approximately 75% were recovered from Neutral sites in southwestern Ontario. Ancestral Wendat sites have yielded just less than 10% of all the decorated beads/tubes; the remaining 15% is distributed in almost equal parts among ancestral Neutral, St. Lawrence Iroquoian, Seneca, and Mohawk sites (Williamson and Veilleux 2005:20–21). An especially

Figure 5.4.   Pendants, Beads, Antler Comb Pendant, and Modified Deer Phalange

interesting and rare artifact from Mantle, therefore, is a composite artifact, likely a pendant, manufactured from two beads, the shorter a piece of bird longbone and the other a fragment of metapodial of a wolf or dog. The beads are of different lengths, both with ground ends and polished surfaces, the longer of which was inserted within the shorter, wider one and fastened permanently (see figure 5.4). The major portion of the inserted bead, which extends below the short one, is marked with two alternating series of short notches on the two margins of the piece, ten visible on one side and eight on the other. It is not known if other notches are present within the seated portion of the bead. Small incised lines or scores are evident between the notches. While the composite construction of the artifact is rare in Iroquoia, the use of transverse incisions or short notches to decorate beads is not, appearing on over 65% of decorated specimens (Williamson and Veilleux 2005:21), often evenly spaced and interpreted to be some sort of tally system.

Another notched bead is manufactured from a mammal longbone, perhaps a dog radius that has been ground considerably and then notched where the bone flattens in circumference. There are four notches on one lateral side of the bead and three on the other (see figure 5.4). The notches on this bead are wide and deep and resemble those on the necks and collar bases of certain ceramic vessels (see chapter 6).

Needs-Howarth (2012) also identified 31 modified deer phalanges and 2 wapiti phalanges, out of 178 individual phalanges, some of which match Karen McCullough's (1978) description of the worked deer phalanges from the Draper site. Very similar artifacts have been found on numerous fourteenth- through sixteenth-century Ontario Iroquoian sites (e.g., Cooper 2010:131; Needs-Howarth 2006:117; C. Ramsden et al. 1998b:133–93). All of the Mantle specimens were ground on their anterior or posterior surfaces, some to the point of creating a hole in the marrow cavity on the posterior surfaces about midway between the epiphysis and the distal condyles; some had also been perforated distally and ground proximally (see figure 5.4). These artifacts have often been linked with a game that involved placing a number of phalanges attached to a leather thong or cord onto a bone pin. Ferris et al. (1985:8–10) have noted, however, that this game was not documented among Iroquoian groups (see also Tooker 1964:114–17) as it was for historic Ojibwa groups and that the modifications found on those game pieces are different than those found on Iroquoian sites. Iroquoian examples more likely functioned as toggles on the ends of cords (J. Wright 1974:100), as clothing fastening devices, or as adornment pieces. Needs-Howarth commented that there was sufficient bone on the site with which to make these kinds of artifacts in that the majority of phalanges were unmodified.

Only one artifact manufactured of antler was recovered; it consisted of a unique three-toothed, comb-shaped pendant found in four pieces from adjacent screened one-meter units in the northwest quadrant of the site (see figure

5.4). While the surface of the body of the piece is evenly polished, there is enhanced wear and polish around the hole from which it was suspended. There are evenly spaced lateral incisions across the body of the artifact from the base of the teeth to its head on one side and from the base of the teeth to the bottom of the hole on the other, the remainder perhaps erased through wear. Carved antler combs, whether intended for use as a comb or pendant, are extremely rare on ancestral and historic Wendat sites; present on Neutral sites, in particular in the historic period; but common from the sixteenth century to the late seventeenth century on Iroquois, especially Seneca, sites (Williamson and Veilleux 2005:8–16).

There were only a few modified shell fragments recovered from the site. In addition to one white discoidal shell bead, presumably manufactured from *Busycon* whelk, documented with one of the burials in the cemetery, two local thick-shelled aquatic snails were modified with small holes. A midsection of a bivalve shell was ground on the margins to form a circular shape and partly perforated, the perforation having been started on the interior surface of the valve. It is of a fairly thin-shelled freshwater taxon.

There is a long tradition of the manufacture and distribution of discoidal shell beads from *Busycon* whelk, along with Marginella and Olivella shells, likely traded from Chesapeake Bay through a number of precontact exchange networks (Bradley 2011:28–31; Fox 2008). George Hammell (1983; 1992) has linked the color white in these shell objects with Aboriginal cosmology and their use as gifts to the living and deceased, given that they frequently occur in mortuary contexts. Bradley (2011:31) documents the beginning of their use in Archaic times but argues that after centuries of absence, there was a dramatic resurgence of the trade in these items on mid-sixteenth-century Susquehannock and some Seneca sites. On Ontario Iroquoian sites, however, shell is not absent but present in small quantities, although local freshwater varieties were used to manufacture both beads and pendants, sometimes in large numbers (Needs-Howarth 2012). In a survey of Iroquoian sites subject to comprehensive excavations along the north shore of Lake Ontario, eight of twenty-one sites dating to between AD 1300 and AD 1500 yielded marine shell: four discoidal, three marginella, and three *Busycon* tubular beads in the fourteenth century; one pendant, one *Busycon* tubular bead, and one olive shell bead from fifteenth-century sites; and one discoidal bead from early-sixteenth-century sites. While similar quantities of beads are present in southwestern Ontario, there appears to have been sporadic presence of larger quantities of marginella shell beads in mortuary contexts (Fox 2008:3). Like Bradley's pattern, sites dating after the mid-sixteenth century yielded increasing numbers of marine shell. The ancestral Wendat late-sixteenth-century Skandatut site, for example, thought to represent the last Wendat occupation of the Humber River drainage, yielded twelve discoidal beads and one tubular bead, all from marine shell, off its surface, and hundreds of discoidal beads were found in its associated Kleinburg ossuary (ASI 2012e).

SUMMARY OF THE MANTLE COMMUNITY SUBSISTENCE SYSTEM

The archaeobotanical, zooarchaeological, isotopic, and material cultural data presented here indicate that the main food products of the Mantle site inhabitants were maize, deer, and fish supplemented by wild plant foods, small mammals, and birds.

The delta C13 values in table 5.1 reflect a pattern of a general increase in maize over time between AD 650 and AD 1300, with an initial peak around the early fourteenth century, which in Ontario is consistent with the very first period of village coalescence. The general trend, however, is consistent with data from Mississippi, Illinois, and Ohio in terms of a gradual increase in maize reliance (Bower 2011; Katzenberg et al. 1995). By the fourteenth century, archaeological and isotopic evidence suggests that 50%–60% of the Iroquoian diet was made up of maize, and on occasion more, as evidenced by the Moatfield data (van der Merwe et al. 2003). This contribution of maize drops slightly before reaching equal if not higher levels at the turn of the sixteenth century as evident in the Mantle, Uxbridge, and MacPherson site values. The rise in contribution might have resulted from agricultural intensification accompanying the second period of significant community coalescence. As at Moatfield, there appear to be intergenerational differences in maize consumption at MacPherson, with higher values for subadults (Katzenberg, Saunders, and Fitzgerald 1993).

The Mantle agricultural system, therefore, provided well over half of the calories to the community's diet and constituted the major ongoing economic activity at and around the site. By the end of the Mantle site's occupation, almost two thousand acres of land would have been under cultivation or abandoned, having lost their fertility. Modeling of the agricultural fields of the fifteenth-century villages on West Duffins Creek suggests modest overlapping of the field systems between sequential communities in order that the most productive fields were closest to the new village. It should also be noted that the trees felled in clearing the fields for agriculture would have been essential for the construction and maintenance of houses and palisade walls, and their limbs and branches dried and used for firewood. This system involved planting, tending, and harvesting crops for ongoing consumption; trade; and surplus for times of scarcity, all of which required coordination among the families in the community to produce, store, and share in foodstuffs. The modeling also revealed that it is unlikely that competition for fields would have been a contributor to any intercommunity tension along the north shore.

Once men had cleared the fields, their primary concern would have been to acquire sufficient hides for their family through hunting and trading. In this regard, our modeling has demonstrated that competition for deer hides among neighboring communities was a distinct possibility, given the enormity of the requirement and the available deer in the broader environment. This may indeed have been a factor in the conflict evidenced in the archaeological record of the late fifteenth century and the abandonment of the Don River drainage. The precoalescent sites all have well less than 35% deer in the identified mammal component, while at Draper and Mantle, the majority of the mammal bone consists of deer (61%). The percentages of dog, garden-hunted taxa, and other miscellaneous species at Draper and Mantle are very similar but considerably less than the earlier sites. From these data, it is evident that the focus in economic strategy shifted considerably between the precoalescent sites and Draper and Mantle—a shift that would also have involved transitioning from individual family or even lineage-based efforts to those organized at the level of focused work groups of individuals from multiple, perhaps clan-based, families.

It is likely, based on the nature of the recovered deer bone, that while some deer were taken close to the community, perhaps in the surrounding agricultural fields, men and some members of their families would have cooperated to engage in long-distance autumnal and winter mass-capture hunts. The fish remains from the site suggest that some energy was also expended in the fall to recover lake fish, when they are most easily taken in large numbers. Yet, the absence of an isotopic signature of a significant contribution to the diet of these fish points to a much greater effort expended to secure the meat and hides associated with the fall deer hunt. Alternatively, while the drop in nitrogen isotope values during the period suggests a decrease in the consumption of lake fish, it may also be true of animal protein more generally (Katzenberg et al. 1995), which itself might be a signal that hides were secured more frequently than meat and that competition for deer hides may have been a factor in the abandonment of the north shore as originally suggested by Gramly (1977).

All of these data suggest that many hides were acquired through trade either with other Iroquoian communities or with northern Algonquian bands, in return for surplus maize. While this is a recorded feature of historic Wendat life in Simcoe County, this study indicates that such trade must have been in place at least a century or two earlier. Those trading relationships and interaction networks would have contributed to a more diverse-looking material culture, possibly through the introduction of marriage partners, captives, or adoptees. These exchange systems would have been crucial in defining the routes by which European trade items first made their appearance in the Lower Great Lakes region at Mantle and contemporaneous communities, and they are explored in the next chapter.

Chapter Six

Production, Consolidation, and Interregional Interaction

In this chapter, we continue to explore the economy of the Mantle community with a specific focus on the material culture produced by the site's inhabitants and perhaps by outsiders or those peripheral to the community. These analyses consider the material culture of the site in the context of the constant requirement to produce and curate the ceramic and stone items that are required by the village inhabitants on a daily basis. These items reflect, however, both local and distant influences in their manufacture and design. We also explore how rare metal objects entered the village through exchange with contemporary communities.

In the latter part of the chapter, we address the burial of those who died during the tenure of the village, and how different mortuary practices existed for those who were the principal occupants of the village and those who were visiting the community when they died or who were simply considered "others." The archival and archaeological record of the region is clear that the community of the living would have designed a community of the dead, whereby they gathered the remains of all those who had died during the tenure of the village, placing them in an ossuary in which their remains were commingled. In this case, a cemetery was also created in which site inhabitants not intended for the ossuary remained interred and which may have been tended regularly after the village's abandonment. Both the site and the cemetery may have been regarded as sacred places long after the village's living inhabitants departed.

These analyses reveal the complex practices and behaviors that signified the construction and consolidation of a coherent community identity and at the same time involvement in far-reaching networks of interaction, trade, and exchange that stretched from the midcontinent to the Atlantic Ocean.

CERAMIC VESSELS

In total, 96,405 ceramic artifacts were recovered from the site, almost all of which are portions of vessel rims, necks, shoulders, and bodies. An additional 550 fragments of miscellaneous fired clay or ceramic objects (e.g., beads, marbles), 548 smoking pipe fragments, and 749 juvenile-manufactured ceramic vessel and pipe fragments were also recovered.

The juvenile ceramics were analyzed and reported on by Aleksandra Pradzynski (2012). The criteria used to distinguish between the juvenile and adult ceramic assemblages included crudeness of form, vessel size, and decorative motifs and techniques. The 193 vessels made by children were usually small or asymmetrical outflaring pinch pots with rounded lips, uneven walls, and a roughly finished, cracked surface. Clear juvenile fingernail and partial fingertip impressions left during the process of creating pots are visible on interior and exterior surfaces. It was clear that young potters and pipe-makers tended to copy the motifs and techniques used to decorate the material culture produced by adults.

The analysis of ceramic vessels produced by adult potters was carried out by Robert B. Wojtowicz (2012). All of the ceramic artifacts were mended prior to analysis, resulting in the identification of 1,914 vessels, which are summarized here. Rims were considered analyzable when they exhibited both interior and exterior surfaces, the lip, and sufficient exterior collar-neck area to ascertain decorative styles and attributes. It is worth noting that 131 fragments featured evidence of red and/or black pigments or slips. These pigments were examined by Brandi Lee MacDonald of McMaster University using a portable X-ray fluorescence device. The red slip was found to originate with iron-based red ochre, while the black was produced by a charred-bone pigment, based on significant calcium content.

Table 6.1 provides the frequencies for a range of ceramic vessel types based on Richard MacNeish (1952) and James Wright (1966). These types use the attributes of neck and collar motif and rim shape to construct classificatory types based upon the assumption that sets of combined attributes (types) represent styles that were in turn thought to reflect trends in time and space, even to the point that similarities and differences in frequencies of types between assemblages might relate to ethnic identity and chronological placement (J. Wright 1966:17). Critics of typological studies (e.g., P. Ramsden 1977:16–18; D. Smith 1983:10–14) questioned the simplistic methodology and inadequate sample used in the original definitions of types. John Hart and William Engelbrecht (2011) have recently used social network analysis to argue that even the most visible attribute combinations of collar development and collar decoration do not reflect traditional Iroquoian ethnic territories and that there are admixtures of design motifs among regions that support a rhizotic rather than dendritic model of northern Iroquoian ethnic evolution—which is fully consistent with the fact that the autonomous, multilineage village represented the maximal political unit prior to communities joining the political confederacies of the late precontact period (Williamson and Robertson 1994; Engelbrecht 2003:113). We should therefore not be surprised by differences in the ceramic assemblages between such autonomous communities, who were employing symbolic means of signifying social boundaries at the local and community level. Each maintained its own trade and exchange networks, which in turn resulted in distinct patterns of material culture at the community and perhaps even household level, assuming one could differentiate at the household level the difference between access to goods and consumer choice (e.g., P. Ramsden 2009).

That does not mean that the broadening social and political networks in which the Mantle community and other contemporary groups were participating are not reflected in the archaeological record of the Great Lakes Region. We would argue that while there are broad similarities in collar development, designs, and motifs across Iroquoia, it requires a much more nuanced approach with examinations of multiple attributes (for example, collar basal and lip notching) to detect regional and community differences. Moreover, expressions of ethnicity at the regional level may be played out through different media. The presence of ossuary burial, in the traditional Wendat form of commingled remains in small pits, from at least the late thirteenth century through the sixteenth century along the north-central shore of Lake Ontario, for example, is evidence of those communities expressing a form of shared identity though their burial patterns. Contemporary ancestral Neutral communities, while participating in secondary multiple burial practice, did not follow the same pattern, nor did New York Iroquois groups. While these north shore populations were all separate communities on their own trajectories, they participated in a burial form that was quite distinct from their more distant neighbors.

Many Iroquoian researchers, while recognizing the advantages of attribute analysis in providing for more detailed and comparative descriptions of assemblages, find it nevertheless useful to report on the frequencies of types in assemblages for comparative purposes, especially if an accurate account of variability in each type is provided. In this case, vessel rims were analyzed using both attribute-based and traditional typological approaches to facilitate future inter- and intrasite comparative studies. This was achieved by grouping the vessels in their traditional types but with subtypes defined on the basis of frequencies of attribute combinations (see Wojtowicz 2012), allowing for the recognition of spatial and temporal patterns in the frequencies of individual attributes or combinations of attributes but in the context of the traditional types.

Of the traditional Wendat types, Huron Incised vessels are most common (56%). These vessels typically have a well-defined outflaring collar with a straight or convex interior collar profile (figure 6.1). Decoration usually consists of a single band of linear stamped obliques on the collar, with undecorated lips and necks, although shoulder decoration is occasionally employed. The difference between Huron and Lawson Incised vessels (7.5%) is the concave, often channeled, interior rim profile on the latter, an attribute thought to be associated with ancestral Neutral populations in southwestern Ontario. In rare cases with both types, collar bases are notched. Sidey Notched vessels (9.5%) typically display motifs similar to those of Huron Incised but also feature a well-defined notched or stamped motif on their lips, often on the front edge and more rarely on the rear edge. Together with the Huron and Lawson Incised pots, these forms represent 73% of the vessels on the site (figure 6.2a).

Three other groups of vessel types were recovered. The first group consists of those types that are common on fourteenth- and fifteenth-century Ontario Iroquoian sites and include Ontario Oblique, Ontario Horizontal, Middleport Oblique, Black Necked (figure 6.2b), Pound Necked, Pound Blank, and Lalonde High Collared vessels. These are all differentiated by collar development and design sequences involving the placement of incised horizontals, bands of incised or stamped oblique or vertical lines in combination or individually on the collars and necks of vessels. The placement of incised horizontals on collars and necks is a temporally sensitive attribute among Ontario Iroquoian assemblages in these centuries. By the early sixteenth century, for example, neck decoration is typically absent and well-developed collars are dominated by incised oblique or vertical lines (J. Wright 1966:71; P. Ramsden 1977:184).

The second group comprises minority but not uncommon vessel types for sixteenth- through early-seventeenth-century ancestral and historic Wendat sites and include the Seed Incised, Niagara Collared, Warminster Horizontal (figure 6.2c), and Ripley Plain types. The Seed Incised–type vessels are generally undecorated, with the exception of frontal lip or basal collar notches or a combination of the two. The Niagara Collared vessels typically have well-defined short collars and no exterior decoration, although lips occasionally feature a single band of oblique or vertical lines or notching. Warminster Horizontal vessels feature horizontal lines on short collars, sometimes with secondary oblique lines above and below the horizontals, and undecorated necks. Ripley Plain vessels all feature collarless rim forms; more than half of the lips are decorated with notching or stamped or incised oblique lines.

The third group, consisting of the remaining types, includes "exotic" vessels that are more commonly associated with Iroquoian-speaking groups along the St. Lawrence River and in central New York State. The task of

Table 6.1.   **Mantle Site Ceramic Vessel Types**

Type	n	%
Huron Incised	1071	55.96
Sidey Notched	182	9.51
Lawson Incised	144	7.52
Dutch Hollow Notched	121	6.32
Seed Incised	88	4.60
Niagara Collared	83	4.34
Black Necked	39	2.04
Untyped	30	1.57
Ripley Plain	25	1.31
Warminster Horizontal	20	1.04
Cayadutta-Otstungo Incised	18	0.94
Roebuck Corn-Ear	16	0.84
Seed Corded	15	0.78
Rice Diagonal	12	0.63
Ontario Horizontal	11	0.57
Chance Incised	11	0.57
Cayuga Horizontal	9	0.47
Neutral Punctate Lip	3	0.16
Ontario Oblique	2	0.10
Pound Blank	2	0.10
Hummel Corded	1	0.05
Thruston Horizontal	1	0.05
Durfee Underlined	1	0.05
Onondaga Triangular	1	0.05
High Collar	1	0.05
Otstungo Notched	1	0.05
Ripley Corded	1	0.05
Lalonde High Collared	1	0.05
Richmond Incised	1	0.05
Middleport Oblique	1	0.05
Pound Necked	1	0.05
Fonda Incised	1	0.05
Total	1914	99.97

Figure 6.1.   Huron Incised Vessel

identifying these vessels is complicated by the fact that New York and St. Lawrence Iroquoian types make their appearance on the north shore at approximately the same time that attributes such as frontal lip and basal collar notching, which are definitive attributes in differentiating between exotic types, are being applied to local ceramic vessels.

Twenty-nine vessels are classified as either Cayadutta-Otstungo Incised (figure 6.2d) or Chance Incised, the former being distinguished from the latter on the basis of the presence of basal collar notching. These vessels have linear stamped vertical or oblique lines on the lip, plain necks, and collars decorated with a variety of motifs involving vertical, horizontal, and opposed lines and punctates. In looking at the attributes documented by Pratt (1976) for these types and comparing them with the Mantle vessels, there are significant variations in the frequencies of interior profile shapes and lip motifs. Convex and straight interior profiles are documented on half of the vessels

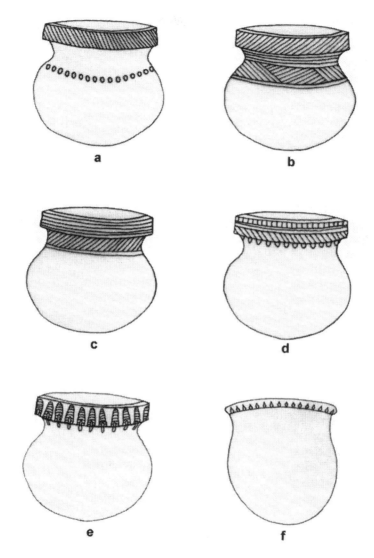

Figure 6.2.   Selection of ceramic vessel types; a) Huron Incised; b) Black Necked; c) Warminster Horizontal; d) Cayadutta-Otstungo Incised; e) Roebuck Corn-Ear; f) Dutch Hollow Notched

typed as Chance Incised from the Mantle site, whereas concave interiors appear to be the norm on the Onondaga Nichols Pond and Buyea sites. Alternatively, the Cayadutta-Otstungo Incised vessels from Mantle display relatively similar frequencies of interior profile shapes. A lip motif of incised obliques or verticals is documented on 42% and 65% of vessels of the

Chanced Incised and Cayadutta-Otstungo Incised types at Mantle, respectively, but is absent on New York pots. Lip motifs of this type were identified on just less than 2% of the other-typed vessels from the Mantle site, either in isolation or in combination with other lip motifs, which is not helpful in determining if this attribute results from local potters making foreign types or simply a blending of attributes in the context of a period of ceramic change. It should be noted that these observations are more accessible to researchers when a combination of traditional type and attribute analyses are undertaken.

The quite distinctive Roebuck Corn-Ear and Durfee Underlined vessels are typically associated with St. Lawrence Iroquoian sites, although both are also present on eastern Iroquois sites. The Roebuck Corn-Ear vessels have distinctive collar motifs that feature deep vertical grooves crossed by interrupted horizontals along with a molded lip, which together imitate a row of corn ears (figure 6.2e). Corn-Ear vessels are present in small numbers in the assemblages of the mid- to late-fifteenth-century Draper and Spang sites, as well as at the mid- to late-fifteenth-century Black Creek and Parsons sites in the Humber Valley (Williamson and Powis 1998:59), the early- to mid-sixteenth-century coalescent Kirche and Coulter sites in the Trent Valley (Damkjar 1990:31–32; C. Ramsden 1989:33), and the early- to mid-sixteenth-century Seed-Barker site in the Humber Valley. Corn-Ear vessels are also present among certain sixteenth-century St. Lawrence Iroquoian site clusters (Chapdelaine 2004:68–69) and increase in frequency until the mid-sixteenth century.

The realignment of various St. Lawrence Iroquoian populations resulted in their abandoning the St. Lawrence Valley in the mid- to late sixteenth century. Their movement to ancestral Wendat sites (e.g., P. Ramsden 1990b; 2009) and eastern Iroquois sites (Engelbrecht 1995, 2004; Petersen et al. 2004; see also J. Jamieson 1990:402–4) is signaled by the presence of St. Lawrence Iroquoian material culture in individual houses or groups of houses suggesting the presence of enclaves. The realignment of these populations, however, may have begun earlier, as evidenced on the north shore of Lake Ontario by a possible enclave at the mid- to late-fifteenth-century Parsons site in the Humber valley (Robertson and Williamson 1998:145–48). It should also be noted that a small discoidal clay bead recovered at Mantle was thought by Pendergast (1981b) to be a St. Lawrence Iroquoian trait, noting they appear in the late precontact period and persist into the protohistoric period. He found that they are often found on Wendat sites in association with St. Lawrence Iroquoian pottery and sometimes with European material.

Fifteen modeled face effigies and fragments were identified in the assemblage on castellations of Cayadutta-Otstungo Incised and Chance Incised vessels. Not only are these exceedingly rare on the north shore of Lake Ontario, they are unique on early-sixteenth-century ancestral Wendat sites. Roughly similar effigies have been found on seventeenth-century Wendat sites in Simcoe County, one at the Auger site (Curtis and Latta 2000:8) and five at the Ball site, the latter of which were described as "pinch face castellations" (Knight and Cameron 1983).

Nine of the human face effigies are complete or nearly complete, while the remaining six fragments vary in completeness and size. All of the effigies appear to be associated with Iroquois vessel types. The complete effigies all appear to have rounded to oval shapes and were most likely molded or, in a few examples, attached as appliqués to the collar surface under the castellation (figure 6.3). At least three additional vessels exhibit scars where effigies had been either removed intentionally or lost through wear.

The effigies depict only the eyes, some with brows, and the nose and mouth. They display a fair amount of variation. The eyes are generally depicted as either a narrow slotted line, oval punctate, or molded surface, or by either three stamped lines or a narrow slot in a molded or punctated depression. The noses are molded and typically damaged; data for only seven are available. Four are well-defined with an incised line for the nostrils, while the three remaining specimens exhibit only short, rounded punctates for the nostrils. The mouth is typically open and most have an oval molded or punctated shape, or more rarely, an open slot or two punctates. These molded

Figure 6.3. Effigy Castellations

facial effigies have been previously found on Oneida, Onondaga, and Seneca sites and more rarely on Mohawk and St. Lawrence Iroquoian sites. The Oneida-Onondaga molded facial effigy forms, identical to the ones at Mantle, were linked by Peter Pratt (1976) to the Iroquois False Face Society and their use in warding off witchcraft and promoting health. More recently, Anthony Wonderley (2002, 2005) has suggested that they represent cornhusk people—mythical, humanlike horticulturalists who represent a visual form of thanks for the three sisters—corn, beans, and squash. Wonderley dates the facial effigies to the early sixteenth century and relates the development of full-bodied effigies with limb elements that are to similarly styled St. Lawrence Iroquoian corn-ear motifs, and suggests that both were part of a shared symbolic system that developed and then flourished around the mid-sixteenth century. The co-occurrence of both facial effigies and Corn-Ear vessels at the early-sixteenth-century Mantle site is consistent with Wonderley's phasing (see also Engelbrecht 2003:86–87). All of the molded facial effigies are completely different in structure and form from the punctate faces that appear on some Early Iroquoian (J. Wright 1966:62) and later St. Lawrence Iroquoian vessels, and their placement is unlikely to be related to the ideological contexts advanced by Wonderley.

Three other vessel types are considered exotic. Cayuga Horizontal vessels display significant variation in rim shape and motif. While the interior surfaces are undecorated, four vessels feature linear stamped or notched oblique or vertical lines. All of the vessels feature a horizontal motif on the collar or neck, a few of which also have oblique or crossing vertical lines. Rice Diagonal vessels typically have a collarless profile with lip motifs consisting of either oblique or vertical lines over frontal lip notching. Dutch Hollow Notched vessels (see figure 6.2f), typically display frontal lip notching on a collarless vessel, although vessels sometimes exhibit a folded lip that gives the appearance of a false collar. Traditionally, these vessels have been identified as a Seneca type, yet they are found on many north shore ancestral Wendat sites in low frequencies as early as the fifteenth century.

The remaining types, all characteristic of New York Iroquois, are represented by single vessels (see Wojtowicz 2012 for detailed descriptions). Of these, thirty vessels displayed shapes and motifs that did not correspond well to any particular defined type. The overall diversity in the ceramic assemblage attests to the cosmopolitan contacts, relationships, or origins of the people who occupied this community.

While many of the "exotic" vessels may have been imported from other communities, some will have been manufactured locally. In an effort to investigate their origin, Linda Howie (2012) conducted a petrographic analysis of a sample of sixty-two vessels from the site. Her work identified significant mineralogical distinctions that relate to their place of manufacture, as well as compositional and textural distinctions that reflect differences in paste recipes, in terms of the choice of the raw material ingredients used to make different groups of vessels.

There was considerable compositional variation with eleven fabric groups distinguished among the sixty-two vessels. The fabric groups were evaluated for their geological consistency with clay samples that were taken from the site environs. Surprisingly, over half (43/62) of the samples are geologically inconsistent with the clay samples taken from around the site. The main geological distinction is the absence of calcitic inclusions (calcites and limestone), which are conspicuous characteristics of the local clay samples and would be expected to appear in the pot samples had local clays been employed in their manufacture.

Some of the groups have subvariants that exhibit subtle compositional differences that could be significant with respect to teaching children how to make pottery. Within the fabric groups that are geologically consistent with local clays, for example, four of the five groups are represented by only one juvenile vessel. These groups differ in inclusions and in abundance and prevalence of segregations, which are related to the compositional properties of the clay component. Together, these may represent novice potters experimenting with mixtures of raw material ingredients to produce pottery successfully. Howie suggests such a scenario might also be expected in instances where potters move into a new area and are unfamiliar with the mechanical performance, drying and firing characteristics of local clays, and the effects of adding tempering materials.

The vessels made of nonlocal fabrics also include compositionally similar regular and "juvenile" pots, although many of the juvenile vessels are untempered. This suggests that these vessels were brought with the families to the site or that task groups continued to acquire nonlocal clays in sufficient quantities to allow for juvenile and adult pot manufacture together.

Some of the nonlocal vessels, however, may have come from far-distant sources. One of the distinctive effigy vessel fragments, for example, was found to be geologically inconsistent with the clay samples prospected from the Mantle area, which suggests that this particular vessel, as well as others belonging to the same fabric group, was produced elsewhere and brought to the Mantle site. It is also possible that the clay itself was brought to the site. In this particular group of effigies, ten of the eleven member vessels were classed as exotic. Similarly, eleven of fourteen vessels identified as having been made of local clays were classed as local types. Of the other nonlocal clay subgroups, there are about as many local as exotic types.

The sources or geological origins of the clay components of the nonlocal fabric groups have yet to be determined. Ongoing research is focused on sampling clays from the Spang and Draper sites, thought to have been occupied immediately prior to Mantle. Samples have also been requested from the assemblages of those sites in eastern Ontario and New York State that bear striking stylistic similarities to the exotic vessels, including the Cayadutta-Otstungo Incised and Chance Incised effigy vessel fragments.

Prior to sampling for thin sectioning, the vessel sherds were laid out according to provenience. An interesting observation to emerge from this analysis was that pottery derived from the same archaeological context formed distinctive clustering in keeping with the different fabric groups. This tendency suggests that patterns of compositional variation are directly related to differences in their archaeological context, implying that different social groups inhabiting areas of the site had different manufacturing processes. The facial effigies, on the other hand, are from contexts across the full extent of the site. Further investigations of both patterns represent an important direction for future research.

All of these data must be considered in evaluating how patterns in ceramic design can be related to settlement trends and the sociopolitical realignments that accompanied community coalescence. Changes in design sequences are not simply a function of the passage of time but may signal or accompany changes in social organization, interaction, and identity formation. Moreover, those changes may differ in community sequences across regions. The Mantle data were, therefore, also considered in relation to the assemblages of the evolving Rouge-Duffins communities and those of neighboring drainages (Pihl, Birch, et al. 2011).

The Rouge-Duffins drainage sequence begins with the early-fifteenth-century precoalescent villages having assemblages dominated by vessels with decorated necks (60%) (see figure 6.2b), followed by types with obliques and verticals on collars with undecorated necks (23%) (see figure 6.2a). The remaining vessels in these assemblages are a small number of other local types (e.g., see figure 6.2c), as well as the first appearance of ceramic types and attributes associated with St. Lawrence Iroquoians (e.g., Corn-Ear) (see figure 6.2e).

With Draper, after the coalescence of the smaller villages, the general trend in local types changes only slightly, with decorated neck wares still accounting for 42% of the assemblage and the number of incised types increasing slightly to 29%. The heterogeneity of the Draper assemblage, however, differs substantially from the earlier, smaller villages, with twenty-seven discrete types as opposed to an average of ten at earlier sites. Mid- to late-fifteenth-century coalescent village assemblages (e.g., Damiani and Parsons) feature, for the first time, types typically associated with New York State, accounting for 2.5% of the total assemblage (e.g., see figure 6.2d). Of the six New York types present at Draper, the most numerous are Onondaga Triangular vessels, which account for 1.65% of the total and more than half of all New York types present. Coronet pipes, a pipe style that appears earlier in the late fourteenth century on Onondaga sites, are also present at Draper, although in very low frequency. Together with the presence of St. Lawrence Iroquoian vessels, these types suggest ties between members of the Draper community and groups to the east and southeast.

The smaller Spang site assemblage, reanalyzed for this study by Aleksandra Pradzynski (Pihl, Birch, et al. 2011), is markedly more homogeneous than the Draper assemblage, containing equal numbers of incised and necked types, which together constitute nearly 90% of the total ceramic assemblage. St. Lawrence Iroquoian and Iroquois types are still present, though in significantly fewer numbers than at Draper.

The assemblage from the Mantle site is different from the villages that preceded it in a number of ways, the most obvious being the virtual disappearance of wares with decorated necks. Instead, the assemblage is dominated by incised designs and includes a marked increase in notched types, a style that appears initially in the mid-fifteenth century on precoalescent villages. Notched varieties are also found in high frequencies in the Humber drainage, thirty-five kilometers to the west. The St. Lawrence Iroquoian presence is marked mainly by the presence of Corn-Ear vessels.

There was also a marked increase in the variety of types associated with New York Iroquois in the Mantle assemblage. Ten discrete types were identified, accounting for more than 3% of the total assemblage. The presence of these vessels suggests a community with multiple exchange systems and external ties that contributed to its cosmopolitan character.

Our preliminary analysis of a small ceramic sample from the Aurora site, thought to postdate Mantle, suggests that Incised vessels dominate its assemblage (60%), followed by notched vessel forms (16%) and a small number of New York Iroquois types, although this latter observation may also reflect the small size of the collection.

As outlined in chapter 3, the upper Humber River was home to Mantle's closest contemporary neighbor at the time of its occupation. The Humber sequence also appears to have featured a number of communities that coalesced in the mid- to late fifteenth century, resulting in the postcoalescent Seed-Barker village, which is approximately coterminous with Mantle. Trends in both locally made and "exotic" wares differ, however, from those in the Rouge-Duffins drainage. While necked types disappear after AD 1500 and incised types increase in frequency, notched types are far more popular, accounting for 56% of the assemblage at the Seed-Barker site (Margie Kennedy, personal communication).

Moreover, when one compares the frequencies of New York Iroquois types at these two sites, different types are present in different frequencies. For example, while the Mantle assemblage contains high frequencies of Cayadutta-Otstungo Incised vessels (some with molded face effigies), these types are noticeably absent at Seed-Barker. The same is true of Dutch Hollow Corded types, which are present in significant quantities at Seed-Barker but not at Mantle. The frequency of the St. Lawrence Iroquoian Corn-Ear variety, however, is the same.

The most striking similarity between these two sites is that Iroquois types represent 3% to 4% of each assemblage and each discrete type occurs in very small frequencies, usually less than 1% of the total assemblage. If the presence of these types is reflective of interaction between individuals or lineages in ancestral Iroquois and Wendat communities, whether they result from trade, diplomacy, intermarriage, or raiding, the direction of interaction differed between the Humber and Rouge-Duffins communities. We should not be surprised that each community was uniquely situated in, and constituted by, a set of interpersonal and historical contingencies.

It is worth noting that this examination of ceramics from Mantle and the other Rouge-Duffins Creek sites, together with ceramic data from across the north shore, has demonstrated that traditional typological analysis is not simply the handmaiden of culture-history. When analyses are situated in contemporary interpretive frameworks and employ large data sets comprised of multiple site sequences with temporal depth and spatial breadth, patterns emerge that produce valuable insights at the intra-site and macroregional levels.

CERAMIC SMOKING PIPES

The ceramic pipe assemblage consists of 548 fragments and was analyzed and reported on by Rob Wojtowicz (2012). Elbow, stem, and mouthpiece fragments represent a little more than half (58%) of the assemblage, while bowl fragments account for 42%. A high proportion of the pipe sample had been burnished, and red pigment, found to be red ochre, was observed on 8 stem fragments.

Of the 146 analyzable bowls, trumpet forms were the most numerous (21.9%), followed by coronet (17.1%); conical (15.6%); anthropomorphic, zoomorphic, and indeterminate effigy (13%); apple bowl (9%); mortice (8.2%); collared ring (6%); plain barrel (3.4%); and other types, including a single disc pipe. Decorations on the bowls include incised horizontal lines or bands of oblique or vertical lines, a few of which were interrupted on decorated trumpet forms; rows of punctates and stamped oblique lines on the coronet pipes; horizontal lines over punctates on apple barrel forms; and combinations of incised horizontal lines, horizontal bands of punctates, and stamped oblique or vertical lines on mortice, conical, collared, and ring barrel types. Six collared, ring barrel pipes display a horizontal motif of one to seven incised lines on their collars.

While many of the pipes are typical for ancestral Wendat sites of the period, a number of observations can be made relating to the development of the smoking pipe complex during the coalescent to postcoalescent period. Coronet pipes appear in small numbers along the north shore of Lake Ontario for the first time at the coalescent sites of Parsons, Keffer, and Draper and are not present on ancestral Neutral or St. Lawrence Iroquoian sites until the sixteenth century. They represent fewer than 2% of the pipes at Draper and over 17% at Mantle, evidencing a significant shift in style during the coalescent period. Proto-coronet types appear in the archaeological record of Iroquoia for the first time on the fourteenth-century Onondaga Kelso and Howlett Hill sites (Tuck 1971:75, 88), and they persist on Onondaga sites into the mid- to late sixteenth century. Their dramatic fluorescence at Mantle during a period of heightened regional interaction, as also indicated by the increased diversity of Iroquois pots, perhaps underscores the direction of interaction between Mantle and the Iroquois as suggested by the Oneida and Onondaga effigy vessels.

One of the coronet pipes recovered from Midden 1 was found with an exceedingly rare native copper insert in one of the corner notches. It is a small piece of sheet copper that had been folded and impressed into the clay, probably before drying and firing, and then removed and wedged back into place after firing (figure 6.4).

Another unique pipe found on the surface of the site is a fragment of a possible ceramic disc pipe resembling those made in the sixteenth century in the midwestern United States out of red stone such as catlinite (see figure 6.4). The disc radius from the edge of the central hole is 35.4 mm, and it is 9.3 mm thick at its edge. These measurements render this specimen quite unlike flattened trumpet pipes, which are far smaller and thinner, although admittedly the diameter of the hole on this piece at approximately 21 mm is significantly larger than those found on most stone pipes. The design on the piece is also quite unique and consists of zoned opposed incised oblique lines meeting at a central vertical line alternating with blank triangles bordered by rows of small punctates.

The surface of the clay appears far redder than the surfaces of other clay pipes. The disc portion of the pipe was subjected to X-ray fluorescence, which identified an iron-based pigment wash (5% iron) on the surface of the artifact, a significantly higher value than has been measured for oxidization of iron in normal clay surfaces (2%).

William Fox has documented evidence for long-distance interaction between Ontario Iroquoian and western Algonquian populations, which in the case of ancestral and historic Wendat groups was facilitated through access to Odawa exchange networks. He noted that a portion of a catlinite disc pipe was recovered from the fifteenth-century ancestral Wendat Quesnel-Deschambault village in Simcoe County and that ancestral Neutral populations

Figure 6.4. Selected ceramic smoking pipes. Coronet pipe with Native copper insert and disc pipe with red ochre wash.

during the coalescent period (e.g., Lawson) also had significant links to Fort Ancient populations in Ohio (Fox 2008:8). A catlinite pendant was also recovered from the Parsons site (Robertson, Monckton, and Williamson 1998:106). While the evidence for interaction to the west for north shore ancestral Wendat populations during this period is slight, the presence of red stone objects that in the next century become far more influential in north-eastern exchange networks suggests that the Mantle ceramic disc pipe had been given an ochre wash to mimic red stone in the absence of the stone itself.

Effigy pipes also increase in frequency throughout the late fifteenth and early sixteenth century (Bradley 1987:38–39; Ramsden 1990a:369). At Mantle they account for 13% of the total pipe assemblage. These include eight anthropomorphic effigies, four zoomorphic effigies, and seven effigies that are typologically indeterminate due to the small fragments recovered. Two pipe stem fragments also display possible partial effigy motifs.

Two spectacular anthropomorphic effigies were recovered, one with a number of other pipe fragments with red ochre slips found in a pit just outside House 64 that, together with the effigy pipe, suggests a place of ritual significance. The bowl fragment consists of half a finely made and decorated human effigy face on one side of a pipe bowl (figure 6.5), which emphasizes recessed eye sockets, a developed chin, a forehead that rises above the pipe bowl, and a prominent single row of fine punctates that dips between the eyes. Within the eye sockets, the eyes are raised and impressed in the center. The nostrils are represented by two punctates, and the mouth is constituted by a horizontal row of fine punctates that from a distance give the impression of a row of teeth. The nose appears to be naturalistic but quite large. The remainder of the bowl is decorated by several bands of punctates that may depict hair. The line of punctates around the face is very similar to the decoration on a head of a Mohawk bone figurine (Snow 1995b:186; fig. 4.49) both of which, in turn, resemble a facial tattoo on an illustration of the grandfather of Joseph Brant, the famous Revolutionary War Mohawk leader.

Another complete and detailed effigy face was recovered (see figure 6.5) that features recessed eye sockets similar to the first effigy, prominent cheeks, a natural nose with two punctates representing the nostrils, a developed chin and mouth, and a prominent, single notch in the forehead. The slit eyes and mouth appear open. The face protrudes slightly from the rest of the bowl. It is one of the most finely detailed anthropomorphic pipes of the period.

Two complete zoomorphic effigies were also recovered, one of which is an owl with a short beak, large eyes, and a radiating row of feathers around its head (see figure 6.5). The eyes are formed by deep depressions, while the beak is molded and incised. A single incised line and a band of short stamped lines that encircle the face and run along the lip of the bowl represent the radiating row of feathers. Another pipe bowl depicts a pileated woodpecker with a long beak and crested head (figure 6.5). This artifact is well burnished and displays post-firing grinding of the sides of the crest, and notches at the peak of the crest and the eyes. Etching was employed to shape the partition of the mouth. Both artifacts were recovered from post molds.

Peter Ramsden (1990a:369) has noted that effigies such as these have been linked variously with totemic symbols, shamanistic paraphernalia, spirit representations, portraiture, or likenesses of important Wendat dignitaries. Chris Watts (2011) has alternatively argued that effigy pipes are a reflection of Wendat cosmology in the sense that inert objects fashioned by people were persons themselves, with which relationships were formed that included the inhabiting of an animal's body in order to assume its viewpoint. Hammell has similarly argued that such objects may have been owed social-ritual obligations in the sense that human and other-than-human beings were linked by reciprocal social responsibilities to maintain their common world (1998:272–73). The rarity of animal effigies compared to the vast majority of pipes, which were used for public smoking as observed at almost all social gatherings and other frequent public rituals, suggests their significance may have been expressed in individual rather than public rituals (see G. Braun 2012).

Figure 6.5.   Effigy pipes. Clockwise from upper left: anthropomorphic effigy with "tattoos;" anthropomorphic effigy; zoomorphic woodpecker effigy; zoomorphic owl effigy.

FLAKED LITHICS

Prior to the contact period and direct trade, when metals replaced chert as the material of choice for the manufacture of projectile points and other tools, access to stone was a good indicator of the direction of exchange routes. The Mantle site flaked lithic assemblage was analyzed by Debbie Steiss (2012). A total of 6,369 flaked lithic artifacts were found at the site. Of these, 351 were formal tools and the remainder of the assemblage was comprised of debitage.

Forty-one cores were identified, all of Onondaga chert. Approximately half of these were "exhausted" or spent, indicating heavy use and conservation of lithic raw materials. Onondaga chert accounted for 98% of the tool stone from the site, indicating that the Mantle site occupants were acquiring most of their chert from ancestral Neutral populations in the Niagara Peninsula, since it outcrops along the northeastern shore of Lake Erie as does Bois Blanc chert, small quantities of which were also found. Other tool stone used includes Kettle Point and Fossil Hill cherts likely acquired through trade with the Odawa living in the Bruce Peninsula area, Balsam Lake chert from the Trent Valley to the east of the site, and a small quantity of Flint Ridge Chalcedony from Ohio. Recovered tools were predominantly made of Onondaga chert; a few tools were made of Kettle Point and Bois Blanc cherts, along with one biface made from Fossil Hill chert.

Fifty-four complete projectile points and 58 fragments were recovered that, with the exception of one side-notched point with a square base, were small, thin, well-made triangular arrow tips with straight or concave bases. Two partial projectile points and one complete point are diagnostic of Middle and Late Archaic time periods and likely represent spear points left by earlier hunting people and found and curated by the Mantle occupants. One specimen, for example, is a base and mid-section of a Late Archaic Genesee point and was found in a pit feature. The recovery of Archaic points from features on Iroquoian villages has been documented elsewhere (Steiss 2010:112).

Thirty-one scrapers were also recovered, a number of which exhibited bilateral denticulation/notching for possible graver use. Combination end-side scrapers and those with multiple graver tips as well as spokeshave edges all suggest exhaustive use of the available tools.

The pattern of the distribution of debitage across the site is interesting in that concentrations of debitage were recovered in the north-central portion of the site, most notably in and around Houses 25 and 27, and within the east end of House 15. While House 25 and House 27 were occupied during the early phase of settlement, House 15 was in use for much of the duration of the occupation (see chapter 4). It is possible that the areas of concentration in and around Houses 25 and 27 may have been outdoor activity areas at some point during the occupation of the site, but given the long tenure of occupation in House 15, it is likely that the processing of flaked lithic artifacts was occurring within the house itself. An additional area of concentration is observable to the south of House 27, within what may have been the main plaza area of the site in the early phase of occupation.

GROUND STONE ARTIFACTS

A total of 458 ground stone artifacts was recovered from the site and analyzed by Martin Cooper (2012). They include 354 celts and celt fragments, twenty-four stone beads and stone bead preforms, thirty-five hammers, eleven stone pendants, and a number of pipe fragments (Cooper 2012). While the pendants, beads, and pipes are of interest here, the enormity of the celt assemblage is of note.

Celts are a category of ground stone woodworking tool that includes axes, adzes, and chisels. Of the 354 celt and celt fragments, 40 were complete enough to determine that they likely functioned as axes used primarily for felling trees; 13 were adzes for gouging and planing wood, perhaps used for the manufacture of canoes; and 23 were hafted chisels or fine woodworking tools based on their small size, undamaged polls, a high degree of use wear, and polish near their working ends. Chloride schist—hard, fine-grained, and easy to work—was the predominant stone used for their manufacture, accounting for approximately 98% of the celt assemblage. It occurs locally in the till and is available as large cobbles in the adjacent creek bed. Evidence of unmodified chloride schist cobbles and the presence of celt preforms indicate that these tools were being manufactured at the site.

An unusual number of celts and celt fragments exhibit thermal alteration. Seventy-one celts and celt fragments (20%) have been thermally altered, as evidenced by noticeable oxidization and discoloration of the schist, and in the cases of prolonged exposure to severe heat, fire cracking producing angular fragments. Thermal alteration has not been observed in other late Iroquoian assemblages, and it may have resulted from intentional deposition of broken celts into hearths. Also, twenty-two celts and celt fragments were found in post molds. Their deposition was perhaps to reinforce or stabilize posts. However, the ceramic pipe bowl effigies described above, a miniature vessel, a number of raptor elements, a raccoon baculum, four cobble hammers, a stone pipe, and a piece of miscellaneous ground stone were also found in posts, some in structural support posts of houses. This pattern of the placement of significant items in support posts was documented at the Parsons site, where scattered human remains were placed in support posts (Robertson and Williamson 1998:148). It is tempting to point to the sacred nature of longhouses (e.g., Engelbrecht 2003:172–73) and the posts used to construct them to explore the deposition of significant items within them, obviously a topic in need of further research.

While ground stone artifacts were recovered throughout the village, a concentration of material in the northeast portion of the site in and around House 25 is coincident with the concentration of flaked lithic material in that area, suggesting that the structure or area constituted a focus for lithic work groups perhaps involved with construction and refurbishment of the village infrastructure.

Ground stone was also used in the manufacture of beads for personal ornamentation. The material used for their manufacture can provide additional evidence of exchange networks for the village or lineages; ornamentation itself was used to signify identity, along with clothing, hairstyle, and tattooing (Joyce 2005:142–43). Twenty-five perforated stone beads, bead preforms, and stone discs were recovered. Complete specimens included twelve discoidal beads made of black shale, one round bead of green steatite, one discoidal bead of black steatite, and two beads of sandstone. Two preforms, both discoidal and made of black shale, were recovered. One of these had the beginning of two centrally placed conical perforations on each face, while the other had only one incipient centrally placed perforation, both of which evidence shale bead manufacturing at the site. One of the stone beads was remarkable due to the pink sandstone from which it was made and its relatively large size. It measured 24 mm in diameter and 13 mm in thickness and had a bidirectional perforation and a series of incised lines encircling the outer edge of the bead.

Five stone discs are similar in size to the discoidal shale beads, but they exhibit no evidence of perforation. While they may be blanks for future bead manufacture, they may also have functioned as gaming pieces. A large pink granite disc is possibly a bead preform or a gaming piece. It has been smoothed over its entire surface with small, centrally placed holes on both faces, perhaps the start of bidirectional perforation.

Twelve stone pendants were also recovered, only three of which were manufactured. The remaining nine pebble pendants have natural, not manmade, perforations. Six are made of limestone, two are sandstone, and one item is of an unidentified material. One of the manufactured pendants is a relatively thin, unfinished black shale pebble pendant with incipient perforations on both faces. The second is a pebble pendant made of orange-red slate and features two notches on one lateral margin and a bidirectional perforation. It exhibits surface polish, possibly from wear, and the bottom portion of the pendant has been removed. The third is a small black shale ovoid pebble pendant with a centrally placed unidirectional perforation.

Black pebble pendants have been found in small numbers in Early through Middle Iroquoian site assemblages along the north shore of Lake Erie (Fox 2004); they become less frequent in the late precontact period, with the exception of the Pound site where more than forty specimens were identified (Fox 2004:205; Lennox and Fitzgerald 1990:423). These pendants have been linked by Fox to the scales of the horned panther-serpent *Mizipiziheu*, suggesting that wearing them protected the individual from the malevolence of the serpent. The anomalous presence of forty-five of these pebbles at the Draper site led Fox to infer a significant ancestral Neutral influence on a portion of the population there, which seems plausible given the fact that they are otherwise rare on north shore sites. The manufacturing of pebble ornaments is replaced at Mantle by black shale and steatite discoidal beads representing a new stone ornament industry.

One half of a winged bannerstone made of Huronia banded slate that was broken at the central perforation was also recovered. After it had broken, there was an attempt to perforate the bannerstone at the top and bottom near the fractured central perforation, perhaps to facilitate suspending the object as a pendant. The surface of the bannerstone has numerous parallel scratches and striations perpendicular to its long axis. While such objects are thought to have functioned as counterweights for atlatls and generally date in Ontario to between 9000 and 3000 BC, it is possible that it was found and curated by a Mantle site villager.

Four crinoid fossils and a portion of a large cephalopod fossil were found, which although not culturally modified, were all found in features and middens, suggesting they had been found and curated by the site occupants.

Two complete and six fragments of stone smoking pipes were also recovered, including two made from shale, four made of limestone, and two from steatite. The first is a complete vasiform pipe bowl made of light brown steatite with a round stem perforation, below which is a suspension perforation that extends on an angle through the bottom of the bowl. While somewhat obscured by the adherence of lime mortar resulting from the construction of a mill structure wall through Midden 1 from where the piece originated, a symmetrical polish pattern is present on one third of the pipe in the region of the stem attachment and along the ridge of the bowl. This may have resulted from a covering of the back of the bowl where it would have been held and polishing only that portion that was exposed. The bowl is rectangular in cross section with rounded corners, and the lip of the bowl is flat with decoration on a short collar consisting of four single horizontal incisions and short vertical incisions at the corners.

Another of the pipes is half of an unfinished black shale vasiform pipe bowl that may have been broken while being manufactured. It has an unfinished stem perforation on one lateral margin and an unfinished suspension hole at the base. The bowl itself has been roughed out, and it is possible that the pipe split during the process of hollowing out the bowl and discarded. A series of horizontal incised lines are located on the edges of the pipe bowl, four on the side with the pipe stem bore (two above and two below the bore) and five on the opposing side. A second black shale pipe bowl is represented by two mended portions. Decoration on the upper zone of the bowl consists of oblique incised lines above two incised horizontal lines.

While ceramic vasiform pipes, some with unusual decorations, are found as a minority presence on most north shore fourteenth- and fifteenth-century Wendat sites, stone varieties do not appear on Iroquoian sites until the post-coalescence period. They appear to be most common on mid-sixteenth- to early-seventeenth-century Seneca (Sempowski and Saunders 2001:257–58; Wray et al. 1987:133) and Oneida sites (Pratt 1976:210, 222, 225) with a few located on Erie and Neutral sites as well. Drooker (2004) has argued that stemmed pipes of this nature are used in group ceremonial settings at the beginning of social and political events such as trade negotiations and adoptions. In this way, the increasing presence of these pipes might be seen as an integrative mechanism for individuals with differing social and political ties, as well as indicating new, larger, and more complex identities based on inter- and intra-village relationships.

A small fragment of a steatite pipe bowl rim was recovered, which featured vertical incising and the remnants of deep vertical grooves. A small complete limestone pipe bowl with horizontal incising near the top of the bowl, a fragment of an outflaring pipe bowl made of a highly fossiliferous white limestone, and two other limestone pipe bowl rim fragments were recovered.

Steatite itself seems to have been a material subject to differential access along the north shore of Lake Ontario. To date, with the exception of a single pebble from the Antrex site (a small, late-thirteenth-century village in the Credit River drainage; see chapter 3), all steatite artifacts date to the fourteenth and fifteenth centuries and are concentrated on sites in the Don River drainage. Numerous steatite artifacts have recently been discovered on the early-fifteenth-century ancestral Wendat Joseph Picard site, situated twenty kilometers east of Mantle in the Lynde Creek drainage. Their complete absence from the Humber drainage and the Rouge-Duffins drainage until the turn of the sixteenth century suggests that communities in these drainages participated in differing trade networks. In that at least three different colors of steatite are found on the north shore, studies aimed at sourcing the material might help delineate those networks.

NATIVE AND EUROPEAN METAL OBJECTS

An iron object was discovered at the bottom of a cultural but otherwise sterile pit at a depth of 41 cm under the bunkline of either House 28 or 29 (as they overlap) (see figure 4.3, figure 6.6). It is also possible that the feature was situated among a cluster of other features in the open plaza during the first occupation of the village. The indistinct nature of the staining in the feature fill suggests that it was excavated for the purpose of burying the object. The archaeological context in which the object was found, together with the techniques employed in its manufacture, indicates that it relates to the village site's occupation rather than the nineteenth-century uses of the property. Due to severe surface accretions, however, the original shape of the object is obscured. Suspecting that the artifact represented either an object cut from an iron axe and reworked (Bradley 1987) or was a stand-alone tool, X-radiography was undertaken to investigate its shape, structure, manufacturing technology, and any surface features (Carnevale 2012; Carnevale et al. 2012).

An initial set of X-rays was undertaken at an industrial facility that produced high-quality radiographs (both digital and film), enabling the interpretation of even the most subtle discontinuities and variations. The tool was found to have a beveled bit with a tapered poll, as well as fibrous patterning resulting from prolonged unidirectional hand hammering during its manufacture, indicating it is a wrought iron object consistent with the manufacturing of European iron tools in the fifteenth and sixteenth centuries.

Using multiple incremental exposures and specifically designed edge and density filters, two forge marks were identified, along with several other possible discontinuities. The first, a horizontal line with an offset square, was the most robust mark impressed into the piece. It was identified at all levels of imaging due to its well-defined depth. The second mark is composed of two circles of common diameter connected by simple lines. This impression

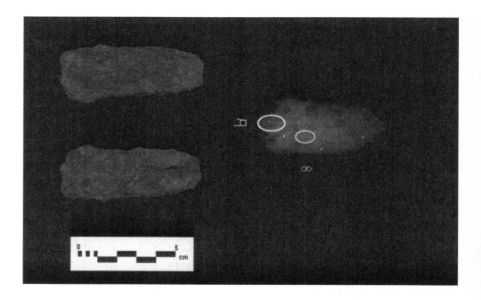

Figure 6.6.   Basque iron object. Photo of object (left), X-radiograph with forge marks (right).

is much shallower in depth and was only identified during the longest exposure times to the X-ray beam and use of a density filter (see figure 6.6). A
second series of X-rays was undertaken at the Royal Ontario Museum with
an experienced metals conservator, Susan Stock, and Heidi Sobol, senior
paintings conservator. The two marks were confirmed and the other discontinuities were provisionally identified as additional marks.

While investigating iron sourcing, mining, processing, and European im-
portation and exportation trends during the late fifteenth and early sixteenth
centuries, Andrea Carnevale was able to determine that a Basque origin is
likely for the Mantle object. Reviewing artifacts recovered from Basque
archaeological sites during the late fifteenth and early sixteenth century, two
marks similar to those identified on the Mantle object were found. These
included one on a meat cleaver and one on sheep shears. There has been
considerable research into the European presence on the east coast of North
America in the late fifteenth and early sixteenth centuries. The site of Red
Bay on the north shore of the Strait of Belle Isle has yielded numerous iron
objects related to Basque whaling stations (Grenier, Bernier, and Stevens
2007). Further investigations into artifacts recovered from Red Bay resulted
in the identification of several similar circular marks on strapping from
wooden casks. Archival sources reveal that combinations of circles were
sometimes used by certain trades as a numerical shorthand, as well as part of
a personal mark (Carnevale et al. 2012).

The iron tool is not the only European item that was found at Mantle.
Until the iron object was demonstrated to be of early European origin, three
copper beads and a piece of bent sheet copper were assumed to be of native
origin. These were subsequently subject to X-ray fluorescence and neutron
activation analyses, resulting in the identification of two of the pieces as
being European in origin. One of the European beads was found in a midden
unit and the other in a post mold in the house adjacent to the one with the iron
tool. To date, Mantle and Seed-Barker appear to be the only pre-1550 ancestral Wendat sites on the north shore to yield European copper (Fox, Hancock,
and Pavlish 1995), although native copper beads are common on mid- to late-
fifteenth-century coalescent sites such as Draper and Parsons; they are less
common on fourteenth-century sites, with only six beads and one awl resulting from the complete excavations of six villages.

The lack of uniform trends in interregional interaction based on the varying frequencies of different kinds of material culture from various communities underscores the importance of considering each community to be
unique in its interactions. While the discovery of European items on this
early-sixteenth-century site, especially a Basque iron object, was surprising
to our team, it was not to James Tuck or Peter Ramsden, who both noted that
if more early-sixteenth-century sites were completely excavated in the Great
Lakes Region, additional such objects would be found, given the consider-

able Basque presence on the east coast by the turn of the sixteenth century and the known interaction of Basque whalers with local Algonquian and/or St. Lawrence Iroquoian groups. The movement of the piece, and presumably the copper, likely followed the same routes that St. Lawrence Iroquoian ceramics and marine shell had a half century earlier. Although conventional wisdom is that it would be unlikely that European material culture would commonly be found on ancestral Wendat sites prior to 1550 (Warrick 2008:117), our discoveries at Mantle suggest we now consider the turn of the sixteenth century as the marker after which European items began to trickle into the lower Great Lakes following centuries-old networks. The burial of the iron piece, however, within a house and under a bunk line, where special objects were sometimes buried (Wrong 1939) is fully in keeping with the ways in which these objects may have been viewed during this period—in the words of George Hamell in a filmed interview regarding the object, "They came from the edge of the world."

BURYING THE DEAD

The main burial ceremony of the ancestral and contact-period Wendat was known as the Feast of the Dead. It involved an event at which the remains of numerous individuals, who were formerly interred within a village, were disinterred and redeposited into ossuaries. Presumably, this act took place upon abandonment of the village in favor of a new site. Ossuaries range in size from those that contain the disarticulated and/or bundled remains of approximately ten individuals, to those that contain the commingled remains of five hundred people or more. The tradition of ossuary burial began in the Early Iroquoian period as a family-oriented rite. By the early fourteenth century, ossuaries had become larger, community-wide features, and by the end of the fourteenth century, their creation sometimes involved the participation of members of different allied villages in a joint burial ceremony (Williamson and Steiss 2003).

Wendat villages were inhabited by the souls of both the living and the recently dead who had not yet been sent on their way by means of the Feast of the Dead. Moreover, living villages also shared the landscape with villages of the dead, as deserted settlements remained inhabited by the souls of those ancestors who, for one reason or another, were unable to make the journey to the Land of the Dead (Trigger 1969:103–4). These spirits remained in the abandoned villages and planted their own crops in the former clearings (von Gernet 1994:42–45; cf. Hall 1976:363). Within such a worldview, ossuaries, and the transformative activities that took place at them, were likely essential to the continued well-being of the community both in life and in death (Robertson 2004). Given this importance, it is likely that the means by which such places are chosen and the locations themselves were rooted in the complex symbolic traditions and worldviews of these communities.

The ossuary for the Mantle site has not yet been found. Based on the locations of nineteen ossuaries in south-central Ontario and the locations of their associated villages, it is likely that it was created at a location within a thousand meters of the village and within three hundred meters of a water source. The lands to the east and south of the site adjacent to Stouffville Creek have yet to be developed and may yet be found to contain the ossuary.

A cemetery, however, containing thirty-seven clustered burial features was found in an area below the top of slope in the valley lands, approximately forty meters southwest of the Mantle site palisade, an area presumed to have little archaeological potential. The cemetery was discovered after the completion of the excavation of the village and was only found due to the need to extend infrastructure through the valley for the subdivision west of the site. It is possible that cemeteries such as that at Mantle are overlooked because they are in contexts rarely chosen for settlement.

Crystal Forrest (2012) undertook an inventory of the skeletal remains in the field as the cemetery was protected in its original location, and the following summary is drawn from her analysis. The features contained the remains of thirty-four individuals, thirty of whom were adults and four juveniles. There were no infants or adolescents (postpubertal individuals younger than eighteen years old) present in the cemetery, although there were four individuals who were probably in their late teens or early twenties who were classified as young adults. Of the adults, twelve were young adults (eighteen to thirty-four), seven were middle-aged adults (thirty-five to forty-nine), five were older adults (fifty plus), and six were of an indeterminate age. It is likely that infants were buried elsewhere, as described in ethnohistoric documents (Thwaites 1896–1901, 10:15) and infant and young juvenile mortality was high in communities such as Mantle due to the synergistic effects of population aggregation, infectious disease, and malnutrition (Forrest 2010b). Of the thirty adults at Mantle, twenty-two were sufficiently preserved such that sex could be estimated; fourteen were male and eight were female. The metric attributes of the individuals in the cemetery are not substantially different than those of other Iroquoian populations (e.g., Stock and Willmore 2003).

Dental disease was common, with most adult and juvenile individuals showing some signs of pathology, including caries, calculus, hypercemetosis, abscess, and antemortem tooth loss, all of which is consistent with the high rates of dental disease observed in other Iroquoian populations (Hartney 1978; Mullen and Hoppa 1992; Crinnion, Merrett, and Pfeiffer 2003). Dental wear, on the other hand, was generally minimal except in older adults. Degenerative joint disease, characterized by osteophyte formation ("lipping"), eburnation, and porosity at joint surfaces, was also present, with twelve of the adults showing signs of osteoarthritis. Other degenerative conditions, including loss of bone mass (osteopenia and osteoporosis) were also observed.

Respiratory disease was common in Iroquoian populations in Ontario (Merrett 2003). Four individuals displayed bony involvement consistent with respiratory conditions including additive and erosive lesions in the thorax, most commonly on the pleural surface of the ribs and sternum, as well as lesions on the bones of the hand (hypertrophic osteoarthropathy). This respiratory disease was generally of an unknown etiology, and while mycobacterium tuberculosis was present in Ontario in the precontact period (Pfeiffer 1991), it was not definitively observed at Mantle.

Two individuals had fractured long bones and another had a healed distal ulnar fracture. Five individuals displayed skeletal changes consistent with nonspecific infection (periostitis), and two showed callus and cloacae formation on their long bones consistent with osteomyelitis (Ortner and Aufderheide 1991). Nutritional stress appears to have been a problem in the early lives of several individuals, given the presence of enamel hypoplasias, linear defects in tooth enamel, and porosity in the orbital portion of the frontal bone, a marker also present in two adults.

Twenty-three of the burials that could be evaluated as to burial form were primary inhumations. All primary burials were flexed, with no obvious pattern to the way in which the burials were oriented or the direction in which they were facing. Six burials were classed as secondary, and all of these burials were of adults. Five were bundle burials, with the appendicular and axial skeletal elements tightly aligned and the crania lying on top of or beside the bundled postcranial skeleton. In one case, an adult female and male of similar age were bundled together, with the female placed on top of the male.

Another secondary burial was that of a young adult male who was interred in a supine position in partial articulation. His head, neck, torso (including pelvis), and left upper arm were still in articulation, but his left leg was folded back under his torso and his left forearm was placed under his head. In addition to being the only burial interred supine and in partial articulation, canine faunal material was recovered from within his pelvic cavity. Two of the other burials had deer phalanges in the burial feature, and one other had deer antler in the fill. Another young adult male had been placed in a flexed position with a circular layer of rocks arranged on top of the feature.

While the above artifacts may be grave goods or objects that were incidentally included in the fill, intentionally deposited objects were only included in three burials. A discoidal shell bead made of Buscyon was found with a cranium—all that remained of a disturbed burial. One individual had a tubular bone bead below the left ear, and another middle adult male in a primary, flexed burial had two bone beads in the cranial area near the forehead and red ochre in the pelvic cavity.

Primary interments and even some multiple secondary burials in cemeteries adjacent to villages are much more common for precontact and postcontact New York Iroquois, Neutral, and St. Lawrence Iroquoian communities (Williamson and Steiss 2003). A cemetery similar to the one at the Mantle site was identified about one hundred meters from the roughly contemporary ancestral Wendat Mackenzie-Woodbridge site in the northern Humber drainage, where a minimum of eighteen individuals were found in a small cemetery (Saunders 1986). The burials comprised both primary and secondary interments of individuals of all ages and both sexes, and included bundles.

The fact that some of the Mantle burials are secondary in nature and that one burial contains the remains of two individuals carefully arranged in a double bundle suggests that these burials were intended to remain in the cemetery. Deaths by violence, drowning, and freezing are given as reasons for exclusion from the ossuary (Thwaites 1896–1901, 39:31). It is also possible that Algonquian ideas may have influenced burial practice. The use of red ochre in burial is uncommon in the Iroquoian tradition, although the use of rocks was documented for an in-house primary inhumation at Draper (Williamson 1978:117).

SUMMARY OF LOCAL CONTINUITY AND REGIONAL INTERACTION

Both the cemetery and the material culture assemblage, therefore, can inform us about the various peoples who inhabited the site. The ceramic and lithic industries reflect both the continuity of locally situated manufacturing practices and the introduction of tool stone or clays, finished products, and sometimes their makers from farther afield.

The presence of juvenile ceramics and innovative clay admixtures suggests the transfer of traditional knowledge and the introduction, encouragement, or experimentation with new techniques and recipes for the manufacturing of ceramic vessels. Yet, increasing uniformity in the design of locally produced ceramic vessels is reflected in the increasing proportions of incised (including notched) varieties compared to the presence of significant quantities of vessels with neck decoration in the Spang, Draper, and earlier assemblages. In that this trend occurs generally at the turn of the sixteenth century across Ontario Iroquoia, this is perhaps a reflection of an increasingly uniform production system shared among fewer, larger communities. The significant diversity in design sequences of only a century or two earlier suggests that coalescence also led to a dampening of individual or lineage-based design expression. However, the diversity in fabrics on the site indicates that people were still involved in multiple manufacturing practices.

The concomitant increasing variety of discrete types associated with groups in the St. Lawrence Valley and New York State suggests ties to populations to the south and east. The differences in those ties between neighboring drainages underscores the basic interpretive framework advanced decades ago by Tuck (1971) that the autonomous community moving through space and time should be our primary focus, at least until their external ties lead them to form formal demonstrable political alliances beyond the village.

In the case of Mantle, it would appear that an easterly-directed network was responsible for the introduction of the earliest European iron object in the Lower Great Lakes region, perhaps the same network by which steatite was introduced. The castellation effigies, in contrast, point directly south to the Oneida and Onondaga as significant partners for this site.

Conversely, the predominance of Onondaga chert as the preferred tool stone at Mantle points to regular exchange networks with nearby ancestral Neutral populations to the west. The presence of limited quantities of Fossil Hill and Kettle Point cherts indicates exchange with Algonquians to the north. That network was no doubt also informed by the likelihood that trade with northern hunters for hides was a prerequisite to the survival of the community. The visits of Algonquians as well as those of the Neutral and/or the Iroquois may be reflected in the interments in the village cemetery. While Wendat persons who were not able to be reinterred in the community ossuary are no doubt buried there, the cemetery mainly points to "others," who, while living lives among the Wendat, were not invited to the Feast of the Dead.

Chapter Seven

Conclusions

After an occupation spanning as long as three decades, the Mantle site was abandoned and the community relocated, most likely to a site on the Upper Rouge River and then sequentially to three other sites in the East Holland River drainage on the other side of the Oak Ridges Moraine, prior to abandoning the north shore region for Wendake (see figure 3.1). The first place to which they relocated is likely the 2.8 ha Radcliffe site, located on the brow of a hill overlooking a steep ravine on a tributary of the Upper Rouge River, just south of the Oak Ridges Moraine and five kilometers northwest of Mantle (Dibb 1979). While the site has only been surface collected, the assemblage includes two shell beads, one discoidal and one tubular; one large steatite bead; one fragment of a black shale pebble pendant; two rolled copper beads; and one large piece of copper or brass with circular cutouts, which has not been tested to determine its origin. One black, round bead, not unlike those found at the late-seventeenth-century Bead Hill and Baby Point Seneca sites, was also reportedly found on the site but is certainly not coterminous with the rest of the assemblage and may represent an item discarded on a visit to the site by a Seneca or Algonquian party during the next century. The ceramic assemblage recovered from the site includes incised varieties along with Roebuck Corn-Ear and Dutch Hollow Notched vessels.

From Radcliffe, the community likely moved westward to the Aurora site, a 3.4 ha village also known as "Old Indian Fort" (Emerson 1954:165). It is situated at the top of a steep-sided hill overlooking a small stream at the headwaters of the East Holland River (J. Wright 1966:70). The initial excavations carried out by the University of Toronto in 1947 yielded charred corn kernels; discoidal stone beads; tubular bone beads; about a dozen stemmed, notched, and triangular chert arrow points; and an assortment of castellated pottery that led Emerson (1947) to conclude that the people "were urban cosmopolitans of their day." While they did not find any European trade goods, later surface collections produced a piece of copper, which has yet to be tested. Recent reanalyses of the ceramics from the site seem to place its occupation in the mid-sixteenth century (Pihl, Birch, et al. 2011; P. Ramsden 1977:65). It is notable that the palisade surrounding the site included an earthen embankment, which was also a feature of the final phase of palisade construction at the Mantle site.

Continuing with a westward relocation, the community may have moved to the Hoshel-Huntley site, located two kilometers west of Aurora. Avocational excavations of the site in the mid-twentieth century yielded "a quantity of Late Woodland ceramics" (Dibb 1979:25). The surface scatter indicated that the site covers approximately one hectare at the top of a gently sloping hill. The collection includes two iron knives and several pieces of brass kettles.

The final site in the sequence is the 4.2 ha Van Nostrand-Wright village (Dibb 1979). The site has only been surface collected but includes a significant number of trade goods, including large quantities of European iron tools and copper or brass tools and scrap, much of which has been modified; one turquoise glass trade bead, along with numerous late-sixteenth-century beads; a netting needle with painted red stripes; three discoidal beads; and a number of incised vessels. The assemblage is similar to that of the Skandatut site in the headwaters of the Humber River and the Benson site in the Upper Trent Valley (see chapter 3). The estimated field systems for the post-Mantle sites are clearly constrained by the presence of the Oak Ridges Moraine, which contains soils unsuitable for agriculture. This may have been a contributing factor in the abandonment of this region by the end of the sixteenth century.

By the turn of the seventeenth century, the north shore of Lake Ontario was devoid of permanent settlement, and the population of south-central Ontario was concentrated in the uplands between Georgian Bay and Lake Simcoe. While the *Attignawantan* (Bear) claimed more than two hundred years of continuous habitation in the country (Thwaites 1896–1901: 16:227–29), the inhabitants of the Benson and associated sites in the Upper Trent Valley, including groups formerly living in the St. Lawrence Valley, migrated west and joined the Wendat Confederacy in the late sixteenth century to form the *Arendarhonon* (Rock) (Trigger 1976:156). The origins of the *Tahontaenrat* (Deer) almost certainly rest with those populations from the north shore of Lake Ontario and specifically in the Humber and Holland River watersheds. The *Tahontaenrat* joined the confederacy in approximately 1610 and were said to have inhabited a single village.

Indigenous societies underwent profound changes in the seventeenth century as they were drawn into the intercontinental economic and cultural dynamics of colonialism (Trigger 1976). After 1634, disease ravaged all of the

Iroquoian societies of the Lower Great Lakes (Warrick 2003), and endemic warfare between the Wendat-Tionontaté and the Iroquois Nations to the south, exacerbated by population loss and the economic motivations of the fur trade, resulted in the abandonment of Huronia by the early 1650s.

WHAT WE LEARNED

The methods of excavation employed at an archaeological site necessarily determine the ways in which that site can be analyzed and interpreted. In this case, the total excavation and detailed analysis of the Mantle site permitted an unprecedented glimpse into the history and culture of a single ancestral Wendat population. By integrating these data with a synthesis of current knowledge about Iroquoian site sequences and patterning of material culture, new insights emerged about the nature of interregional interaction and multi-linear evolution of Iroquoian nations. The near complete excavation of the Mantle site was prompted by the development of the lands it occupied and was conducted by Archaeological Services Inc., a private consulting firm. As such, this project has also provided an excellent example of how research conducted in the context of cultural resource management can be integrated into theoretically informed research designs that contribute to big-picture questions in anthropology.

The detailed reconstructions of the occupational histories of the Mantle site and the villages that preceded it point to the creation of new community-based identities, corporate decision making structures, and increasing social integration over time. Analyses of the built environment of the site have revealed the specifics of how people constructed, inhabited, and negotiated domestic and public spaces. The results demonstrate that while settlement aggregation can be documented at the regional level, only detailed intrasite analyses can identify the small-scale changes in practice that reflect the lived experience of coalescence.

Our desire to understand how the Mantle community sustained itself in terms of building materials and necessary foodstuffs, including both gathered and cultivated plants, led to the modeling of the agricultural field systems around the Mantle site and its predecessors. The recognition that the acquisition of hides for clothing may have presented a singular challenge for such a large population led us to the realization that the hide requirements of this community could not have been met locally. This very well may have had significant implications for fifteenth-century conflict and the extension of trading networks with both their Iroquoian and Algonquian neighbors.

While the frequencies of fish bone in the site's faunal assemblage suggest that the mass capture of fall-spawning fish was of some importance, the relatively low mean nitrogen isotope values in teeth recovered from the village suggest that the contribution of lake fish to the diet of the Mantle inhabitants was markedly low when compared to earlier or later populations. With the intensification of agricultural production and a growing requirement for deer hides, other hunting and fishing activities may have become largely opportunistic. These new insights have permitted a much more nuanced understanding of the nature of human-environment interaction than has previously been explored for a single Iroquoian community.

As new mechanisms for maintaining this community were evolving within the village, the residents would also have been negotiating their place within a macroregional landscape that changed dramatically during the fifteenth and sixteenth centuries. The relationship between population pressure, conflict, and settlement aggregation appears to have differed between tribal clusters. In the first half of the fifteenth century, the number of village sites on the north shore of Lake Ontario more than doubled. This increasingly dense regional population and settlement distribution may have created scalar stress (G. Johnson 1982) and external pressures on and between communities. It has been thought that until the large-scale conflicts and dispersals of the seventeenth century, Northern Iroquoian warfare was not waged to control resources or territory and did not include attacks en masse or involve the siege of entire villages (Warrick 1984:129). This may not be the case. Tensions relating to underlying material conditions and resource shortages, particularly with respect to deer-hunting territories, likely contributed to an increase in violence in precontact southern Ontario (Gramly 1977).

Large, defensible settlements seem to appear on the north shore of Lake Ontario earlier than elsewhere in Iroquoia, suggesting that conflict and coalescence may have first developed in the Toronto area. The western end and north shore of Lake Ontario contains some of the earliest evidence for sustained violent conflict in the Lower Great Lakes. The early-fifteenth-century Black Creek site on the middle Humber River was palisaded at a time when others were not. The former Black Creek community and other local groups coalesced at the Parsons site in the mid-fifteenth century, where evidence for warfare includes hundreds of pieces of burnt human bone recovered from midden deposits and two isolated crania that were morphologically similar to those of the Uxbridge ossuary located approximately eighty kilometers northeast (Dupras and Pratte 1998; Pfeiffer 1983; see chapter 3). The Parsons village may have been either engaged in warfare with groups to the east, including those occupying the Draper or Keffer sites; groups to the south and west, as suggested by burials indicative of violent trauma and trophy-taking at the early-fifteenth-century Alhart and Van Oordt sites; or both, as it is entirely possible that communities on the north shore of Lake Ontario were engaged in warfare with both distant and adjacent populations.

It is possible that the militarization of a few local groups led to cycles of raiding and retaliation that, by the late fifteenth to early sixteenth century, had spread throughout the Lower Great Lakes. The formation of "big players" in the late fifteenth to early sixteenth century seems to have displaced and/or absorbed lesser players. For example, in south-central Ontario, the fifteenth-century occupants of the Don River Valley seem to have been displaced by the larger communities forming to the west and east, in the Humber and Duffins Creek drainages. Likewise, populations east of Duffins Creek may have migrated farther east, amalgamating with extant groups in the Trent Valley. The Lower St. Lawrence Valley was likewise abandoned, and these populations were incorporated into the Trent Valley, the Toronto area, and the eastern Iroquois nations.

In the fifteenth century, the formation of larger communities may have served a dual function in terms of warfare and sociopolitical reorganization. First, large, fortified settlements would have had an increased chance of success thanks to stronger defenses against enemy raids and larger war parties and would have been better able to absorb losses (Keeley 1996:129). Second, conflict against mutual enemies may have served an integrative function in communities by quelling internal tensions and directing hostilities outward (Birch 2010b). Because warfare was one of the primary means by which Iroquoian men acquired prestige, the intensification of performances and symbolic displays related to warfare, including ornamentation made of the human bone of captives, would have also provided an avenue for negotiating status and leadership in these newly formed village aggregates. However, over time, the decision to mount an attack or retaliate against a rival village may have been complicated by the larger numbers of people that would have had to agree to the action, which could have had negative consequences for the group down the road. A small number of large villages may have helped to alleviate external tensions by concentrating people in the landscape and opening up buffer zones between communities.

By the early to mid-sixteenth century, levels of conflict in south-central Ontario declined, possibly as a result of increasing organizational complexity and alliance-building between consolidated community aggregates. Increasing population density is correlated with greater social and economic complexity (Carniero 1970; Keeley 1988). Innovations in economic and sociopolitical behaviors are required in order to permit larger numbers of people to be supported by the same resource base and share smaller physical spaces. Larger villages require the creation of the organizational structures necessary to manage larger coresidential populations (village councils, internal ordering of constituent groups, and cooperative economic functions), as well as leaders and organizations which can better manage external relationships (trade and alliances). While large village aggregates may have initially formed in the interests of common defense, they gave rise to new forms of social, political, and economic organization.

The formation of large village aggregates was one strategy adopted to deal with specific external pressures (e.g., increasing settlement density and violent conflict) at particular times and places (cf. Kowalewski 2006:117). While on the north shore of Lake Ontario, community coalescence occurred in the mid- to late fifteenth century, in some parts of New York State and northern Simcoe County, it would seem that the preference was to move together into clusters of villages located a few kilometers from one another, as opposed to forming single large communities that would quickly stress local resources (Engelbrecht 2003:113). Another major difference in precontact and postcontact settlement in Ontario and New York State is that whereas Wendat settlements relocated to Simcoe County over the course of approximately three hundred years (ca. AD 1300–1600) and concentrated or coalesced there in the decades preceding direct European contact, communities belonging to particular Iroquois nations remained, more or less, in their traditional, precontact territories during the same period. Yet, recent perspectives on the ethnogenesis of ancestral Iroquois populations have shown that the development of Iroquoian cultures and ethnic groups is not a one-way evolutionary path (Engelbrecht 2003:112–13). Instead, there were multiple occasions in which social, cultural, technological, and linguistic developments converged and/or separated during the Late Woodland period. It is possible that this ethnogenesis included populations from throughout the Lower Great Lakes. The presence of New York State Iroquoian pottery on sixteenth-century ancestral Wendat sites (for example, the Oneida-like castellation effigies at Mantle) suggests that the relationships between these groups are more complex than we have perhaps recognized. The shadow of the historic conflict between the Wendat and Iroquois has been projected back in time in such a way that archaeologists have restrained themselves from seeking evidence of more amicable relations between Iroquoian communities in Ontario and New York State, such as ties of kinship and intermarriage or trade and exchange.

In order to understand how societies changed over time, we need to adopt multiscalar research designs that focus on changes in practice at the local and community level situated within broader trajectories of cultural development at the macroregional scale, including the movement of materials, ideas, and people. One important question arising from this research concerns questions about the development of organizational diversity in eastern North America. Specifically, given the existence of a similar set of Middle Woodland cultural traditions and Late Woodland socioenvironmental preconditions throughout eastern North America, including the intensification of horticulture, population growth, and increasing conflict, why was it that societies in southeastern

North America developed chiefdoms and vertically integrated societies whereas those in the Northeast developed councils, confederacies, and horizontally integrated societies? This is a question that has significant implications for the study of precontact societies beyond eastern North America.

The evidence for complex corporate organizational structures operating at the Draper and Mantle sites calls into question the categorization of precontact Iroquoians as "simple" tribal or egalitarian societies. This settlement also pushes the boundaries of what constitutes a "village" as opposed to a "town" or "regional center," and in so doing, causes us to rethink common taxonomies for both societal types and settlement hierarchies. This study has therefore contributed to the growing body of literature on middle-range societies, intermediate social formations, and the problems inherent in attempts to classify them into ideal types (cf. Crumley 1995; Feinman and Neitzel 1984; McGuire and Saitta 1996).

CLAIMING THE MANTLE SITE

This project began as a routine cultural resource management project involving an assessment of a private subdivision development, and it quickly evolved into a multiyear analysis and writing effort that was centered not only on meeting the requirements of a government regulatory agency, but also those of the academy and the descendants of the past we were investigating. While our team had worked very closely with the Huron-Wendat Nation of Wendake, Quebec, for the past several years on this and other projects, including discussions around the sampling of teeth for scientific analyses in the context of their long-term objectives, this particular enterprise truly came to fruition when we met one of the Wendat's firm requirements. On a beautiful early fall day in 2011, a ceremony was held near the Mantle cemetery, at which time the village and cemetery were renamed Jean-Baptiste Lainé, in honor of a late community elder. With this simple and moving act, the Wendat reclaimed at least this moment and this place in their complex and storied past on the north shore of Lake Ontario.

References

Abel, Timothy James. 2001. "The Clayton Cluster: Cultural Dynamics of a Late Prehistoric Village Sequence in the Upper St. Lawrence Valley." PhD diss., State University of New York at Albany.

Adler, Michael A., and Richard H. Wilshusen. 1990. "Large-Scale Integrative Facilities in Tribal Societies: Cross-Cultural and Southwestern US Examples." *World Archaeology* 22(2):133–46.

Agriculture and Agri-Food Canada. 1971. *Canada Land Inventory Map: Land Capability for Wildlife—Ungulates.* Toronto 30M, 1:250,000 scale. Last modified August 6, 2011. http://res.agr.ca/cansis/publications/maps/cli/250k/ung/index.html

———. 2012. *Soil Survey Reports for Ontario.* Soil Survey of York County. Last modified January 1, 2012. http://sis.agr.gc.ca/cansis/publications/surveys/on/index.html

AM Archaeological Associates. 1997. "An Archaeological Assessment of the Highway 407/ Transitway from Markham Road Easterly to Highway 7 (W.P. 282-86-01)." Report on file. Toronto: Ontario Ministry of Transportation.

Anderson, Jacob M. 2009. *The Lawson Site: An Early Sixteenth-Century Neutral Iroquoian Fortress.* Special Publication No. 2. London: Museum of Ontario Archaeology.

Andreae, Christopher, Robert H. Pihl, and Ronald F. Williamson. 1998. "Consulting Activities: Summary of 1997 Research by Archaeological Services Inc." *Annual Archaeological Report, Ontario (New Series)* 9:7–16. Toronto: Ontario Heritage Foundation.

Archaeologix. 2006. "Archaeological Assessment (Stage 4), The Settlement at St. Davids, vol. 1: The Steele Village (AgGs-3), Town of Niagara-on-the-Lake, Regional Municipality of Niagara, Ontario." Report on file. Toronto: Ontario Ministry of Tourism, Culture, and Sport.

Armelagos, George J., Alan H. Goodman, and Kenneth H. Jacobs. 1991. "The Origins of Agriculture: Population Growth during a Period of Declining Health." *Population and Environment* 13:9–22.

ASI (Archaeological Services Inc.). 1998. "Final Report on Archaeological Salvage Excavation of the Murphy-Goulding Site (AlGu-3), Town of Richmond Hill, Regional Municipality of York." Report on file. Toronto: Ontario Ministry of Tourism, Culture, and Sport.

———. 2001. "Final Report on the Human Remains Recovered during the 1999 Stage 4 Salvage Excavations at the Jarrett-Lahmer Site (AlGv-18), Lot 17, Concession 5 (WYS), Former Township of Vaughan, Regional Municipality of York, Ontario." Report on file. Toronto: Ontario Ministry of Tourism, Culture, and Sport.

———. 2002. "Stage 1 and 2 Archaeological Assessment Village Securities Property Proposed Plan of Subdivision SC-T19990003 Part Lot 12, Concession 4 (Former City of Scarborough), City of Toronto." Revised Interim Report. Report on file. Toronto: Ontario Ministry of Tourism, Culture, and Sport.

————. 2003. "McGaw Site (AlGu-88) Archaeological Interpretive Program Results of the 2003 Field Season." Report on file. Toronto: Ontario Ministry of Tourism, Culture, and Sport.

————. 2004. "Stage 3 Archaeological Assessment of the Burkholder 1 Site (AlGt-19) on the Cornell-Jennora Lands Parts Lots 9 and 10, Concession 9, Town of Markham, Regional Municipality of York, Ontario." Report on file. Toronto: Ontario Ministry of Tourism, Culture, and Sport.

————. 2005a. "The Stage 3–4 Salvage Excavations of the Burkholder 2 Site (AlGt-35) Lot 8, Concession 9, Geographic Township of Markham Box Grove Secondary Planning Area, Box Grove Hill Development Lands, Town of Markham, Regional Municipality of York, Ontario." Report on file. Toronto: Ontario Ministry of Tourism, Culture, and Sport.

————. 2005b. "Archaeological Investigation of the Teston Site Ossuary, City of Vaughan, Regional Municipality of York, Ontario." Report on file. Toronto: Cemeteries Registrar and Archaeological Services Inc.

————. 2006a. "Stage 4 Archaeological Assessment of the New Site (AlGt-36), Ibrans Box Grove Property, Draft Plan of Subdivision 19TM-04001, Town of Markham, Regional Municipality of York, Ontario." Report on file. Toronto: Ontario Ministry of Tourism, Culture, and Sport.

————. 2006b. "Stage 4 Archaeological Excavation of the Mill Street Site (AlGu-77), Block 12 OPA 400, Draft Plan 19T-99V08, Part of Lot 23, Concession 2, City of Vaughan, Regional Municipality of York, Ontario." Report on file. Toronto: Ontario Ministry of Tourism, Culture, and Sport.

————. 2006c. "The Stage 4 Salvage Excavation of the Baker Site (AkGu-15) Lot 11 Concession 2 (WYS) Block 10 O.P.A. 400 Former Township of Vaughan, City of Vaughan, Regional Municipality of York, Ontario." Report on file. Toronto: Ontario Ministry of Tourism, Culture, and Sport.

————. 2006d. "Stages 1–3 Investigation of the Mantle Site (AlGt-334) Part of Lot 33, Concession 9, Town of Whitchurch-Stouffville, Regional Municipality of York, Ontario." Report on file. Toronto: Ontario Ministry of Tourism, Culture, and Sport.

————. 2008a. "Report on the Stage 3–4 Salvage Excavation of the Alexandra Site (AkGt-53) Draft Plan of Subdivision SC-T20000001 (55T-00601), Geographic Township of Scarborough, Now in the City of Toronto, Ontario." Report on file. Toronto: Ontario Ministry of Tourism, Culture, and Sport.

————. 2008b. "The Stage 4 Salvage Excavation of the Orion Site (AlGu-45) Lot 56, Concession 1 W.Y.S. Town of Richmond Hill, Regional Municipality of York, Ontario." Report on file. Toronto: Ontario Ministry of Tourism, Culture, and Sport.

————. 2010a. "The Archaeology of the Robb Site (AlGt-4), A Report on the Stage 4 Mitigative Excavation of the Angus Meadows Subdivision 19T-95030 (Revised) Part of Lot 1, Concession 8 Town of Markham Regional Municipality of York, Ontario." Report on file. Toronto: Ontario Ministry of Tourism, Culture, and Sport.

————. 2010b. "The Archaeology of the Walkington 2 Site (AlGu-341), A Report on the Stage 3 and Stage 4 Mitigative Excavations of the Nine-Ten Property, Draft Plan of Subdivision 19T-95066 (Revised) Part of Lots 16 and 17, Concession 2, City of Vaughan, Regional Municipality of York, Ontario." Report on file. Toronto: Ontario Ministry of Tourism, Culture, and Sport.

————. 2010c. "The Archaeology of the Hidden Spring Site (AlGu-368), Stage 4 Salvage Excavation of the Hidden Spring Site, Oxford West Subdivision Development, Part of Lots 13–16 and 37–40, Registered Plan 1931, Town of Richmond Hill, Regional Municipality of York, Ontario." Report on file. Toronto: Ontario Ministry of Tourism, Culture, and Sport.

————. 2010d. "Report on the Salvage Excavation of the Antrex Site (AjGv-38), City of Mississauga, Regional Municipality of Peel, Ontario." Report on file. Toronto: Ontario Ministry of Tourism, Culture, and Sport.

————. 2011a. "Stage 3 Archaeological Assessment (Site-Specific Assessment) of the Wonowin Site (AlGs-329), City of Pickering, Regional Municipality of Durham, Ontario." Report on file. Toronto: Ontario Ministry of Tourism, Culture, and Sport.

———. 2011b. "Stage 3 Archaeological Assessment (Site-Specific Assessment) of the Sebastien Site (AlGs-341), City of Pickering, Regional Municipality of Durham, Ontario." Report on file. Toronto: Ontario Ministry of Tourism, Culture, and Sport.

———. 2011c. "The Stage 3–4 Archaeological Excavation of the Hope Site (AlGv-199), Draft Plan of Subdivision 19T-02V07 and 19T-02V08, City of Vaughan, Regional Municipality of York, Ontario." Toronto: Ontario Ministry of Tourism, Culture, and Sport.

———. 2012a. "The Archaeology of the Mantle Site (AlGt-334), Report on the Stage 3–4 Mitigative Excavation of Part of Lot 22, Concession 9, Town of Whitchurch-Stouffville, Regional Municipality of York, Ontario." Report on file. Toronto: Ontario Ministry of Tourism, Culture, and Sport.

———. 2012b. "Stage 3 Archaeological Assessment (Site-Specific Assessment) of the Wilson Park Site (AlGt-28), City of Pickering, Regional Municipality of Durham, Ontario." Report on file. Toronto: Ontario Ministry of Tourism, Culture, and Sport.

———. 2012c. "Report on the Stage 3–4 Mitigative Excavation of the McNair Site (AlGu-8), City of Vaughan, Regional Municipality of York, Ontario." Report on file. Toronto: Ontario Ministry of Tourism, Culture, and Sport.

———. 2012d. "Report on the Stage 3–4 Mitigative Excavation of the Damiani Site (AlGv-231), City of Vaughan, Regional Municipality of York, Ontario." Report on file. Toronto: Ontario Ministry of Tourism, Culture, and Sport.

———. 2012e. "Stage 3 Archaeological Resource Assessment to Define the North Limits of the Skandatut Site (AlGv-193), Lot 24, Concession 7, Geographic Township of Vaughan, City of Vaughan, Ontario." Report on file. Toronto: Ontario Ministry of Tourism, Culture, and Sport.

Baden, William W. 1987. "A Dynamic Model of Stability and Change in Mississippian Agricultural Systems." PhD diss., University of Tennessee.

Baden, William W., and Christopher S. Beekman. 2001. "Culture and Agriculture: A Comment on Sissel Schroeder, Maize Productivity in the Eastern Woodlands and Great Plains of North America." *American Antiquity* 66(3):505–15.

Banfield, Alexander W. F. 1981. *The Mammals of Canada*. Toronto: University of Toronto Press.

Berg, Debbie. 1976. "The Sewell Site (AlGt-9) Final Report." Report on file. Department of Anthropology, University of Toronto.

Biggar, Henry P., ed. 1922–36. *The Works of Samuel de Champlain*, 6 vols. Toronto: Champlain Society.

Birch, Jennifer. 2008. "Rethinking the Archaeological Application of Iroquoian Kinship." *Canadian Journal of Archaeology* 32:194–213.

———. 2010a. "Coalescent Communities in Iroquoian Ontario." PhD diss., McMaster University.

———. 2010b. "Coalescence and Conflict in Iroquoian Ontario." *Archaeological Review from Cambridge* 25(1):29–48.

———. 2012. "Coalescent Communities: Settlement Aggregation and Social Integration in Iroquoian Ontario." *American Antiquity.* 77(4). 646–70.

Bolstad, Paul V., and Ted L. Gragson. 2008. "Resource Abundance Constraints on the Early Post-Contact Cherokee Population." *Journal of Archaeological Science* 35:563–76.

Boulware, Tyler. 2011. *Deconstructing the Cherokee Nation: Town, Region, and Nation among Eighteenth-Century Cherokees*. Gainesville: University Press of Florida.

Bourbou, Chryssi, Benjamin T. Fuller, Sandra J. Garvie-Lok, and Michael P. Richards. 2011. "Reconstructing the Diets of Greek Byzantine Populations (6th–15th Centuries AD) Using Carbon and Nitrogen Stable Isotope Ratios." *American Journal of Physical Anthropology* 146:569–81.

Bourdieu, Pierre. 1970. "The Berber House or the World Reversed." *Social Science Information* 9:151–70.

———. 1977. *Outline of a Theory of Practice*. Cambridge: Cambridge University Press.

Bower, Megan A. 2011. "An Osteological and Stable Isotopic Investigation of Diet and Health during the Late Woodland Period at Hidden Spring in Richmond Hill, Ontario." MA thesis, Trent University.

Bowser, Brenda J., and John Q. Patton. 2004. "Domestic Spaces as Public Places: An Ethnoar-chaeological Case Study of Houses, Gender, and Politics in the Ecuadorian Amazon." *Journal of Archaeological Method and Theory* 11(2):157–81.

Bradley, James W. 1987. *Evolution of the Onondaga Iroquois: Accommodating Change 1500–1655.* Syracuse, NY: University of Syracuse Press.

———. 2011. "Revisiting Wampum and Other Seventeenth-Century Shell Games." *Archaeology of Eastern North America* 39:25–51.

Braun, David P. 1995. "Style, Selection, and Historiocity." In *Style, Selection, and Person: Archaeological and Ethnological Perspectives.* Edited by Christopher Carr and Jill E. Neitzel, 123–41. New York: Plenum.

Braun, Gregory V. 2012. "Petrography as a Technique for Investigating Iroquoian Ceramic Production and Smoking Rituals." *Journal of Archaeological Science* 39:1–10.

Braund, Kathryn E. Holland. 1993. *Deerskins and Duffels.* Lincoln: University of Nebraska Press.

Buckley, Brendan M., Robert J. S. Wilson, Peter E. Kelly, Douglas W. Larson, and Edward R. Cook. 2004. "Inferred Summer Precipitation for Southern Ontario back to AD 610, as Reconstructed from Ring Widths of *Thuja occidentalis.*" *Canadian Journal of Forestry Research* 34:2541–2553.

Burgar, Robert W. C. 1990. "Boyd Archaeological Field School." *Annual Archaeological Report, Ontario* (new series) 1:119–21.

———. 1993. "The Archaeological Resource Management Program of the Metropolitan Toronto and Region Conservation Authority: The 1992 Field Season." *Annual Archaeological Report, Ontario* (new series) 4:58–62.

Burns, James A. 1979. "Faunal Analysis of the Draper Site." In *Settlement Patterns of the Draper and White Sites, 1973 Excavations.* Edited by Brian Hayden. Simon Fraser University, Department of Anthropology, Publication No. 6. Vancouver: Simon Fraser University.

Cadman, Michael D., Donald A. Sutherland, Gregor G. Beck, Denis Lepage, and Andrew R. Couturier, eds. 2007. *Atlas of the Breeding Birds of Ontario, 2001–2005.* Toronto: Bird Studies Canada, Environment Canada, Ontario Field Ornithologists, Ontario Ministry of Natural Resources, and Ontario Nature.

Canuto, Marcello A., and Jason Yaeger, eds. 2000. *The Archaeology of Communities: A New World Perspective.* New York: Routledge.

Carnevale, Andrea. 2012. "The Archaeology of the Mantle Site (AlGt-334), Report on the Stage 3–4 Mitigative Excavation of Part of Lot 22, Concession 9, Town of Whitchurch-Stouffville, Regional Municipality of York, Ontario." Report on file. Toronto: Ontario Ministry of Tourism, Culture, and Sport.

Carnevale, Andrea, Ronald F. Williamson, Martin S. Cooper, and Jennifer Birch. 2012. "Hidden from View: The Story of an Early Sixteenth-Century Iron Tool in Eastern North America." Paper presented at the Seventy-Seventh Annual Meeting of the Society for American Archaeology, Memphis, Tennessee.

Carniero, Robert L. 1970. "A Theory on the Origin of the State." *Science* (new series) 169(3947):733–73.

Carter, Jaqueline E. 1981. "Spang: A Sixteenth-Century Huron Village Site, Pickering, Ontario." MA thesis, University of Toronto.

Casselberry, Samuel E. 1974. "Further Refinement of Formulae for Determining Population from Floor Area." *World Archaeology* 6:117–22.

Ceci, Lynn. 1990. "Radiocarbon Dating 'Village' Sites in Coastal New York: Settlement Pattern Change in the Middle to Late Woodland." *Man in the Northeast* 39:1–28.

Chapdelaine, Claude. 1989. *Le Site Mandeville à Tracy: Variabilité culturelle des Iroquoiens du Saint-Laurent.* Montréal: Amérindiennes au Québec.

———. 2004. "A Review of the Latest Developments in St. Lawrence Iroquoian Archaeology." In *A Passion for the Past: Papers in Honour of James F. Pendergast.* Edited by James V. Wright and Jean Luc Pilon, 63–75. Archaeological Survey of Canada Mercury Series Paper No. 164. Gatineau: Canadian Museum of Civilization.

Chapman, Lyman J., and Donald F. Putnam. 1984. *The Physiography of Southern Ontario.* Ontario Geological Survey, special vol. 2, ed. 3. Sudbury: Ontario Geological Survey.

Churcher, C. S., and Walter A. Kenyon. 1960. "The Tabor Hill Ossuaries: A Study in Iroquois Demography." *Human Biology* 32:249–73.

Cohen, Anthony Paul. 1985. *The Symbolic Construction of Community*. New York: Routledge.

Cook, Edward, and Paul Krusic. 2004. *North American Drought Atlas*. Lamont-Doherty Earth Observatory and the National Science Foundation.

Cooper, Martin S. 1984. "An Analysis of Scattered Human Bone from Ontario Iroquoian Sites." Report on file. Mississauga: University of Toronto, Department of Anthropology.

———. 2010. "Bone Artifacts." In "Report on the Salvage Excavation of the Antrex Site (AjGv-38), City of Mississauga, Regional Municipality of Peel, Ontario." Report on file. Toronto: Ontario Ministry of Tourism, Culture, and Sport.

———. 2012. "Groundstone." In "The Archaeology of the Mantle Site (AlGt-334), Report on the Stage 3–4 Mitigative Excavation of Part of Lot 22, Concession 9, Town of Whitchurch-Stouffville, Regional Municipality of York, Ontario." Report on file. Toronto: Ontario Ministry of Tourism, Culture, and Sport.

Cowgill, Ursula M.1962. "An Agricultural Study of the Southern Maya Lowlands." *American Anthropologist* 64:273–86.

Crawford, Gary. 2003. "The Wallace Site (AkGx-1), 1984 and 1985." Report on file. Mississauga: University of Toronto, Department of Anthropology.

Crawford, Gary W., David G. Smith, and Vandy E. Bowyer. 1997. "Dating the Entry of Corn (Zea Mays) into the Lower Great Lakes Region." *American Antiquity* 62(1):112–19.

Crinnion, Catherine, Deborah C. Merrett, and Susan Pfeiffer. 2003. "The Dentition of the Moatfield People." In *Bones of the Ancestors: The Archaeology and Osteobiography of the Moatfield Site*. Edited by Ronald F. Williamson and Susan Pfeiffer, 223–39. Archaeological Survey of Canada Mercury Series Paper No. 163. Gatineau: Canadian Museum of Civilization.

Crumley, Carole L. 1995. "Heterarchy and the Analysis of Complex Societies." *Archeological Papers of the American Anthropological Association* 6(1):1–5.

Curtis, Jenneth E., and Martha A. Latta. 2000. "Ceramics as Reflectors of Social Relationship: The Auger Site and Ball Site Castellations." *Ontario Archaeology* 70:1–15.

Damkjar, Eric. 1990. *The Coulter Site and Late Iroquoian Coalescence in the Upper Trent Valley*. Occasional Papers in Northeastern Archaeology No. 2. Dundas: Copetown Press.

Diaz, Henry F., and David W. Stahle. 2007. "Climate and Cultural History in the Americas: An Overview." *Climatic Change* 83:1–8.

Dibb, Gordon. 1979. *An Archaeological Survey of the East Holland River and Its Environs*. Manuscript on file. Toronto: Ontario Ministry of Tourism, Culture, and Sport.

Dincauze, Dena F., and Robert J. Hasenstab. 1989. "Explaining the Iroquois: Tribalization in a Prehistoric Periphery." In *Centre and Periphery: Comparative Studies in Archaeology*. Edited by T. C. Champion, 67–87. London: Unwin Hyman.

Dodd, Christine. 1984. *Ontario Iroquois Tradition Longhouses*. Archaeological Survey of Canada, Mercury Series Paper No. 124. Ottawa: National Museum of Man.

Dodd, Christine F., Dana Poulton, Paul A. Lennox, David G. Smith, and Gary Warrick. 1990. "The Middle Ontario Iroquois Stage." In *The Archaeology of Southern Ontario to A.D. 1650*. Edited by Chris J. Ellis and Neal Ferris, 321–60. Occasional Publication of the London Chapter, No. 5. London: Ontario Archaeological Society.

Donaldson, William S. 1962. "The Boyd Site: Report and Appraisal." *Ontario Archaeology* 7:1–20.

DPA (D. R. Poulton and Associates Inc.). 1994. "Report on the 1992–1993 Archaeological Investigations of the Mackenzie Glen Community Development Plan, City of Vaughan, Ontario." Report on file. Toronto: Ontario Ministry of Tourism, Culture, and Sport.

———. 1996. "The 1992–1993 Stage 3–4 Archaeological Excavations of the Over Site (AlGu-120) (W.P. 233-89-00)," vol. 1. Report on file. Toronto: Ontario Ministry of Tourism, Culture, and Sport.

———. 2003. "The 2000 Stage 3 Archaeological Test Excavations of the Jarrett-Lahmer Site (AlGv-18), Draft Plan 19T-99079 City of Vaughan, Ontario." Report on file. Toronto: Ontario Ministry of Tourism, Culture, and Sport.

Drooker, Penelope. 2004. "Pipes, Leadership, and Interregional Interaction in Protohistoric Midwestern and Northeastern North America." In *Smoking and Culture: The Archaeology of Tobacco Pipes in Eastern North America*. Edited by Sean M. Rafferty and Rob Mann, 73–124. Knoxville: University of Tennessee Press.

Dupras, Tosha L., and David G. Pratte. 1998. "Craniometric Study of the Parsons Crania from Midden 4/Feature 245." *Ontario Archaeology* 65/66:140–45.

Ellis, Chris J., and Neal Ferris, eds. 1990. *The Archaeology of Southern Ontario to A.D. 1650*. Occasional Publication of the London Chapter, No. 5. London: Ontario Archaeological Society.

Emerson, J. Norman. 1947. "A Preliminary Report to the Committee for Research in the Humanities and Social Sciences: The Archaeological Investigation of the 'Old Indian Fort' Site, Whitchurch Township, York County, Ontario." Report on file. Toronto: University of Toronto: Department of Anthropology.

———. 1954. "The Archaeology of the Ontario Iroquois." PhD diss., University of Chicago.

———. 1967. "The Payne Site: An Iroquoian Manifestation in Prince Edward County, Ontario." In *Contributions to Anthropology V: Archaeology and Physical Anthropology*, 126–257. Museum of Canada Bulletin No. 206. Ottawa: National Museum of Canada.

Engelbrecht, William. 1985. "New York Iroquois Political Development." In *Cultures in Contact*. Edited by William W. Fitzhugh, 163–83. Washington: Smithsonian Institution.

———. 1995. "The Case of the Disappearing Iroquoians: Early Contact Period Superpower Politics." *Northeast Anthropology* 50:35–59.

———. 1999. "Iroquoian Ethnicity and Archaeological Taxa." In *Taming the Taxonomy: Toward a New Understanding of Great Lakes Archaeology*. Edited by Ronald F. Williamson and Christopher M. Watts, 51–59. Toronto: eastendbooks.

———. 2003. *Iroquoia: The Development of a Native World*. Syracuse, NY: Syracuse University Press.

———. 2004. "Northern New York Revisited in St. Lawrence Iroquoian Archaeology." In *A Passion for the Past: Papers in Honour of James F. Pendergast*. Edited by James V. Wright and Jean Luc Pilon, 63–76. Archaeological Survey of Canada Mercury Series Paper No. 164. Gatineau: Canadian Museum of Civilization.

———. 2009. "Defense in an Iroquois Village." In *Iroquoian Archaeology and Analytical Scale*. Edited by Laurie E. Miroff and Timothy D. Knapp, 179–88. Knoxville: University of Tennessee Press.

Fecteau, Rudolphe D. 1978. "A Preliminary Report on the Seed Remains from Longhouse Features at the Draper Site." Museum of Indian Archaeology, Research Report No. 4. London: University of Western Ontario.

Feinman, Gary, and Jill Neitzel. 1984. "Too Many Types: An Overview of Sedentary Prestate Societies in the Americas." *Advances in Archaeological Method and Theory* 7:39–102.

Fenton, William N. 1978. "Northern Iroquoian Culture Patterns." In *Handbook of North American Indians*, vol. 15, *Northeast*. Edited by Bruce G. Trigger, 296–321. Washington, DC: Smithsonian Institution Press.

———. 1998. *The Great Law and the Longhouse: A Political History of the Iroquois Confederacy*. Norman: University of Oklahoma Press.

Ferris, Neal. 1999. "Telling Tales: Interpretive Trends in Southern Ontario Late Woodland Archaeology." *Ontario Archaeology* 68:1–62.

Ferris, Neal, Ian Kenyon, Rosemary Prevec, and Carl Murphy. 1985. "Bellamy: A Late Historic Ojibwa Habitation." *Ontario Archaeology* 44:3–22.

Ferris, Neal, and Michael W. Spence. 1995. "The Woodland Traditions in Southern Ontario." *Revista de Arqueología Americana* 9:83–138.

Fiedel, Stuart. 1999. "Algonquians and Iroquoians: Taxonomy, Chronology, and Archaeological Implications." In *Taming the Taxonomy: Toward a New Understanding of Great Lakes Archaeology*. Edited by Ronald F. Williamson and Christopher M. Watts, 193–204. Toronto: eastendbooks.

Finlayson, William D. 1977. *The Saugeen Culture: A Middle Woodland Manifestation in Southwestern Ontario*. Archaeological Survey of Canada, Mercury Series Paper No. 61. Ottawa: National Museum of Man.

———. 1985. "The 1975 and 1978 Rescue Excavations at the Draper Site: Introduction and Settlement Pattern." Archaeological Survey of Canada Mercury Series Paper No. 130. Ottawa: Canadian Museum of Civilization.

———. 1998. *Iroquoian Peoples of the Land of Rock and Water, A.D. 1000–1650: A Study in Settlement Archaeology*, vol. 3. London: London Museum of Archaeology.

Finlayson, William D., David G. Smith, Michael W. Spence, and Peter A. Timmins. 1987. "The 1985 Salvage Excavations at the Keffer Site: A License Report." Report on file. Toronto: Ontario Ministry of Tourism, Culture, and Sport.

Fitzgerald, William R. 1990a. "Chronology to Cultural Process: Lower Great Lakes Archaeology, 1500–1650." PhD diss., McGill University.

———. 1990b. "Preliminary Observations on the Ivan Elliot (AiHa-16) Village and the Raymond Reid (AiHa-4) Hamlet, Wellington County, Ontario." *Kewa* 90(6):2–16.

———. 2001. "Contact, Neutral Iroquoian Transformation, and the Little Ice Age." In *Societies in Eclipse: The Archaeology of the Eastern Woodland Indians, A.D. 1400–1700*. Edited by David S. Brose, C. Wesley Cowan, and Robert C. Mainfort Jr., 37–47. Washington, DC: Smithsonian Institution Press.

Flannery, Kent V., ed. 1976. *The Early Mesoamerican Village*. New York: Academic Press.

Fogt, Lisa, and Peter Ramsden. 1996. "From Timepiece to Time Machine: Scale and Complexity in Iroquoian Archaeology." In *Debating Complexity: Proceedings of the Twenty-Sixth Annual Conference of the Archaeological Association of the University of Calgary*. Edited by Daniel A. Meyer, Peter C. Dawson, and Donald T. Hanna, 39–45. Calgary, AB: Archaeological Association of the University of Calgary.

Fontaine, Adriana. 2004. "Scattered Bone: Fragmentary Human Remains from the Lawson Site (AgHh-1)." MA thesis, University of Western Ontario.

Forge, Anthony. 1972. "Normative Factors in Settlement Size of Neolithic Cultivators." In *Man, Settlement, and Urbanism*. Edited by Peter J. Ucko, Ruth Tringham, and G. W. Dimbleby, 363–76. London: Duckworth.

Forrest, Crystal. 2010a. "The In-house Burials at the Late Ontario Iroquoian Draper Site (AlGt-2): A Multidirectional Approach to Interpretation." *Ontario Archaeology* 89–90: 97–119.

———. 2010b. "Iroquoian Infant Mortality and Juvenile Growth 1250 to 1700 AD." PhD diss., University of Toronto.

———. 2012. "Cemetery Investigation and Analysis." In "The Archaeology of the Mantle Site (AlGt-334) Report on the Stage 3–4 Mitigative Excavation of Part of Lot 22, Concession 9, Town of Whitchurch-Stouffville, Regional Municipality of York, Ontario." Report on file. Toronto: Ontario Ministry of Tourism, Culture, and Sport.

Foster, Gary. 1990. *The Wolfe Creek Site, AcHm-3: A Prehistoric Neutral Frontier Community in Southwestern Ontario*. Monographs in Ontario Archaeology No. 3. Toronto: Ontario Archaeological Society.

Fox, William A. 1990. "The Middle Woodland to Late Woodland Transition." In *The Archaeology of Southern Ontario to A.D. 1650*. Edited by Chris J. Ellis and Neal Ferris, 171–88. Occasional Publication of the London Chapter, No. 5. London: Ontario Archaeological Society.

———. 2004. "Horned Panthers and Erie Associates." In *A Passion for the Past: Papers in Honour of James F. Pendergast*. Edited by James V. Wright and Jean-Luc Pilon. Archaeological Survey of Canada Mercury Series Paper No. 164. Gatineau: Canadian Museum of Civilization.

———. 2008. "Ontario Iroquois Long-Distance Contacts." *Northeast Anthropology* 75–76:1–22.

Fox, William A., Ron G. V. Hancock, and Larry A. Pavlish. 1995. "Where East Met West: The New Copper Culture." *Wisconsin Archaeologist* 76(3–4): 269–93.

Free, Melissa, and Alan Robock. 1999. "Global Warming in the Context of the Little Ice Age." *Journal of Geophysical Research* 104(D16):19057–19070.

Gerritsen, Fokke. 2004. "Archaeological Perspectives on Local Communities." In *A Companion to Archaeology*. Edited by John Bintliff, 141–54. Oxford: Blackwell Publishing.

Giddens, Anthony. 1984. *The Constitution of Society: Outline of the Theory of Structure*. Berkeley: University of California Press.

Godfrey, W. Earl. 1966. *The Birds of Canada*. National Museum of Canada Bulletin No. 203. Ottawa: National Museum of Canada.

Gramly, Richard M. 1977. "Deerskins and Hunting Territories: Competition for a Scarce Resource of the Northeastern Woodlands." *American Antiquity* 42(4):601–5.

Grenier, Robert, Marc-André Bernier, and Willis Stevens, eds. 2007. *The Underwater Archaeology of Red Bay: Basque Shipbuilding and Whaling in the Sixteenth Century*. Ottawa: Parks Canada.

Griffin, James. 1944. "The Iroquois in American Prehistory." *Papers of the Michigan Academy of Science, Arts, and Letters* 29:357–74.

Gruspier, Katherine. 1999. "Subadult Growth and Health from Ossuary Samples of Prehistoric Southern Ontario Iroquoian Populations." PhD diss., University of Toronto.

Hall, Robert L. 1976. "Ghosts, Water Barriers, Corn, and Sacred Enclosures in the Eastern Woodlands." *American Antiquity* 41(3):360–64.

Hamell, George. 1983. "Trading in Metaphors: The Magic of Glass Beads." In *Proceedings of the 1986 Shell Bead Conference, Selected Papers*. Edited by Charles F. Hayes, 5–28. Rochester Museum and Science Centre, Research Record No. 20, Rochester, New York.

———. 1992. "The Iroquois and the World's Rim: Speculation on Colour, Culture, and Contact." *American Indian Quarterly: Journal of American Indian Studies* 16:151–69.

———. 1998. "Long-tail: The Panther in Huron-Wendat and Seneca Myth, Ritual, and Material Culture." In *Icons of Power: Feline Symbolism in the Americas*. Edited by Nicholas J. Saunders, 258–91. New York: Routledge.

Harris, Marvin. 1968. "Comments." In *New Perspectives in Archaeology*. Edited by Sally R. Binford and Lewis R. Binford, 359–61. Chicago: Aldine.

Harrison, Roman G., and M. Anne Katzenberg. 2003. "Paleodiet Studies Using Stable Carbon Isotopes from Bone Bio Apatite and Collagen: Examples from Southern Ontario and San Nicolas Island, California." *Journal of Anthropological Archaeology* 22:227–44.

Hart, John P. 2001. "The Origin of the Iroquois as Suggested by Their Archaeology." *American Anthropologist* 18:479–507.

Hart, John P., and Hetty Jo Brumbach. 2003. "The Death of Owasco." *American Antiquity* 68:737–52.

Hart, John P., and William Engelbrecht. 2011. "Northern Iroquoian Ethnic Evolution: A Social Network Analysis." *Journal of Archaeological Method and Theory* 19(2):322–49.

Hart, John P., Robert G. Thompson, and Hetty Jo Brumbach. 2003. "Phytolith Evidence for Early Maize (*Zea mays*) in the Northern Finger Lakes Region of New York." *American Antiquity* 68:619–40.

Hartney, Patrick C. 1978. "Palaeopathology of Archaeological Aboriginal Populations from Southern Ontario and Adjacent Region." PhD diss., University of Toronto.

Hawkins, Alicia L. 2004. "Report on the 2004 Investigations at the Emmerson Springs Village (AkGx-5), Town of Halton Hills, Ontario, under License P081-002 and P081-004." Report on file. Toronto: Ontario Ministry of Tourism, Culture, and Sport.

Haxell, Jonathan. 2002. "Ancient Settlements and Modern Technology: Excavations at the Middle Iroquoian Lougheed and Gregor Sites." Paper presented at the annual meeting of the Canadian Archaeological Association. Ottawa.

Hayden, Brian. 1979. "The Draper and White Sites: Preliminary and Theoretical Considerations." In *Settlement Patterns of the Draper and White Sites, 1973 Excavations*. Edited by Brian Hayden, 1–28. Department of Archaeology, Publication No. 6. Burnaby, BC: Simon Fraser University.

Hayden, Brian, and Aubrey Cannon. 1982. "The Corporate Group as an Archaeological Unit." *Journal of Anthropological Archaeology* 1:132–58.

Hegmon, Michelle. 1989. "Social Integration and Architecture." In *The Architecture of Social Integration in Prehistoric Pueblos*. Edited by William D. Lipe and Michelle Hegmon, 5–14. Occasional Papers of the Crow Canyon Archaeological Center. Cortez, CO: Crow Canyon Archaeological Center.

Heidenreich, Conrad E. 1971. *Huronia: A History and Geography of the Huron Indian, 1600–1650*. Toronto: McClelland and Stewart.

————. 1974. "A Relict Indian Corn Field near Creemore, Ontario." *Canadian Geographer* 18(4):379–94.

Helmuth, Hermann. 1993. "The Quackenbush Skeletons: Osteology and Culture." Trent University Occasional Papers in Anthropology No. 9. Peterborough: Trent University.

Hickerson, Harold. 1965. "The Virginia Deer and Intertribal Buffer Zones in the Upper Mississippi Valley." In *Man's Culture and Animals*. Edited by A. Leeds and A. P. Vayda, 43–66. Washington, DC: American Association for the Advancement of Science.

Hillier, Bill, and Julienne Hanson. 1984. *The Social Logic of Space*. Cambridge: Cambridge University Press.

Hodge, Fredrick Webb. 1971 [1913]. *Handbook of the Indians of Canada*. Toronto: Coles Publishing.

Howie, Linda. 2012. "Mantle Site: Report on Possible Implications of Ceramic Compositional Variation at the Microscopic Level." Report on file. Toronto: Archaeological Services Inc.

Ingold, Tim. 2000. *The Perception of the Environment: Essays in Livelihood, Dwelling, and Skill*. London: Routledge.

Isbell, William H. 2000. "What We Should Be Studying: The 'Imagined Community' and the 'Natural Community.'" In *The Archaeology of Communities: A New World Perspective*. Edited by Marcello A. Canuto and Jason Yaeger, 243–66. New York: Routledge.

Jackson, Lawrence J. 1988. "Dawson Creek Site Feature Analysis: 4,000 Years of Ontario Prehistory." Trent University Occasional Papers in Anthropology, No. 5. Peterborough: Trent University.

Jamieson, J. Bruce. 1983. "An Examination of Prisoner Sacrifice and Cannibalism at the St. Lawrence Iroquoian Roebuck Site." *Canadian Journal of Archaeology* 7:159–75.

————. 1990. "The Archaeology of the St. Lawrence Iroquoians." In *The Archaeology of Southern Ontario to A.D. 1650*. Edited by Chris J. Ellis and Neal Ferris, 385–404. Occasional Publication of the London Chapter, No. 5. London: Ontario Archaeological Society.

Jamieson, Susan M. 1992. "Regional Interaction and Ontario Iroquois Evolution." *Canadian Journal of Archaeology* 16:70–88.

Jenkins, Tara. 2011. "Contexts, Needs, and Social Messaging: Situating Iroquoian Human Bone Artifacts." Major Research Paper, Department of Anthropology, McMaster University.

Johnson, Dave S. 1980. "The McKenzie or Woodbridge Site (AkGv-2), and Its Place in the Late Ontario Iroquois Tradition." *Archaeology of Eastern North America* 8:77–87.

Johnson, Gregory A. 1982. "Organizational Structure and Scalar Stress." In *Theory and Explanation in Archaeology*. Edited by Colin Renfrew, Michael J. Rowlands, and Barbara Abbott Seagraves, 389–421. New York: Academic Press.

Jones, Eric E. 2010a. "Population History of the Onondaga and Oneida Iroquois, A.D. 1500–1700." *American Antiquity* 75(2):387–407.

————. 2010b. "An Analysis of Factors Influencing Sixteenth and Seventeenth Century Haudenosaunee (Iroquois) Settlement Locations." *Journal of Anthropological Archaeology* 29:1–14.

Joyce, Rosemary A. 2005. "Archaeology of the Body." *Annual Review of Anthropology* 34:139–58.

Kapches, Mima. 1981. "The Middleport Pattern in Ontario Iroquoian Prehistory." PhD diss., University of Toronto.

————. 1984. "Cabins on Ontario Iroquois Sites." *North American Archaeologist* 5:63–71.

————. 1987. "The Auda Site: An Early Pickering Iroquois Component in Southeastern Ontario." *Archaeology of Eastern North America* 15:155–75.

Katzenberg M. Anne, Olga Goriunova, and Andrezj Weber. 2009. "Paleodiet Reconstruction of Bronze Age Siberians from the Mortuary Site of Khuzhir-Nuge XIV, Lake Baikal." *Journal of Archaeological Science* 36:663–74.

Katzenberg, M. Anne, Shelley R. Saunders, and William R. Fitzgerald. 1993. "Age Differences in Stable Carbon and Nitrogen Isotope Ratios in a Population of Prehistoric Maize Horticulturalists." *American Journal of Physical Anthropology* 90:267–81.

Katzenberg, M. Anne, Henry Schwarcz, M. Knyf, and F. Jerry Melbye. 1995. "Stable Isotope Evidence for Maize Horticulture and Paleodiet in Southern Ontario, Canada." *American Antiquity* 60(2):335–50.

Keeley, Lawrence H. 1988. "Hunter-Gatherer Economic Complexity and 'Population Pressure': A Cross-Cultural Analysis." *Journal of Anthropological Archaeology* 7(4):373–411.

———. 1996. *War before Civilization.* New York: Oxford University Press.

Keene, Arthur S. 1981. *Prehistoric Foraging in a Temperate Forest: A Linear Programming Model.* New York: Academic Press.

Kent, Susan. 1990. "Activity Areas and Architecture: An Interdisciplinary View of the Relationship between Use of Space and Domestic Built Environments." In *Domestic Architecture and the Use of Space: An Interdisciplinary Cross-Cultural Study.* Edited by Susan Kent, 1–8. Cambridge: New Directions in Archaeology, Cambridge University Press.

Kenyon, Walter A. 1968. *The Miller Site.* Art and Archaeology Occasional Paper No. 14. Toronto: Royal Ontario Museum.

Knight, Dean H., and Sally Cameron. 1983. "The Ball Site, 1975–1982." Report on file. Waterloo: Wilfrid Laurier University.

Kolb, Michael J., and James E. Snead. 1997. "It's a Small World after All: Comparative Analyses of Community Organization in Archaeology." *American Antiquity* 62:609–28.

Konrad, Victor A. 1973. *The Archaeological Resources of the Metropolitan Toronto Planning Area: Inventory and Prospect.* Discussion Paper No. 10. Toronto: York University Department of Geography.

Konrad, Victor A., and W. A. Ross. 1974. *An Archaeological Survey for the North Pickering Project, Part 1: North Pickering Archaeology.* Research Report No. 4. Toronto: Ontario Ministry of Tourism, Culture, and Sport and Recreation Historical Planning and Research Branch.

Kowalewski, Stephen A. 2006. "Coalescent Societies." *In Light on the Path: The Anthropology and History of the Southeastern Indians.* Edited by Thomas J. Pluckhahn and Robbie Ethridge, 94–122. Tuscaloosa: University of Alabama Press.

Kroeber, Alfred L. 1939. *Cultural and Natural Areas of Native North America.* University of California Publications in American Archaeology and Ethnology, vol. 38. Berkeley: University of California Press.

Kuhn, Robert D. 2004. "Reconstructing Patterns of Interaction and Warfare between the Mohawk and Northern Iroquoians during the A.D. 1400–1700 Period." In *A Passion for the Past: Papers in Honour of James F. Pendergast.* Edited by James V. Wright and Jean-Luc Pilon, 145–66. Archaeological Survey of Canada, Mercury Series Paper No. 164. Gatineau: Canadian Museum of Civilization.

Latta, M. A. 1980. "Controlling the heights: The Iroquoian occupations of the Albion Pass region." *Archaeology of Eastern North America* 8:71–77.

Lawrence, Denise L., and Setha M. Low. 1990. "The Built Environment and Spatial Form." *Annual Review of Anthropology* 19:453–505.

Lee, Thomas E. 1952. "Preliminary Report on an Archaeological Survey of Southwestern Ontario for 1950." *National Museum of Canada Bulletin* 126:64–75. Ottawa: National Museum of Canada.

Lee-Thorp, Julia A., Judith C. Sealy, and Nikolaas J. van der Merwe. 1989. "Stable Carbon Isotope Ratio Differences between Bone Collagen and Bone Apatite, and Their Relationship to Diet." *Journal of Archaeological Science* 16:585–99.

Lenig, Donald. 1965. *The Oak Hill Horizon and Its Relation to the Development of Five Nations Iroquois Culture.* Researches and Transactions of the New York State Archaeological Association 15(1).

Lennox, Paul A. 1984. "The Hood Site: A Historic Neutral Town of 1640 A.D." Archaeological Survey of Canada, Mercury Series Paper No. 121:1–183. Ottawa: Canadian Museum of Civilization.

Lennox, Paul A., Christine F. Dodd, and C. R. Murphy. 1986. *The Wiacek Site: A Late Middleport Component in Simcoe County, Ontario.* London: Ontario Ministry of Transportation and Communications, Environmental Unit, Planning and Design Section.

Lennox, Paul A., and William R. Fitzgerald. 1990. "The Culture History and Archaeology of the Neutral Iroquoians." In *The Archaeology of Southern Ontario to A.D. 1650.* Edited by Chris J. Ellis and Neal Ferris, 405–56. Occasional Publication of the London Chapter, No. 5. London: Ontario Archaeological Society.

Lightfoot, Kent G., Antoinette Martinez, and Ann M. Schiff. 1998. "Daily Practice and Material Culture in Pluralistic Social Settings: An Archaeological Study of Culture Change and Persistence from Fort Ross, California." *American Antiquity* 63:199–222.

Lipe, William D., and Michelle Hegmon. 1989. "Historical and Analytical Perspectives on Architecture and Social Integration in the Prehistoric Pueblos." In *The Architecture of Social Integration in Prehistoric Pueblos.* Edited by William D. Lipe and Michelle Hegmon, 15–34. Occasional Paper No. 1. Cortez: Crow Canyon Archaeological Centre.

Lounsbury, Floyd G. 1978. "Iroquoian Languages." In *Handbook of North American Indians,* Volume 15, *Northeast.* Edited by Bruce G. Trigger, 334–343. Washington, DC: Smithsonian Institution Press.

Mac Sweeney, Naoíse. 2011. *Community Identity and Archaeology: Dynamic Communities at Aphrodisias and Becyesultan.* Ann Arbor: University of Michigan Press.

MacDonald, Robert I. 1986. "The Coleman Site (AiHd-7): A Late Prehistoric Iroquoian Village in the Waterloo Region." MA thesis, Trent University.

———. 1988. "Ontario Iroquoian Sweat Lodges." *Ontario Archaeology* 48:17–26.

———. 2002. "Late Woodland Settlement Trends in South-Central Ontario: A Study of Ecological Relationships and Culture Change." PhD diss., McGill University.

MacDonald, Robert I., and Ronald F. Williamson. 1995. "The Hibou Site (AlGo-50): Investigating Ontario Iroquoian Origins in the Central North Shore Area of Lake Ontario." In *Origins of the People of the Longhouse.* Edited by André Bekerman and Gary Warrick, 9–42. Proceedings of the Twenty-First Annual Symposium of the Ontario Archaeological Society Inc. Toronto: Ontario Archaeological Society.

———. 2001. "Sweatlodges and Solidarity: The Archaeology of the Hubbert Site." *Ontario Archaeology* 71:29–78.

MacKay, Hector H. 1963. *Fishes of Ontario.* Toronto: Bryant Press.

MacNeish, Richard S. 1952. *Iroquois Pottery Types: A Technique for the Study of Iroquois Prehistory.* National Museum of Canada Bulletin No. 124, Anthropological Series No. 31. Ottawa: National Museum of Canada.

McCabe, Richard E. 2002. "Elk and Indians: Then Again." In *North American Elk: Ecology and Management.* Edited by Dale E. Toweill and Jack Ward Thomas, 121–97. Washington, DC: Smithsonian Institution Press.

McCullough, Karen M. 1978. *Modified Deer Phalanges at the Draper Site.* Museum of Indian Archaeology Research Reports No. 5. London: Museum of Indian Archaeology, University of Western Ontario.

McGuire, Randall H., and Dean J. Saitta. 1996. "Although They Have Petty Captains, They Obey Them Badly: The Dialectics of Prehispanic Western Pueblo Social Organization." *American Antiquity* 61(2):197–216.

Merrett, Deborah C. 2003. "Maxillary Sinusitis among the Moatfield People." In *Bones of the Ancestors: The Archaeology and Osteobiography of the Moatfield Site.* Edited by Ronald F. Williamson and Susan Pfeiffer, 241–61. Archaeological Survey of Canada Mercury Series Paper No. 163. Gatineau: Canadian Museum of Civilization.

Merritt, Lisa. 2001. "The Bidmead Site (BeGv-4): An Historic Wendat Village in Simcoe County, Ontario." MA thesis, University of Toronto.

Molto, J. Eldon, Michael Spence, and William Fox. 1986. "The Van Oordt Site: A Case Study in Salvage Archaeology." *Canadian Review of Physical Anthropology* 5(2):49–61.

Monckton, Stephen G. 1992. *Huron Paleoethnobotany.* Ontario Archaeological Reports, No. 1. Toronto: Ontario Heritage Foundation.

———. 1998. "Myers Road Plant Remains." In *The Myers Road Site: Archaeology of the Early to Middle Iroquoian Transition.* Edited by Ronald F. Williamson, 109–132. Occasional Publication of the London Chapter No. 7. London: Ontario Archaeological Society.

Monckton, Stephen G., and Crystal L. Forrest. 2012. "Plant Remains." In "The Archaeology of the Mantle Site (AlGt-334), Report on the Stage 3–4 Mitigative Excavation of Part of Lot 22, Concession 9, Town of Whitchurch-Stouffville, Regional Municipality of York, Ontario." Report on file. Toronto: Ontario Ministry of Tourism, Culture, and Sport.

Moore, John H. 1994. "Putting Anthropology Back Together Again: The Ethnogenetic Critique of Cladistic Theory." *American Anthropologist* (new series) 96(4):925–48.

MPP (Mayer, Pihl, Poulton, and Associates). 1986a. "Report on Phase 1 of an Archaeological Master Plan for the Town of Vaughan: Background Research and Feasibility Study." Report on file. Toronto: Ontario Ministry of Tourism, Culture, and Sport.

———. 1986b. "Mitigative Investigations at Three Archaeological Sites on the Proposed Parkway Belt West Pipeline." Report on file. Toronto: Ontario Ministry of Tourism, Culture, and Sport.

———. 1987. "The 1984 Salvage Excavation at the Boyle-Atkinson Site (AlGu-1), Town of Richmond Hill, Ontario." Report on file. Toronto: Ontario Ministry of Tourism, Culture, and Sport.

———. 1988. *The Archaeological Facility Master Plan Study of the Northeast Scarborough Study Area.* Report on file. Toronto: Ontario Ministry of Tourism, Culture, and Sport.

Mt Pleasant, Jane. 2006. "The Science behind the Three Sisters Mound System: An Agronomic Assessment of an Indigenous Agricultural System in the Northeast." In *Histories of Maize: Multidisciplinary Approaches to Prehistory, Linguistics, Biogeography, Domestication, and Evolution of Maize.* Edited by John Staller, Robert Tykot, and Bruce Benz, 529–37. Burlington, MA: Elsevier Press.

Mt Pleasant, Jane, and Robert F. Burt. 2010. "Estimating Productivity of Traditional Iroquoian Cropping Systems from Field Experiments and Historical Literature." *Journal of Ethnobiology* 30(1):52–79.

Mullen, Grant J., and Robert D. Hoppa. 1992. "Rogers Ossuary (AgHb-131): An Early Ontario Iroquois Burial Feature from Brantford Township." *Canadian Journal of Archaeology* 16:32–47.

Murdock, George P. 1949. *Social Structure.* New York: Macmillan.

Needs-Howarth, Suzanne. 2006. "Zooarchaeological Remains." In "The Stage 4 Salvage Excavation of the Baker Site (AkGu-15), Lot 11 Concession 2 (WYS) Block 10 O.P.A. 400 Former Township of Vaughan, City of Vaughan, Regional Municipality of York, Ontario." Report on file. Toronto: Ontario Ministry of Tourism, Culture, and Sport.

———. 2012. "Zooarchaeological Remains." In "The Archaeology of the Mantle Site (AlGt-334), Report on the Stage 3–4 Mitigative Excavation of Part of Lot 22, Concession 9, Town of Whitchurch-Stouffville, Regional Municipality of York, Ontario." Report on file. Toronto: Ontario Ministry of Tourism, Culture, and Sport.

Needs-Howarth, Suzanne, and Ronald F. Williamson. 2010. "Feeding and Clothing the Masses: The Role of White-Tailed Deer in Community Planning in Sixteenth-Century Ontario." In *Bone Commons,* Item 1419. Accessed January 17, 2012. http://alexandriaarchive.org/bonecommons/items/show/1419

Niemczycki, Mary-Ann P. 1984. "The Origin and Development of the Seneca and Cayuga Tribes of New York State." PhD diss., State University of New York at Buffalo.

———. 1991. "Cayuga Archaeology: Where Do We Go from Here?" *The Bulletin: Journal of the New York State Archaeological Association* 102:27–33.

———. 1995. "Ceramics and Ethnicity in West-Central New York: Exploring Owasco-Iroquois Connections." *Northeast Anthropology* 49:43–54.

Noble, William C. 1974. "The Jackes (Eglinton) Site: Another Facet of Southern Huron Development in the Toronto Region." *Ontario Archaeology* 22:3–22.

Ortner, Donald J., and Arthur C. Aufderheide. 1991. *Human Paleopathology: Current Syntheses and Future Options.* Washington, DC: Smithsonian Institution Press.

Parker, Arthur C. 1916. "The Origin of the Iroquois as Suggested by Their Archaeology." *American Anthropologist* 18:479–507.

———. 1922. *The Archaeological History of New York.* Albany: State University of New York Press.

Parker Pearson, Michael, and Colin Richards. 1994. "Ordering the World: Perceptions of Architecture, Space, and Time." In *Architecture and Order: Approaches to Social Space.* Edited by Michael Parker Pearson and Colin Richards, 1–37. New York: Routledge.

Pauketat, Timothy R. 2001. "Practice and History in Archaeology: An Emerging Paradigm." *Anthropological Theory* 1:73–98.

————. 2003. "Material and the Immaterial in Historical-Processual Archaeology." In *Essential Tensions in Archaeological Method and Theory*. Edited by Todd L. VanPool and Christine S. VanPool, 41–54. Salt Lake City: University of Utah Press.

Pauketat, Timothy R., and Susan Alt. 2005. "Agency in a Postmould? Physicality and the Agency of Culture-Making." *Journal of Archaeological Method and Theory* 12:213–36.

Pearce, Robert J. 1978a. "A Preliminary Report on the Draper Site Rim Sherds." Museum of Indian Archaeology Research Report No. 1. London: Museum of Indian Archaeology.

————. 1978b. "A Description of the Miscellaneous Ceramic Objects Recovered during the 1975 Field Season at the Draper Site." Museum of Indian Archaeology Research Report No. 2. London: Museum of Indian Archaeology.

————. 1978c. "A Description of the Juvenile Ceramics Recovered during the 1975 Field Season at the Draper Site." Museum of Indian Archaeology Research Report No. 3. London: Museum of Indian Archaeology.

————. 1983. "A Summary Description and Analysis of the Ground and Rough Stone Tools." In "Progress Report on the Draper Site Analysis, 1980–1983." Edited by William D. Finlayson. Report on file. London: Museum of Indian Archaeology.

————. 1996. "Mapping Middleport: A Case Study in Societal Archaeology." London Museum of Archaeology Report 25. London: London Museum of Archaeology.

————. 1997. "The Watford Site (AlGu-5), Richmond Hill, License Report. East Half, Lot 23, Concession 2, E.Y.S., Town of Richmond Hill." Report on file. London: Museum of Ontario Archaeology.

Pearce, Robert, Robert MacDonald, David Smith, Peter Timmins, and Gary Warrick. 2006. "Bruce Trigger's Impact on Ontario Iroquoian Studies." In *The Archaeology of Bruce Trigger: Theoretical Empiricism*. Edited by Ronald F. Williamson and Michael S. Bisson, 114–34. Montreal and Kingston: McGill-Queen's University Press.

Pendergast, James F. 1963. *The Payne Site*. National Museum of Canada Bulletin No. 193. Ottawa: National Museum of Man.

————. 1964. "The Waupoos Site: An Iroquois Component in Prince Edward County, Ontario." *Pennsylvania Archaeologist* 34:69–89.

————. 1972. "The Lite Site: An Early Southern Division Site near Belleville, Ontario." *Ontario Archaeology* 17:24–61.

————. 1981a. "Origins of the St. Lawrence Iroquoian Pottery on the Draper Site." Manuscript on file. Toronto: Archaeological Services Inc.

————. 1981b. "Distribution of Iroquoian Discoidal Clay Beads." *Ontario Archaeology* 36:57–72.

————. 1988. "The Maynard-McKeown Site, BeFv-1: A Sixteenth-Century St. Lawrence Iroquoian Village Site in Grenville County, Ontario; A Preliminary Report." *Ottawa Archaeologist* 15(4):1–12.

————. 1993. "More on When and Why the St. Lawrence Iroquoians Disappeared." In *Essays in St. Lawrence Iroquoian Archaeology*. Edited by James F. Pendergast and Claude Chapdelaine, 9–48. Occasional Papers in Northeast Archaeology No. 8. Dundas: Copetown Press.

Petersen, James B., John G. Crock, Ellen R. Cowie, Richard A. Boisvert, Joshua R. Toney, and Geoffery Mandel. 2004. "St. Lawrence Iroquoians in Northern New England: Pendergast Was 'Right' and More." In *A Passion for the Past: Papers in Honour of James F. Pendergast*. Edited by James V. Wright and Jean-Luc Pilon, 87–123. Mercury Series, Archaeology Paper No. 164. Gatineau: Canadian Museum of Civilization.

Peterson, Randolph L. 1966. *The Mammals of Eastern Canada*. Toronto: Oxford University Press.

Pfeiffer, Susan. 1983. "Demographic Parameters of the Uxbridge Ossuary Population." *Ontario Archaeology* 40:9–14.

————. 1991. "Rib Lesions and New World Tuberculosis." *International Journal of Osteoarchaeology* 1:191–98.

Pfeiffer, Susan, Ronald F. Williamson, Judith Sealey, and Crystal L. Forrest. 2013. "Report on the Stable Isotopes from Selected Ontario Iroquoian Sites." Report on file at Archaeological Services Inc.

Pihl, Robert H. 1984. "Final Report on the Draper Rim Sherd Collection: 1975/1978 Excavated Samples." Report on file at Toronto: Archaeological Services Inc.

————. 2002. "Public Archaeology and the OAS: Results of the 2001 Field Season at the McGaw Site," 132–141. Annual Archaeological Report 13, new series. Toronto: Ontario Heritage Trust.

Pihl, Robert H., Jennifer Birch, Aleksandra Pradzynski, and Rob Wojtowicz. 2011. "Multi-Scalar Perspectives on Iroquoian Ceramics: A Re-examination of the West Duffins Creek Site Sequence." Paper presented at the Seventy-Sixth Annual Meeting of the Society for American Archaeology, Sacramento.

Pihl, Robert H., S. G. Monckton, D. A. Robertson, and R. F. Williamson. 2008. "Settlement and Subsistence Change at the Turn of the First Millennium: The View from the Holmedale Site, Brantford, Ontario." In *Current Northeast Paleoethnobotany II*. Edited by John P. Hart, 151–172.The New York State Education Department, New York State Museum Bulletin Series No. 512. Albany: State University of New York Press.

Popham, Robert E. 1950. "Late Huron Occupations of Ontario: An Archaeological Survey of Innisfil Township." *Ontario History* 42(2):81–90.

Poulton, Dana R. 1979. "The Prehistory of the New Toronto International Airport Property: The 1976–1978 Surveys." Report on file. London: Museum of Indian Archaeology

————. 1984. "An Analysis of the Draper Site Chipped Lithic Artifacts." Report on file. London: Museum of Indian Archaeology

Powis, Terry G., and Ronald F. Williamson. 1998. "Parsons Site Ceramic Vessels." *Ontario Archaeology* 65/66:53–71.

Pradzynski, Aleksandra. 2012. "Juvenile Manufactured Ceramic Vessels and Pipes." In "The Archaeology of the Mantle Site (AlGt-334), Report on the Stage 3–4 Mitigative Excavation of Part of Lot 22, Concession 9, Town of Whitchurch-Stouffville, Regional Municipality of York, Ontario." Report on file. Toronto: Ontario Ministry of Tourism, Culture, and Sport.

Pratt, Peter P. 1976. *Archaeology of the Oneida Iroquois,* vol. 1. Occasional Publications in Northeastern Anthropology No. 1. Albany: Man in the Northeast.

Puric-Mladenovic, Danijela. 2003. "Predictive Vegetation Modeling for Forest Conservation and Management in Settled Landscapes." PhD diss., University of Toronto.

Rainey, Dori L. 2002. "Challenging Assumptions: An Analysis of the Scattered Human Remains from the Keffer Site (AkGv-14)." MA thesis, University of Western Ontario, London.

Ramsden, Carol Nasmith. 1989. *The Kirche Site.* Dundas: Copetown Press.

Ramsden, Carol N., Ronald F. Williamson, Robert I. MacDonald, and Carol Short. 1998a. "Settlement Patterns." In *The Myers Road Site: Archaeology of the Early to Middle Iroquoian Transition.* Edited by Ronald F. Williamson, 11–84. Occasional Publication of the London Chapter, No. 7. London: Ontario Archaeological Society.

Ramsden, Carol N., Ronald F. Williamson, Stephen Cox Thomas, and Tony Hanley. 1998b. "Artifact Analysis." In *The Myers Road Site: Archaeology of the Early to Middle Iroquoian Transition.* Edited by Ronald F. Williamson, 133–93. Occasional Publication of the London Chapter, No. 7. London: Ontario Archaeological Society.

Ramsden, Peter G. 1968. "The Draper Site: A Late Ontario Iroquois Component." MA thesis, University of Calgary.

————. 1977. *A Refinement of Some Aspects of Huron Ceramic Analysis.* Archaeological Survey of Canada Mercury Series Paper No. 63. Ottawa: Canadian Museum of Civilization.

————. 1978. "Late Iroquoian Occupations of South-Central Ontario: A Preliminary Report on the 1977 Field Season." Manuscript submitted to the Canada Council.

————. 1988. "Palisade Extension, Village Expansion and Immigration in Iroquoian Sites in the Upper Trent Valley." *Canadian Journal of Archaeology* 12:177–83.

————. 1990a. "The Hurons: Archaeology and Culture History." In *The Archaeology of Southern Ontario to A.D. 1650*. Edited by Chris J. Ellis and Neal Ferris, 361–84. Occasional Paper of the London Chapter. London: Ontario Archaeological Society.

————. 1990b. "Saint Lawrence Iroquoians in the Upper Trent River Valley." *Man in the Northeast* 39:87–95.

————. 1996. "The Current State of Huron Archaeology." *Northeast Anthropology* 51:101–12.

————. 2006. "But Once the Twain Did Meet: A Speculation about Iroquoian Origins." In *From the Arctic to Avalon: Papers in Honour of Jim Tuck*. Edited by Lisa Rankin and Peter Ramsden, 27–32. *British Archaeological Reports International Series* 1507.

————. 2009. "Politics in a Huron Village." In *Painting the Past with a Broad Brush: Papers in Honor of James Valliere Wright*. Edited by David L. Keenlyside and Jen-Luc Pilon, 299–318. Archaeological Survey of Canada, Mercury Series Paper No. 170. Gatineau: Canadian Museum of Civilization.

Rapoport, Amos. 1990. *The Meaning of the Built Environment: A Nonverbal Communication Approach*. Tucson: University of Arizona Press.

————. 1994. "Spatial Organization and the Built Environment." In *Companion Encyclopedia of Anthropology: Humanity, Culture, and Social Life*. Edited by Tim Ingold, 460–502. London: Routledge.

Rautman, Alison E. 2000. "Population Aggregation, Community Organization, and Plaza-Oriented Pueblos in the American Southwest." *Journal of Field Archaeology* 27:271–83.

Reed, Patricia. 1993. "The MacLeod Site (AlGr-1) and a Preliminary Delineation of the Lake Ontario Iroquois." In *North and South: Two Views of the Black Creek–Lalonde Period*. Edited by Peter G. Ramsden, 2–62. Occasional Papers in Northeast Archaeology No. 7. Dundas: Copetown Press.

Reid, C. S. 1975. *The Boys Site and the Early Ontario Iroquois Tradition*. Archaeological Survey of Canada Mercury Series Paper No. 42. Ottawa: Canadian Museum of Civilization.

Reimer, Paula J., Mike G. L. Baillie, Edouard Bard, Alex Bayliss, J. Warren Beck, C. Bertrand, P. G. Blackwell, et al. 2009. "Intcal09 and Marine09 Radiocarbon Age Calibration Curves." *Radiocarbon* 51:1111–1150.

Renfrew, Colin. 1986. "Introduction." In *Peer-Polity Interaction and Socio-Political Change*. Edited by Colin Renfrew and John F. Cherry, 1–18. New Directions in Archaeology. Cambridge: Cambridge University Press.

Richards, Cara. 1967. "Huron and Iroquois Residence Patterns." In *Iroquois Culture, History, and Prehistory: Proceedings of the 1965 Conference on Iroquois Research*. Edited by E. Tooker, 51–56. Albany: State University of New York Press, State Education Department, and New York State Museum and Science Service.

Ritchie, William A. 1944. *The Pre-Iroquoian Occupations of New York State*. Memoir No. 1. Rochester: Rochester Museum of Arts and Sciences.

————. 1969. *The Archaeology of New York State*. Revised edition. Garden City: Natural History Press.

Ritchie, William A., and Richard S. MacNeish. 1949. "The Pre-Iroquoian Pottery of New York State." *American Antiquity* 15:97–124.

Robb, John. 2008. "Meaningless Violence and the Lived Body: The Huron Jesuit Collision of World Orders." In *Past Bodies: Body-centered Research in Archaeology*. Edited by Dusan Borić and John Robb, 89–100. Oxford: Oxbow Books.

Robertson, David A. 2004. "The Hutchinson Site: A Place to Prepare for the Final Journey." *Ontario Archaeology* 77/78:95–120.

————. 2010. "Conclusions. Report on the Salvage Excavation of the Antrex Site (AjGv-38), City of Mississauga, Regional Municipality of Peel, Ontario." Report on file. Toronto: Ministry of Culture.

Robertson, David A., Stephen G. Monckton, and Ronald F. Williamson. 1995. "The Wiacek Site Revisited: The Results of the 1990 Excavations." *Ontario Archaeology* 60:40–91.

————. 1998. "Parsons Site Exotica and Archaeometry." *Ontario Archaeology* 65/66:104–10.

Robertson, David A., and Ronald F. Williamson. 1998. "The Archaeology of the Parsons Site: Summary and Conclusions." *Ontario Archaeology* 65/66:146–50.

————. 2003. "The Archaeology of the Dunsmore Site: Fifteenth-Century Community Trans-formations in Southern Ontario." *Canadian Journal of Archaeology* 27(1):1–61.

Robertson, David A., Ronald F. Williamson, and Bruce M. Welsh. 1998. "Settlement Patterns at the Parsons Site." *Ontario Archaeology* 65/66:21–51.

Robinson, Percy James. 1933. *Toronto during the French Régime: A History of the Toronto Region from Brûlé to Simcoe, 1615–1793.* Toronto: University of Toronto Press.

Rutherford, A. A., J. Wittenberg, and R. Wilmeth. 1979. "University of Saskatchewan Radio-carbon dates III." *Radiocarbon* 21:48–94.

Rutledge, Linda Y., Kristen I. Bos, Robert J. Pearce, and Bradley N. White. 2010. "Genetic and Morphometric Analysis of Sixteenth-Century Canis Skull Fragments: Implications for His-toric Eastern and Gray Wolf Distribution in North America." *Conservation Genetics* 11(4):1273–1281.

Sahlins, Marshall. 1963. "Poor Man, Big Man, Rich Man, Chief: Political Types in Melanesia and Polynesia." *Comparative Studies in Society and History* 5:285–303.

Saunders, Shelley R. 1986. "The Mackenzie Site Human Skeletal Material." *Ontario Archaeol-ogy* 45:9–26.

Schoeninger, Margaret J., and Michael J. DeNiro. 1984. "Nitrogen and Carbon Isotopic Com-position of Bone Collagen from Marine and Terrestrial Animals." *Geochimica et Cosmo-chimica Acta* 48:625–39.

Schoeninger, Margaret J., Michael J. DeNiro, and Henrik Tauber. 1983. "Stable Nitrogen Isotope Ratios Reflect Marine and Terrestrial Components of Prehistoric Human Diet." *Science* 220:1381–1383.

Schroeder, Sissel. 1999. "Maize Productivity in the Eastern Woodlands and Great Plains of North America." *American Antiquity* 64(3):499–516.

Schwarcz, Henry P., Jerome Melbye, M. Anne Katzenberg, and Martin Knyf. 1985. "Stable Isotopes in Human Skeletons of Southern Ontario: Reconstructing Palaeodiet." *Journal of Archaeological Science* 12:187–206.

Sempowski, Martha L., and Lorraine P. Saunders. 2001. *The Dutch Hollow and Factory Hol-low Sites: The Advent of Dutch Trade among the Seneca.* Charles F. Wray Series in Seneca Archaeology, vol. 3. Research Records No. 24. Rochester, NY: Rochester Museum and Science Center.

Sempowski, Martha L., Lorraine P. Saunders, and Gian Carlo Cervone. 1988. "The Adams and Culbertson Sites: A Hypothesis for Village Formation." *Man in the Northeast* 35:95–108.

Severinghaus, C. W., and E. L. Cheatum. 1956. "Life and Times of the White-Tailed Deer." In *The Deer of North America: Their History and Management.* Edited by Walter P. Taylor, 57–186. Harrisburg, PA: Stackpole.

Shelford, Victor E. 1963. *The Ecology of North America.* Urbana: University of Illinois Press.

Shennan, Stephen. 1993. "After Social Evolution: A New Archaeological Agenda?" In *Archae-ological Theory: Who Sets the Agenda?* Edited by Norman Yoffee and Andrew Sherratt, 53–59. Cambridge: Cambridge University Press.

Shook, Beth Alison Schultz, and David Glenn Smith. 2008. "Using Ancient mtDNA to Con-struct the Population History of Northeastern North America." *American Journal of Physi-cal Anthropology* 137(1):14–29.

Sioui, Georges E. 1999. *Huron-Wendat: The Heritage of the Circle.* Translated by J. Brierley. Vancouver: University of British Columbia Press.

Smith, Bruce D. 1975. "Middle Mississippi Exploitation of Animal Populations." Museum of Anthropology, University of Michigan, Anthropological Papers No. 57. Ann Arbor: Univer-sity of Michigan.

Smith, David G. 1977. *The Archaeological Investigations at the Southwold Earthworks, 1935 and 1976.* Parks Canada Manuscript Report No. 314.

————. 1983. "An Analytical Approach to the Seriation of Iroquoian Pottery." Museum of Indian Archaeology, Research Report No. 12. London: Museum of Indian Archaeology.

————. 1990. "Iroquoian Societies in Southern Ontario: Introduction and Historical Over-view." In *The Archaeology of Southern Ontario to A.D. 1650.* Edited by Chris J. Ellis and Neal Ferris, 279–90. Occasional Publication of the London Chapter. London: Ontario Ar-chaeological Society.

Smith, Huron H. 1933. "Ethnobotany of the Potawatomi." Milwaukee Public Museum, Bulletin No. 7, 32–127. Milwaukee: Milwaukee Public Museum.

Snow, Dean R. 1994. *The Iroquois*. New York: Taylor & Francis.

———. 1995a. "Migration in Prehistory: The Northern Iroquoian Case." *American Antiquity* 60:59–79.

———. 1995b. *Mohawk Valley Archaeology: The Sites*. Occasional Papers in Anthropology No. 23, Matson Museum of Anthropology. University Park: Pennsylvania State University.

———. 1996. "More on Migration in Prehistory: Accommodating the New Evidence in the Northern Iroquoian Case." *American Antiquity* 61:791–96.

———. 2007. "Iroquois-Huron Warfare." In *North American Indigenous Warfare and Ritual Violence*. Edited by Richard J. Chacon and Rubén G. Mendoza, 149–59. Tucson: University of Arizona Press.

Spence, Michael W. 1999. "Comments: The Social Foundations of Archaeological Taxonomy." In *Taming the Taxonomy*. Edited by Ronald F. Williamson and Christopher M. Watts, 275–82. Toronto: eastendbooks.

Spence, Michael W., Robert H. Pihl, and J. E. Molto. 1984. "Hunter-Gatherer Social Group Identification: A Case Study from Middle Woodland Southern Ontario." In *Exploring the Limits: Frontiers and Boundaries in Prehistory*. Edited by Suzanne P. DeAtley and Frank J. Findlow, 117–42. British Archaeological Reports International Series 223.

Spence, Michael, Robert Pihl, and Carl Murphy. 1990. "Cultural Complexes of the Early and Middle Woodland Periods." In *The Archaeology of Southern Ontario to A.D. 1650*. Edited by Christopher Ellis and Neal Ferris, 125–69. Occasional Papers of the London Chapter, Ontario Archaeological Society No. 5. London: Ontario Archaeological Society.

Stahle, David W., and Malcolm K. Cleaveland. 1994. "Tree-Ring Reconstructed Rainfall over the Southeastern USA during the Medieval Warm Period and the Little Ice Age." *Climatic Change* 26:199–212.

Staski, Edward, and Livingston D. Sutro, eds. 1991. *The Ethnoarchaeology of Refuse Disposal*. Arizona State University Anthropological Research Papers No. 42. Tempe: Arizona State University.

Steckley, John. 2007. *Words of the Huron*. Waterloo: Wilfrid Laurier University Press.

———, ed. 2009. *Sagard's Dictionary of Huron*. ALR Supplement Series, vol. 2. Merchantville, NJ: Evolution Publishing.

Steiss, Deborah A. 2010. "Flaked Lithics." In "Report on the Salvage Excavation of the Antrex Site (AjGv-38), City of Mississauga, Regional Municipality of Peel, Ontario." Report on file. Toronto: Ontario Ministry of Tourism, Culture, and Sport.

———. 2012. "Flaked Lithics." In "The Archaeology of the Mantle Site (AlGt-334), Report on the Stage 3–4 Mitigative Excavation Part of Lot 22, Concession 9, Town of Whitchurch-Stouffville, Regional Municipality of York, Ontario." Report on file. Toronto: Ontario Ministry of Tourism, Culture, and Sport.

Stewart, Frances L. 1991. "Faunal Remains from the Keffer Site (AkGv-14), a Southern Ontario Iroquois Village." Museum of Indian Archaeology Research Report No. 21. London: Museum of Indian Archaeology.

Stock, Jay, and Katherine Willmore. 2003. "Body Size, Bone Mass, and Biomechanical Analyses of the Adult Post-Cranial Remains." In *Bones of the Ancestors: The Archaeology and Osteobiography of the Moatfield Site*. Edited by Ronald F. Williamson and Susan Pfeiffer, 309–29. Archaeological Survey of Canada Mercury Series Paper No. 163. Gatineau: Canadian Museum of Civilization.

Stothers, David. 1977. *The Princess Point Complex*. Archaeological Survey of Canada Mercury Series Paper No. 58. Ottawa: Canadian Museum of Civilization.

Sublett, Audrey J., and Charles F. Wray. 1970. "Some Examples of Accidental and Deliberate Human Skeletal Modification in the Northeast." *The Bulletin: Journal of the New York State Archaeological Association* 50:14–26.

Suttles, Gerald D. 1972. *The Social Construction of Communities*. Chicago: University of Chicago Press.

Sutton, Richard E. 1990. *Hidden amidst the Hills: Middle and Late Iroquoian Occupations in the Middle Trent Valley.* Occasional Papers in Northeastern Archaeology No. 3. Dundas: Copetown Press.

————. 1999. "The Barrie Site: A Pioneering Iroquoian Village Located in Simcoe County, Ontario." *Ontario Archaeology* 67:40–87.

Thomas, Stephen C. 1998. "Zooarchaeology of the Parsons Site." *Ontario Archaeology* 65/66:121–139.

Thomas, Stephen C., C. E. J. Carscallen, and Suzanne Needs-Howarth. 1998. "Faunal Analysis." In *The Myers Road Site: Archaeology of the Early to Middle Iroquoian Transition.* Edited by R. F. Williamson. Occasional Publication of the London Chapter No. 7. London: Ontario Archaeological Society.

Thompson, Robert G., John P. Hart, Hetty J. Brumbach, and Robert Lusteck. 2004. "Phytolith Evidence for Twentieth-Century B.P. Maize in Northern Iroquoia." *Northeast Anthropology* No. 68:25–40.

Thwaites, Reuben Gold. 1896–1901. *The Jesuit Relations and Allied Documents.* 73 vols. Cleveland, OH: Burrows Brothers Company.

Tieszen, L. L., and T. Fagre. 1993. "Effect of Diet Quality on the Isotopic Composition of Respiratory CO_2, Bone Collagen, Bioapatite, and Soft Tissues." In *Prehistoric Human Bone: Archaeology at the Molecular Level.* Edited by J. B. Lambert and G. Grupe, 121–55. Berlin: Springer-Verlag.

Timmins, Peter A. 1997. *The Calvert Site: An Interpretive Framework for the Early Iroquoian Village.* Archaeological Survey of Canada Mercury Series Paper No. 156. Gatineau: Canadian Museum of Civilization.

Tooker, Elizabeth. 1964. *An Ethnography of the Huron Indians, 1615–1649.* Smithsonian Institution, Bureau of American Ethnology, Bulletin 190. Washington, DC: U.S. Government Printing Office.

TRCA (Toronto and Region Conservation Authority). 2002. *Duffins Creek State of the Watershed Report: Aquatic Habitat and Species.* Toronto: Toronto and Region Conservation Authority.

Trigger, Bruce G. 1969. *The Huron: Farmers of the North.* Holt, Rinehart and Winston.

————. 1976. *The Children of Aataentsic: A History of the Huron People to 1660,* 2 vols. Montreal: McGill-Queen's University Press.

————. 1978. "Iroquoian Matriliny." *Pennsylvania Archaeologist* 48(1+2):55–65.

————. 1981a. "Prehistoric Social and Political Organization: An Iroquoian Case Study." In *Foundations of Northeast Archaeology.* Edited by Dean R. Snow, 1–50. New York: Academic Press.

————. 1981b. "Webster vs. Champlain." *American Antiquity* 46(2):420–21.

————. 1985. *Natives and Newcomers: Canada's "Heroic Age" Reconsidered.* Montreal: McGill-Queen's University Press.

————. 1990. "Maintaining Economic Equality in Opposition to Complexity: An Iroquoian Case Study." In *The Evolution of Political Systems.* Edited by Steadman Upham, 119–45. Cambridge: Cambridge University Press.

————. 2007. *A History of Archaeological Thought.* 2nd ed. Cambridge: Cambridge University Press.

Tripp, Grant. 1978. "The White Site: A Southern Division Huron Component." Manuscript on file. London: Museum of Indian Archaeology, University of Western Ontario.

Tuck, James A. 1971. *Onondaga Iroquois Prehistory: A Study in Settlement Archaeology.* Syracuse, NY: Syracuse University Press.

Turchin, Peter, and Andrew V. Korotayev. 2006. "Population Dynamics and Internal Warfare: A Reconsideration." *Social Evolution & History* 5(2):112–47.

Turner, E. Randolph, and Robert S. Santley. 1979. "Deer Skins and Hunting Territories Reconsidered." *American Antiquity* 44(4):810–15.

Turner, Lucien M. 1894. "Ethnology of the Ungava District." In *Eleventh Annual Report, Bureau of Ethnology,* 167–350. Washington, DC: Smithsonian Institution.

URS Canada Inc. 2011. "Stage 3 Archaeological Assessment of the Miindaamiin Site Part of Lots 16 & 17, Concession V, Geographic Township of Pickering, Ontario." Report on file. Toronto: Ontario Ministry of Tourism, Culture, and Sport.

van der Merwe, Nikolaas J., Susan Pfeiffer, Ronald F. Williamson, and Stephanie C. Thomas. 2003. "Isotopic Analysis and the Diet of the Moatfield Community." In *Bones of the Ancestors: The Archaeology and Osteobiography of the Moatfield Site.* Edited by R. F. Williamson and S. Pfeiffer, 205–22. Archaeological Survey of Canada Mercury Series Paper No. 163. Gatineau: Canadian Museum of Civilization.

Varley, Colin, and Aubrey Cannon. 1994. "Historical Inconsistencies: Huron Longhouse Length, Hearth Number, and Time." *Ontario Archaeology* 58:85–96.

Veilleux, Annie. 2011. "Knowing Landscape: Living, Discussing, and Imagining the Toronto Carrying Place." MA thesis, York University.

Voigt, Dennis, Greg Deyne, Mike Malhiot, Bruce Ranta, Barry Snider, Ray Stefanski, and Midge Strickland. 1992. *White-Tailed Deer in Ontario: Background to a Policy.* Ontario Ministry of Natural Resources, Wildlife Policy Branch, draft document.

von Gernet, Alexander D. 1982. "Interpreting the Intrasite Spatial Distribution of Artifacts: The Draper Site Pipe Fragments." *Man in the Northeast* 23:49–60.

———. 1985. *Analysis of Intrasite Artifact Spatial Distributions: The Draper Site Smoking Pipes.* Research Report No. 16. London: Museum of Indian Archaeology, University of Western Ontario.

———. 1994. "Saving the Souls: Reincarnation Beliefs of the Seventeenth-Century Huron." In *Reincarnation Belief among North American Indians and Inuit.* Edited by Antonia Mills and Richard Slobodin, 38–54. Toronto: University of Toronto Press.

Warrick, Gary A. 1984. "Reconstructing Ontario Iroquois Village Organization." Archaeological Survey of Canada Mercury Series Paper No. 124:1–180. Ottawa: Canadian Museum of Civilization.

———. 1988. "Estimating Ontario Iroquoian Village Duration." *Man in the Northeast* 36: 21–60.

———. 1996. "Evolution of the Iroquoian Longhouse." In *People Who Lived in Big Houses: Archaeological Perspectives on Large Domestic Structures.* Edited by Gary Coupland and Edward B. Banning, 11–26. Monographs in World Archaeology, no. 27. Madison, WI: Prehistory Press.

———. 2000. "The Precontact Occupation of Southern Ontario." *Journal of World Prehistory* 14:415–66.

———. 2008. *A Population History of the Huron-Petun, A.D. 500–1650.* Cambridge: Cambridge University Press.

Watts, Christopher M. 2011. "Points of Passage / Points of View: Iroquoian Animal Effigy Pipes and the Crossing of Corporeal Borders." Paper presented at the Seventy-Sixth Annual Meeting, Society for American Archaeology, Sacramento.

Waugh, Frederick W. 1916. *Iroquois Foods and Food Preparation.* Anthropological Series No. 12, Memoirs of the Canadian Genaeological Survey No. 86. Ottawa: Government Printing Bureau.

Webster, Gary S. 1979. "Deer Hides and Tribal Confederacies: An Appraisal of Gramly's Hypothesis." *American Antiquity* 44(4):816–20.

White, Marian E. 1978a. "Erie." In *Handbook of North American Indians*, vol. 15, *Northeast.* Edited by Bruce G. Trigger, 412–17. Washington, DC: Smithsonian Institution.

———. 1978b. "Neutral and Wenro." In *Handbook of North American Indians*, vol. 15, *Northeast.* Edited by Bruce G. Trigger, 407–11. Washington, DC: Smithsonian Institution.

Whitney, Theodore. 1970. "The Buyea Site OND 13-3." *The Bulletin: Journal of the New York State Archaeological Association* 50:1–14.

Willey, Gordon R., and Jeremy Sabloff. 1980. *A History of American Archaeology.* 2nd ed. San Francisco: W. H. Freeman and Co.

Williamson, Ronald F. 1978. "Preliminary Report on Human Interment Patterns at the Draper Site." *Canadian Journal of Archaeology* 2:117–21.

————. 1983. *The Robin Hood Site: A Study in Functional Variability in Late Iroquoian Settlement Patterns*. Vol. 1 of Monographs in Ontario Archaeology. Toronto: Ontario Archaeological Society.

————. 1985. "Glen Meyer: People in Transition." PhD diss., McGill University.

————. 1990. "The Early Iroquoian Period of Southern Ontario." In *Archaeology of Southern Ontario to A.D. 1650*. Edited by Chris J. Ellis and Neal Ferris, 291–320. Occasional Publication of the London Chapter, OAS No. 5. London: Ontario Archaeological Society.

————, ed. 1998. *The Myers Road Site: Archaeology of the Early to Middle Iroquoian Transition*. Occasional Publication No. 7. London: Ontario Archaeological Society.

————. 1999. "Toward a Grounded Archaeology." In *Taming the Taxonomy*. Edited by Ronald F. Williamson and Christopher M. Watts, 3–8. Toronto: eastendbooks.

————. 2007. "'Ontinontsiskiaj ondaon' (The House of Cut-off Heads): The History and Archaeology of Northern Iroquoian Trophy Taking." In *The Taking and Displaying of Human Body Parts as Trophies*. Edited by Richard J. Chacon and David H. Dye, 190–221. New York: Springer.

————. 2012. "What Will Be Has Always Been: The Past and Present of Northern Iroquoians." In *The Oxford Handbook of North American Archaeology*. Edited by Timothy Pauketat, 273–84. Oxford: Oxford University Press.

Williamson, Ronald F., Shaun J. Austin, and Stephen Cox Thomas. 2003. "The Archaeology of the Grandview Site: A Fifteenth-Century Community on the North Shore of Lake Ontario." *Arch Notes* 8(5):5–49.

Williamson, Ronald F., Martin S. Cooper, and David A. Robertson. 1998. "The 1989–90 Excavations at the Parsons Site: Introduction and Retrospect." *Ontario Archaeology* 65/66:4–16.

Williamson, Ronald F., and Susan Pfeiffer, eds. 2003. *Bones of the Ancestors: The Archaeology and Osteobiography of the Moatfield Ossuary*. Archaeological Survey of Canada Mercury Series Paper No. 163. Gatineau: Canadian Museum of Civilization.

Williamson, Ronald F., and Robert H. Pihl. 2002. "Foragers and Fishers on the Credit: The Scott-O'Brian Site." In *Mississauga: The First 10,000 Years*. Edited by Frank A. Dieterman, 73–90. Mississauga Heritage Foundation. Toronto: eastendbooks.

Williamson, Ronald F., and Terry G. Powis. 1998. "Parsons Site Ceramic Vessels." *Ontario Archaeology* 65/66:53–71.

Williamson, Ronald F., and Carol Nasmith Ramsden. 1998. "Conclusions." In *The Myers Road Site: Archaeology of the Early to Middle Iroquoian Transition*. Edited by Ronald F. Williamson, 193–204. Occasional Publication No. 7. London: Ontario Archaeological Society.

Williamson, Ronald F., and David A. Robertson. 1994. "Peer Polities beyond the Periphery: Early and Middle Iroquoian Regional Interaction." Ontario Archaeology 58:27–40.

————, eds. 1998. "The Archaeology of the Parsons Site: A Fifty-Year Perspective." *Ontario Archaeology* 65/66.

Williamson, Ronald F., and Debbie A. Steiss. 2003. "A History of Iroquoian Burial Practice." In *Bones of the Ancestors: The Archaeology and Osteobiography of the Moatfield Ossuary*. Edited by Ronald F. Williamson and Susan Pfeiffer, 89–132. Archaeological Survey of Canada Mercury Series Paper No. 163. Gatineau: Canadian Museum of Civilization.

Williamson, Ronald F., Stephen C. Thomas, and Robert I. MacDonald. 2003. "The Archaeology of the Moatfield Village Site." In *Bones of the Ancestors: The Archaeology and Osteobiography of the Moatfield Ossuary*. Edited by R. F. Williamson and S. Pfeiffer, 19–88. Archaeological Survey of Canada Mercury Series Paper No. 163. Gatineau: Canadian Museum of Civilization.

Williamson, Ronald F., and Annie Veilleux. 2005. "A Review of Northern Iroquoian Bone and Antler Artifacts: A Search for Meaning." *Ontario Archaeology* 79/80:3–37.

Williamson, Ronald F., and Christopher M. Watts, eds. 1999. *Taming the Taxonomy: Toward a New Understanding of Great Lakes Archaeology*. Toronto: eastendbooks.

Wilson, Jim. 1991. "A Bad Analogy? Northern Algonquian Models and the Middle Woodland Occupations of Southwestern Ontario." *Kewa* 91(4):9–22.

Wintemberg, William J. 1928. *Uren Prehistoric Village Site, Oxford County, Ontario.* National Museum of Canada Bulletin No. 51. Ottawa: National Museum of Canada.

———. 1936. *The Roebuck Prehistoric Village Site, Grenville County, Ontario.* National Museum of Canada Bulletin 83. Ottawa: National Museum of Canada.

———. 1939. *Lawson Prehistoric Village Site, Middlesex County, Ontario.* National Museum of Canada Bulletin No. 94. Ottawa: National Museum of Canada.

———. 1948. *The Middleport Prehistoric Village Site.* National Museum of Canada Bulletin No. 109. Ottawa: National Museum of Canada.

Wojtowicz, Robert. 2012. "Ceramic Artifact Analysis." In "The Archaeology of the Mantle Site (AlGt-334), Report on the Stage 3–4 Mitigative Excavation of Part of Lot 22, Concession 9, Town of Whitchurch-Stouffville, Regional Municipality of York, Ontario." Report on file. Toronto: Ontario Ministry of Tourism, Culture, and Sport.

Wonderley, Anthony. 2002. "Oneida Ceramic Effigies: A Question of Meaning." *Northeast Anthropology* 63:23–48.

———. 2005. "Effigy Pipes, Diplomacy, and Myth: Exploring Interactions between St. Lawrence Iroquoians and Eastern Iroquoians in New York State." *American Antiquity* 70(2):211–40.

Wray, Charles F., and Harry L. Schoff. 1953. "A Preliminary Report on the Seneca Sequence in Western New York, 1550–1687." *Pennsylvania Archaeologist* 23(2):53–63.

Wray, Charles F., Martha L. Sempowski, and Lorraine P. Saunders. 1991. *Two Early Contact Era Seneca Sites.* Research Records No. 21. Rochester, NY: Rochester Museum and Science Center Research.

Wray, Charles F., Martha L. Sempowski, Lorraine P. Saunders, and G. Cervone. 1987. *The Adams and Culbertson Sites.* Research Records No. 19. Rochester, NY: Rochester Museum and Science Center Research.

Wright, James V. 1966. *The Ontario Iroquois Tradition.* National Museum of Canada Bulletin No. 210. Ottawa: National Museum of Canada.

———. 1974. "The Nodwell Site." Archaeological Survey of Canada Mercury Series Bulletin No. 22. Ottawa: Canadian Museum of Civilization.

———. 1979. *Quebec Prehistory.* Toronto: Van Nostrand Reinhold.

Wright, Joyce. 2004. "Ouatit's People: The Cosmological Significance of Dogs in Wendat Society." In *A Passion for the Past: Papers in Honour of James F. Pendergast,* edited by James V. Wright and Jean-Luc Pilon, 305–320. Mercury Series, Archaeology Paper 164.

Wright, Milton J. 1986. *The Uren Site (AfHd-3): An Analysis and Reappraisal of the Uren Substage Type Site.* Vol. 2 of Monographs in Ontario Archaeology. Toronto: Ontario Archaeological Society.

Wrong, G. M., ed. 1939. *The Long Journey to the Country of the Hurons, by Gabriel Sagard (1632).* Toronto: Champlain Society.

Wylie, Alison. 1989. "Archaeological Cables and Tacking: The Implications of Practice for Bernstein's 'Options beyond Objectivism and Relativism.'" *Philosophy of the Social Sciences* 19:1–18.

Wymer, Dee. 1993. "Cultural Change and Subsistence: The Middle and Late Woodland Transition in the Mid-Ohio Valley." In *Foraging and Farming in the Eastern Woodlands.* Edited by C. Margaret Scarry, 13–26. Gainesville: University Press of Florida.

Index

abandonment: of Huronia, 159; of the Mantle site, 157; of the north shore of Lake Ontario, 113, 117, 124, 157, 158; of the St. Lawrence Valley, 24, 134, 161; of the Trent Valley, 43, 158; of villages, 9, 29, 35, 36, 39, 61, 87, 127, 152

Adams site, 48–49

adoption, 4, 82, 149

adornment, 26, 103, 121

adzes. *See* celts

agency, 7

aggregation, 18, 21, 23, 25, 51, 53, 54, 61, 81, 85, 89, 159, 160; at the Draper site, 56–61, 79; Early and Middle Iroquoian aggregation, 17, 18–19, 19, 28, 31, 34; Early and Middle Woodland aggregation, 13, 16; effects on health, 153; historic Wendat aggregation, 22; in New York State, 48, 49, 50; Late Iroquoian aggregation, 35, 36, 37, 38, 39, 42, 43, 53, 56, 61, 85, 160; relationship to conflict, 35, 36, 37, 39, 161–162. *See also* coalescence

agriculture, 91–101; adoption of, 13–15; clearing fields, 102, 123; modeling of agricultural field systems, 93–101. *See also* maize

Alexandra site, 28

Alhart site, 48, 161

Algonquian, 3, 4, 12, 74, 88, 98, 111, 141, 151, 155, 156, 159; trade with, 18, 88, 91, 98, 113, 118, 124, 156, 159

alliances, 22, 24, 39, 44, 156, 161–162

antler, 44, 50, 111, 112, 120

Antrex site, 40, 149

Archaic, 145

Arendarhonon, 2, 158

Archaeological Services, Inc., 64, 159

Archie Little 2 site, 28

architecture. *See* built environment

Atingeennonniahak, 2

Attignawantan, 2, 157, 158

Auda site, 14

Aurora site, 75, 139

awls, 24, 112, 118, 120

axes. *See* celts: iron axe; metals, European

Baden, William W., 97

Baillargeon, Morgan, 114

Baker site, 31, 34, 38

Ball site,, Table5.1, Table5.2 135

Balsam Lake, 42

bannerstone, 148

bark, 2, 21, 87, 90, 91

Barnes site, 50

Basque, 63, 151

beads: bone, 50, 103, 120, 120–121, 154, 157; bone, human, 44; ceramic, 134; copper. *See* metals; glass, 158; shell, 122, 154, 157; stone, 146, 147, 157, 158

About the Authors

Jennifer Birch is assistant professor of anthropology at the University of Georgia. Her current research projects include a cross-cultural study of aggregated social formations and investigating the development of organizational complexity in eastern North America. She also teaches and conducts research on the archaeology of warfare, cultural resource management, and the intersection of archaeology and contemporary society. Her articles have appeared in the *Canadian Journal of Archaeology*, the *Archaeological Review from Cambridge*, and *American Antiquity*.

Ronald F. Williamson is founder and managing partner of Archaeological Services Inc., a cultural resource management firm based in Toronto, Ontario. He has published extensively on the precontact and colonial history of the Great Lakes Region. Recent publications include an edited volume honoring the lifelong work of Canada's preeminent prehistorian, Bruce G. Trigger, titled *The Archaeology of Bruce Trigger: Theoretical Empiricism* (2006), and an edited volume titled *Toronto: An Illustrated History of Its First 12,000 Years* (2008).